IMAGES
of America

CARVER

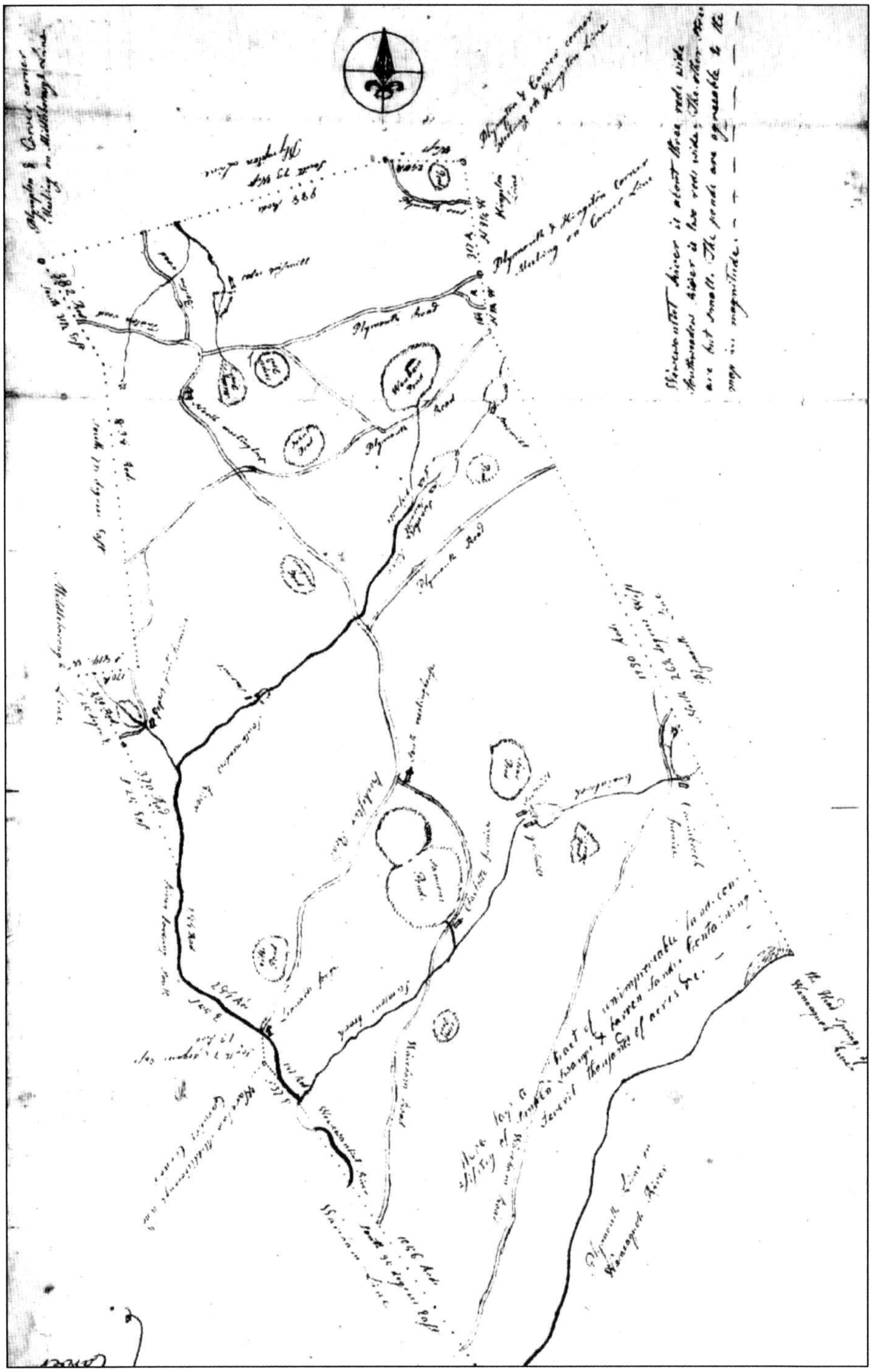

The statement on this map begins, "Agreeable to a Resolve of the Commonwealth of Massachusetts of June 18th, 1794 requiring each town in said Commonwealth to take an accurate map of their respective town. . . . " The selectmen—Nehemiah Cobb, Bartlett Murdock, and Benjamin Shurtleff—signed their names to the map.

IMAGES
of America

CARVER

Constance Jenney Shaw
and Amy B. Sheperdson

ARCADIA
PUBLISHING

ISBN 978-0-7385-3518-0

Published by Arcadia Publishing
Charleston, South Carolina

Printed in the United States of America

Library of Congress Catalog Card Number: 2003116187

For all general information, contact Arcadia Publishing:
Telephone 843-853-2070
Fax 843-853-0044
E-mail sales@arcadiapublishing.com
For customer service and orders:
Toll-free 1-888-313-2665

Visit us on the Internet at www.arcadiapublishing.com

On the cover: Philander Holmes stands by a wagonload of barrel tops in front of his cooper shop on Holmes Street in 1909. (Courtesy of William Holmes.)

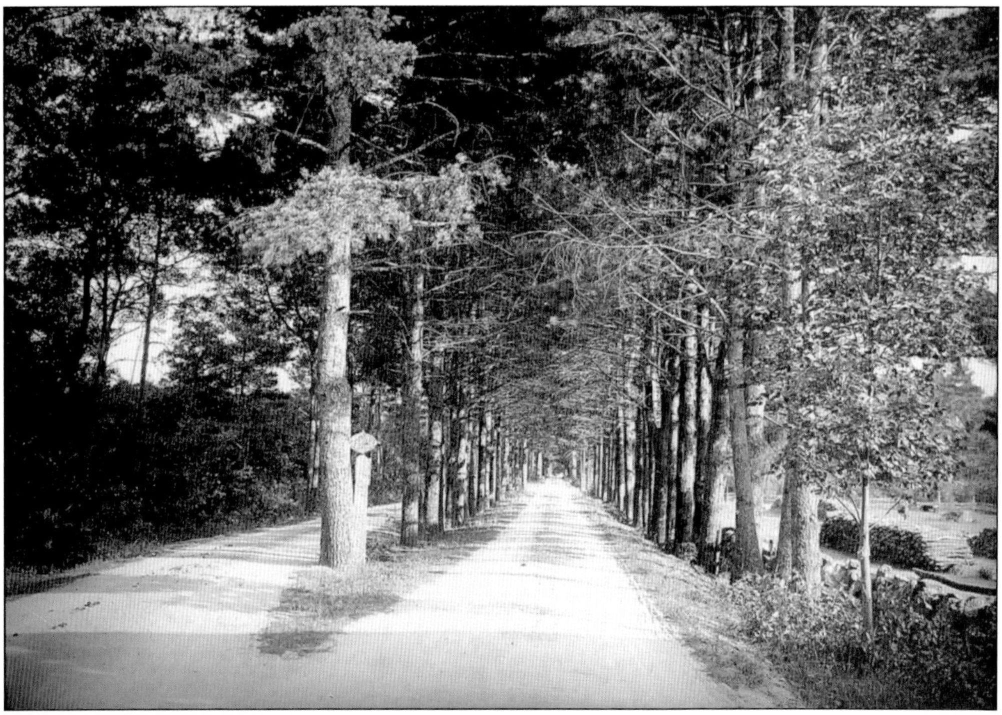

Savery Avenue runs for a half-mile within a grove of trees in South Carver. It was the main road between Center and South Carver until the 1960s, when Main Street was diverted around the avenue.

Contents

Acknowledgments

We would like to extend a heartfelt thank you to all of the people and groups who have made this book possible. To begin, we thank Carole Julius, director of the Carver Public Library, and Rick LaFond, town administrator, for their support of this project. The staff and trustees of the Carver Public Library, the Carver Historical Commission, and the Friends of the Carver Public Library have all been extremely helpful and supportive. Without the donations of local residents, our collection would not be what it is today. We have Nancy Bailey Davison to thank for many photographs and other materials, and Elaine Shurtleff to thank for the valuable William Murdock Collection. Larry Cole, William Holmes, and Dana Ward have not only donated materials to the Carver Room but also given us much information about the past and have helped in identifying mysterious photographs. Marsha Penti has provided valuable information, and Eileen Maki, our resident genealogist, has been invaluable in her ongoing work. We thank Richard LaBerge for the loan of photographs from the Edaville USA Collection.

We also want to thank photographers Wesley Ennis and James Nauen for their help and expertise. Finally, we want to acknowledge all of the people who have loaned their treasured photographs to us so that they may be shared with the world.

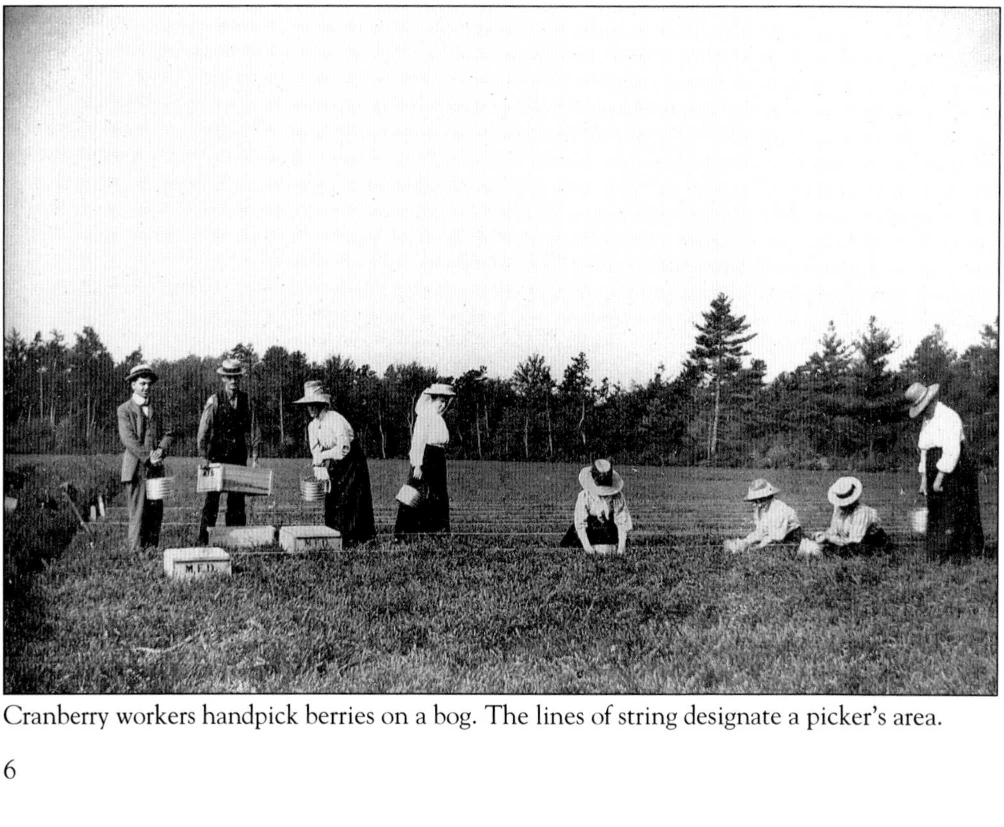

Cranberry workers handpick berries on a bog. The lines of string designate a picker's area.

INTRODUCTION

Carver is located in southeastern Massachusetts and is bordered by Plymouth, Kingston, Wareham, Middleborough, and Plympton. The town is named after the first governor of Plymouth Colony, John Carver. The area now known as Carver was referred to as the South Precinct in 1707, when it became part of the town of Plympton. Residents in the South Precinct started agitating for a separate town immediately. It was not until 1790, however, that Carver was finally incorporated as its own town.

The first settlement was located in North Carver, in and around the North Carver Green. This area has become the Lakenham Historic District. Cole's Mill, built *c.* 1706 in North Carver, was in almost continuous operation, beginning as a grist mill and then producing lumber, tacks, boxes, and barrels until 1947. Center Carver was the next area to grow into a village.

Iron foundries soon appeared in the area, as iron ore was plentiful in and around the various water sources of Carver. The first furnace, Pope's Point Furnace, was located in West Carver on Pope's Point Road. This furnace ran from 1735 to 1837 and was the second-longest running furnace in Carver after the Charlotte Furnace. It is believed that the first tea kettle in the United States was made in Carver. West Carver was a thriving village toward the end of the 1700s with Pope's Point Furnace and several other industries, as well as homes and a school; although there is little evidence there now to indicate the area once prospered.

The Charlotte Furnace in South Carver was built by Bartlett Murdock in the 1760s and stayed in business under various names until 1904. Federal Furnace, also located in South Carver, was built in 1793. South Carver was called Furnace Village for many years; it was not until after the Civil War that the village became known as South Carver. Benjamin Ellis, who began working for Bartlett Murdock at the Charlotte Furnace, eventually became owner of the furnace and the most prosperous man in Carver. He was considered a "Captain of Industry" in the words of Henry Griffith, author of *History of the Town of Carver, Massachusetts*. The Honorable Benjamin Ellis also became a member of the Massachusetts legislature, where he was known as "the Cast Iron Senator" because of the cannonballs he made for the War of 1812.

The men who owned the iron foundries built mansions on the west side of Sampson's Pond, now part of the Savery Historic District. The unique Union Church and cemetery are also part of the historic district. The families who made their fortunes from the foundries are buried there. Their graves are marked by elaborate monuments that are now part of Monument Row. William Savery, who was born in Carver but worked for 20 years in New York and New Jersey in the foundry business, financed and directed the construction of the historic Savery Avenue, which is believed to be the first divided highway in the United States. Savery also made his mark upon the community by donating a library of books to every school in the town and coordinating the building of the Union Church.

The cranberry industry began after the Civil War. In 1940, more cranberries came from Carver than from any other town in the United States. Many immigrants from Finland and the Cape Verde Islands came to Carver to work in the cranberry industry. They were joined by families from nearby cities arriving to harvest the year's crop. Shanties housed many of the workers; most dwellings were not as accommodating as those pictured at the Cranebrook Cranberry Company. Many workers remained in the community and eventually acquired their own bogs, thereby contributing to the town's economic, social, and civil life over the years.

This book captures only a short period of time in Carver's history beginning in the late 1800s and ending in the mid-1900s. From the 1600s onward, the area that is now Carver progressed from being land seasonally inhabited by American Indians to a town with several busy villages. Much of the information in the book comes from materials and sources in the Carver Room at the Carver Public Library. People are invited to come visit, explore, and learn about Carver's rich past.

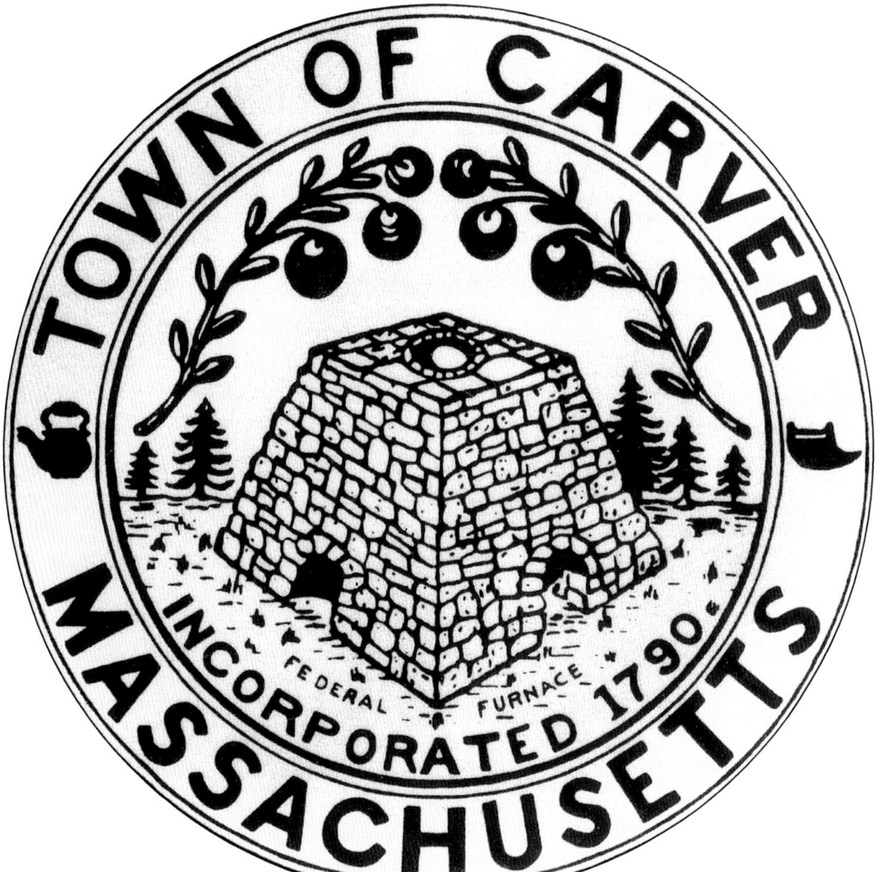

The Carver town seal was designed by Earl Boardway, who was then the president of the Carver Historical Society, and accepted at a town meeting on March 5, 1946. Federal Furnace graces the center of the seal depicting blast furnaces and foundries that operated in Carver from 1735 to 1904. Since it is thought that the first tea kettle in America was made here in Carver, the tea kettle is located on the left side of the seal. Cranberry vines are found in the center of the seal, representing Carver's importance in the cranberry industry, and the cranberry scoop on the right of the seal complements the cranberry vines. The pine trees that are located in the center of the seal represent the native trees that were made into barrels and boxes at Carver sawmills. Finally, the town of Carver's incorporation date of 1790 is located on the seal, indicating Carver's independence from the town of Plympton.

One

North Carver

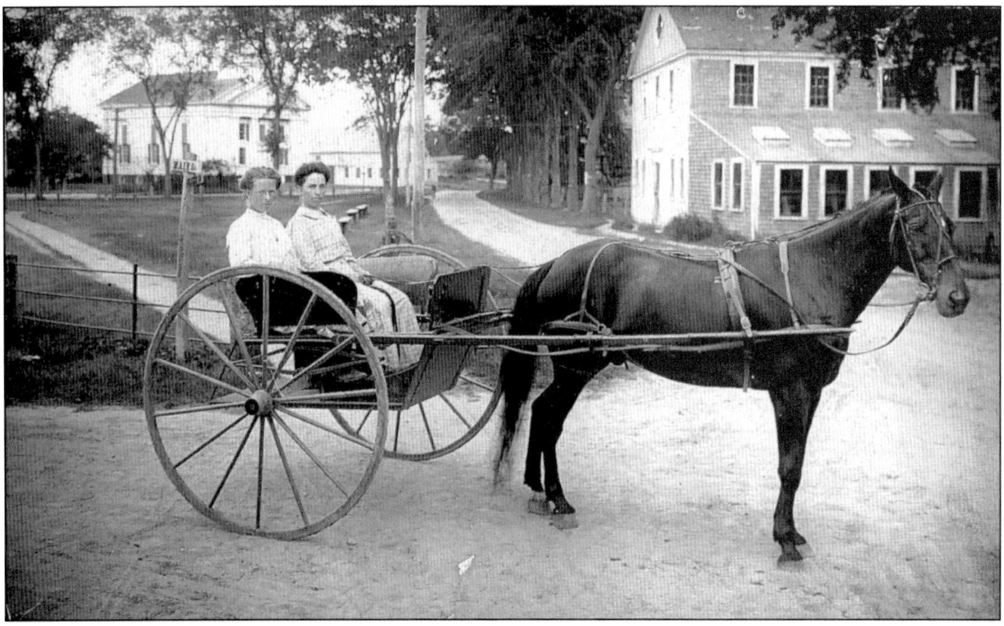

Mildred (left) and Lena Vaughan (right) are shown on the North Carver Green on August 12, 1909. The Veterans of All Wars Memorial Park, more commonly known as the North Carver Green, was given to the town by Benoni and Jonathan Shaw c. 1737. Originally known as Lakenham Green, it was used as a common for grazing animals and later as a training ground for the militia. (Courtesy of Holly Peay.)

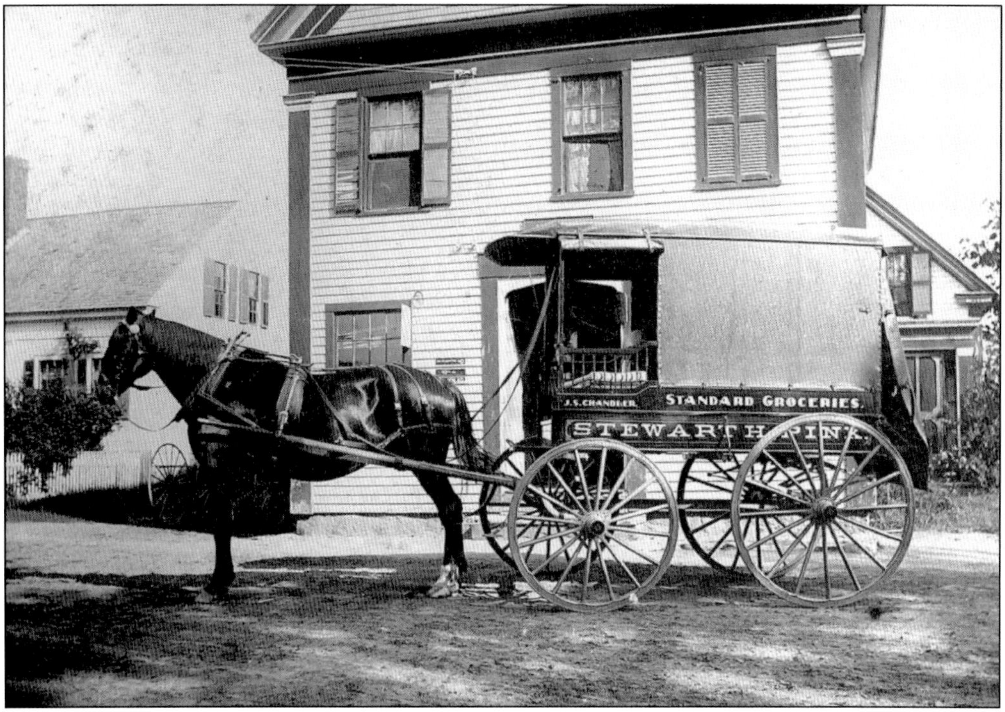

Stewart H. Pink's delivery wagon sits in front of his store in North Carver *c.* 1900. (Courtesy of Dana Ward.)

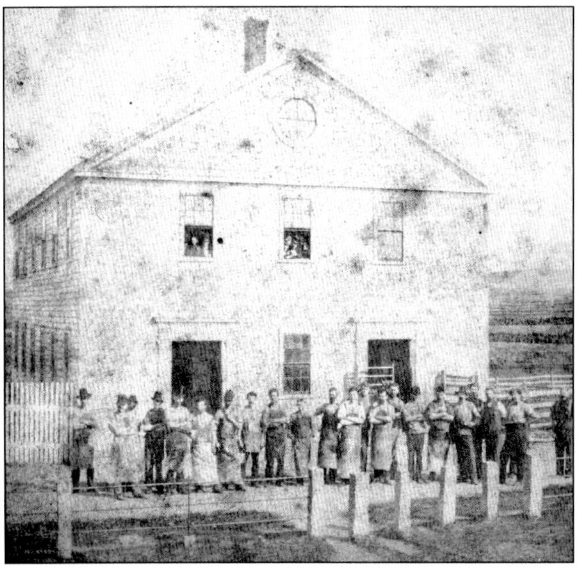

Workers assemble outside King Philip's Hall on the North Carver Green in the 1870s. King Philip's Hall was originally built as a church in 1732 near the Lakenham Cemetery, and it was called Second Church. The church was moved to the green in 1823. When a new church was built on the green *c.* 1859, the building became known as King Philip's Hall. It had a shoe shop on the first floor, and the second floor was used for dances. Cranberry growers later used the building for storage of equipment and boarding for workers. (Courtesy of Michael Mazalewski.)

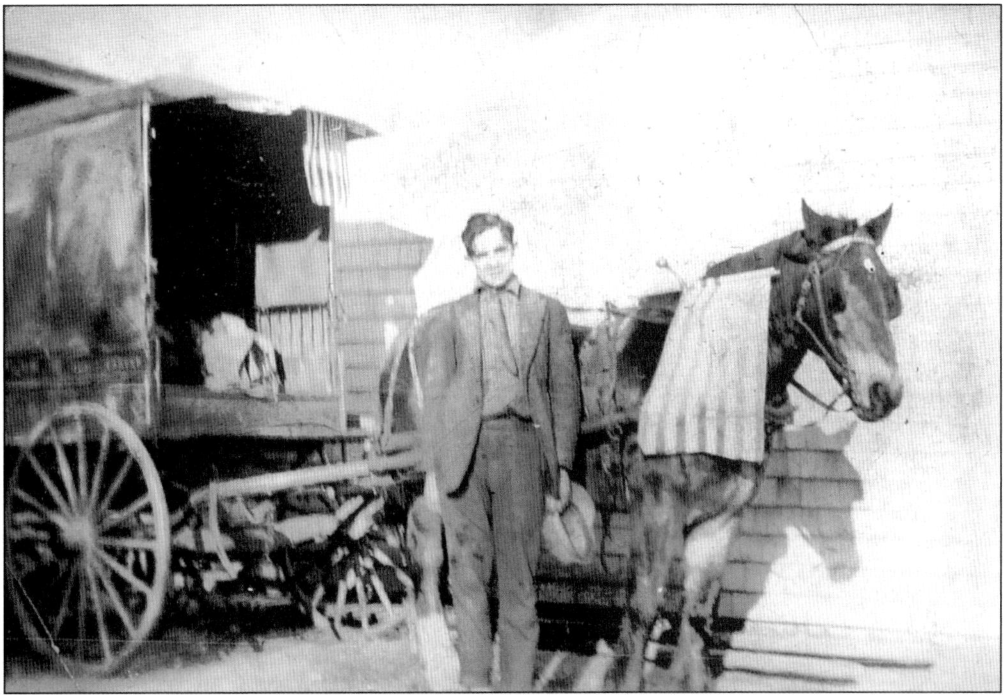

Clarence Burgess readies to deliver supplies to customers of Pink's Store in North Carver. (Courtesy of Dana Ward.)

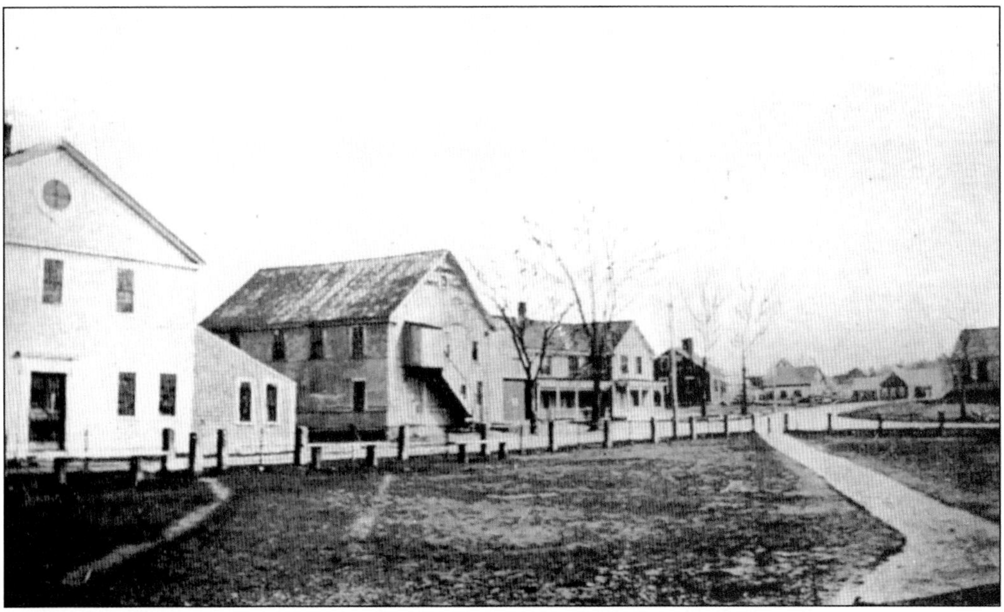

In this southerly view of North Carver Green, the building to the right of King Philip's Hall was originally Roswell Shurtleff Hall and was built *c.* 1907. The second floor was a community room used for entertainment, and the first floor held Shurtleff's store. It was later used as a Grange Hall.

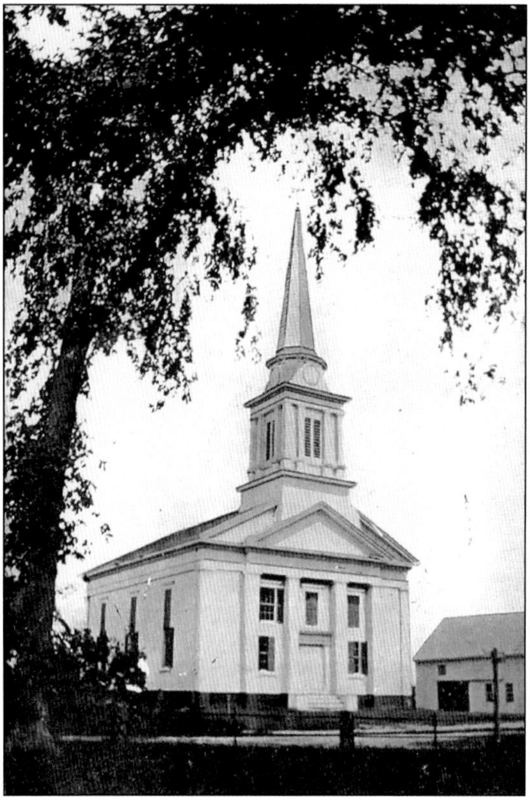

The Congregational church in North Carver was built on the green in 1859. Before that time, religious services and town meetings were held in Second Church, which later became known as King Philip's Hall.

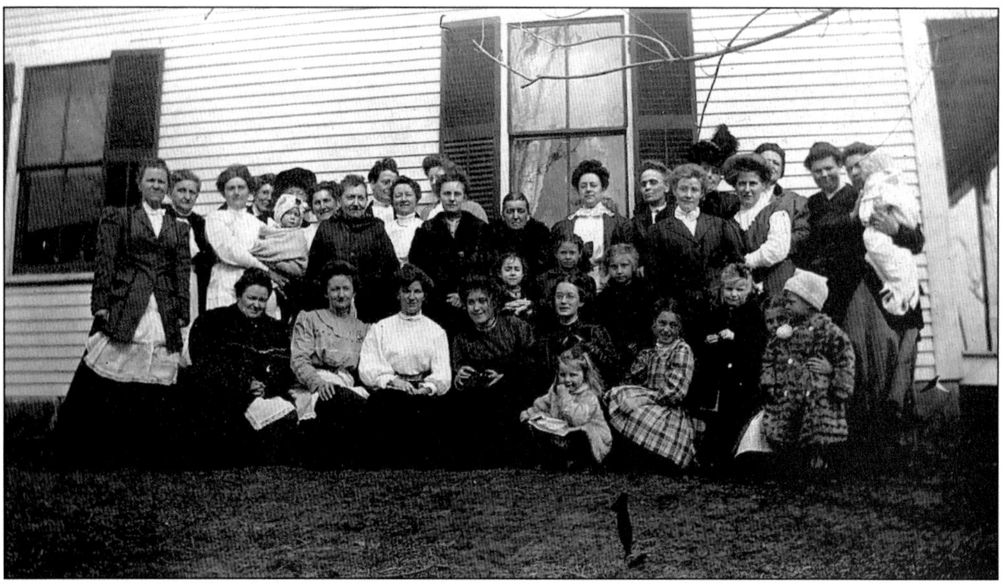

The North Carver Ladies' Aid meets at the home of Charlotte Cole *c.* 1900. (Courtesy of Dana Ward.)

Henry Pink, proprietor of Pink's Store in North Carver, steps up to bat for the Carver Athletics at McKay's Field in 1912. McKay's Field was on the north side of Plymouth Street and on the east end of what is now the Lakenham Historic District. (Courtesy of Dana Ward.)

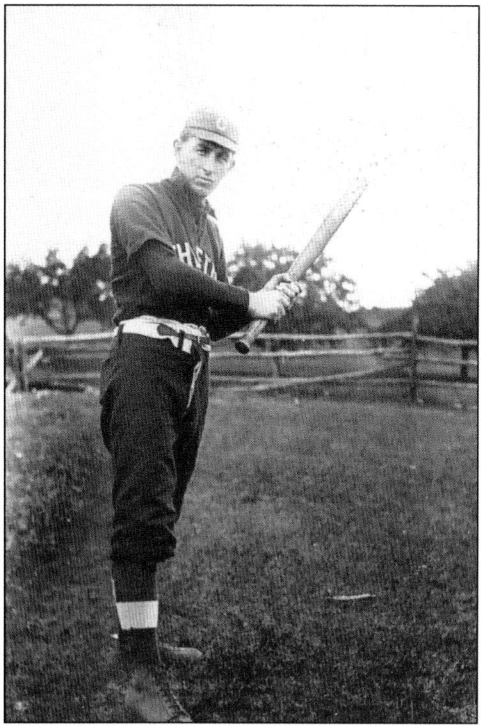

S. H. PINK'S CASH STORE.

GROCERIES,
PROVISIONS,
FLOUR,

Hay and Grain,
Fine Teas, Coffees and Pure Spices,
Dry Goods, Boots, Shoes and Rubbers,
Hardware, Patent Medicines, Etc.

PLYMOUTH STREET AT CARVER GREEN,
NO. CARVER, MASS.

An advertisement for S. H. Pink's Cash Store appears in *The 1902–1903 Resident and Business Directory of Carver, Halifax, Hanson, and Plympton*.

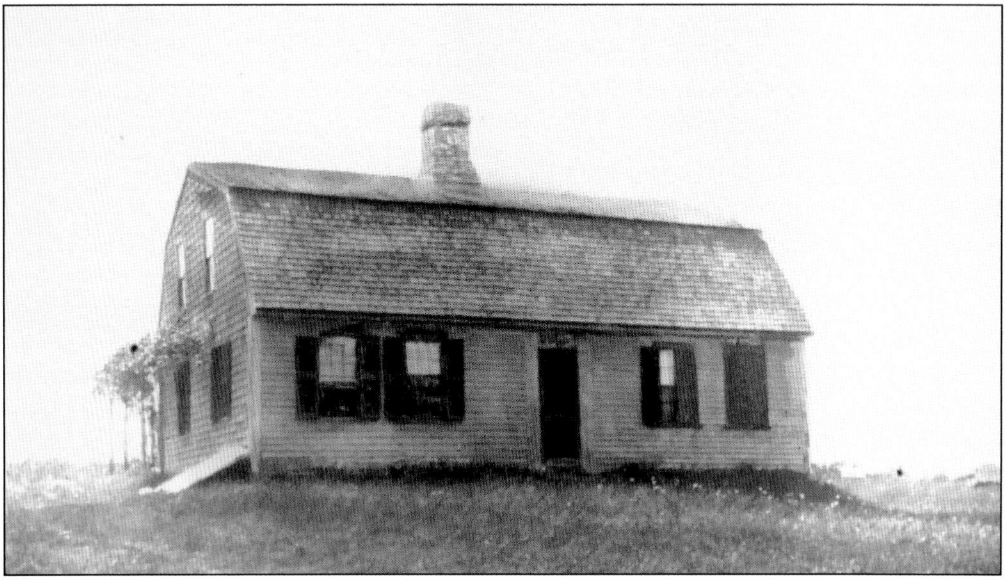

The land upon which the Sturtevant House sits, on the south side of the North Carver Green, is considered to be the site of Carver's first house, built *c.* 1660 by Jonathan Shaw, Carver's first permanent resident. It is unknown what happened to the first home, but Shaw's descendant and namesake, Jonathan Shaw, built the current home known as the Sturtevant House *c.* 1770. Built *c.* 1700, the Waterman House on High Street is considered the oldest remaining home in Carver.

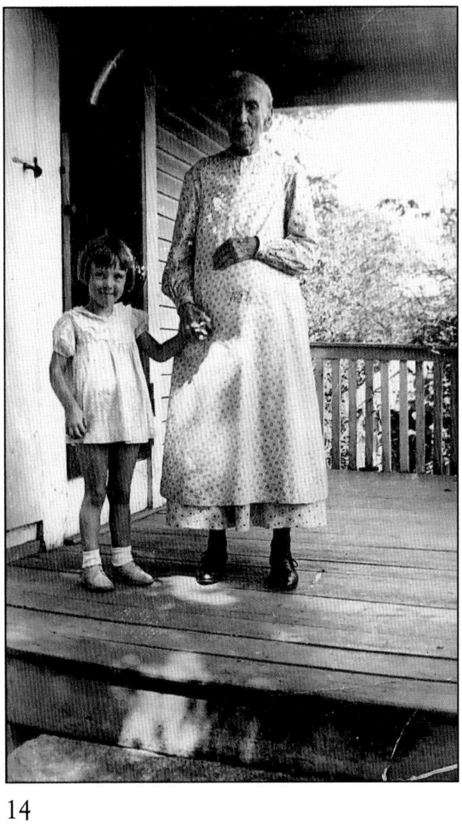

Lucinda Morse, at 100 years of age, is pictured with a young relative. Her husband was Dr. George F. Morse, who practiced medicine in North Carver. According to Ellsworth Braddock, author of *Memories of North Carver*, Dr. Morse charged 50¢ for an office visit and $1 for a house call. (Courtesy of Dana Ward.)

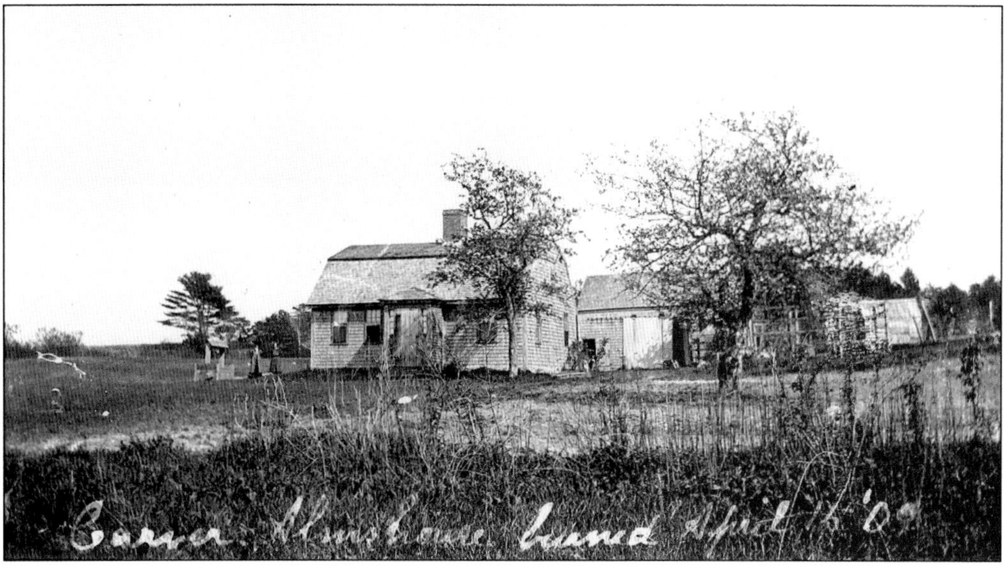

The almshouse was originally the home of the town's first selectman, Thomas Savery, and was situated on Green Street just behind the present location of the North Carver Fire Station. The town purchased the home in 1845. Previously, the town had either housed people in need in other town-owned homes and farms or provided financial assistance to families who took the needy into their own homes. The house burned in 1909.

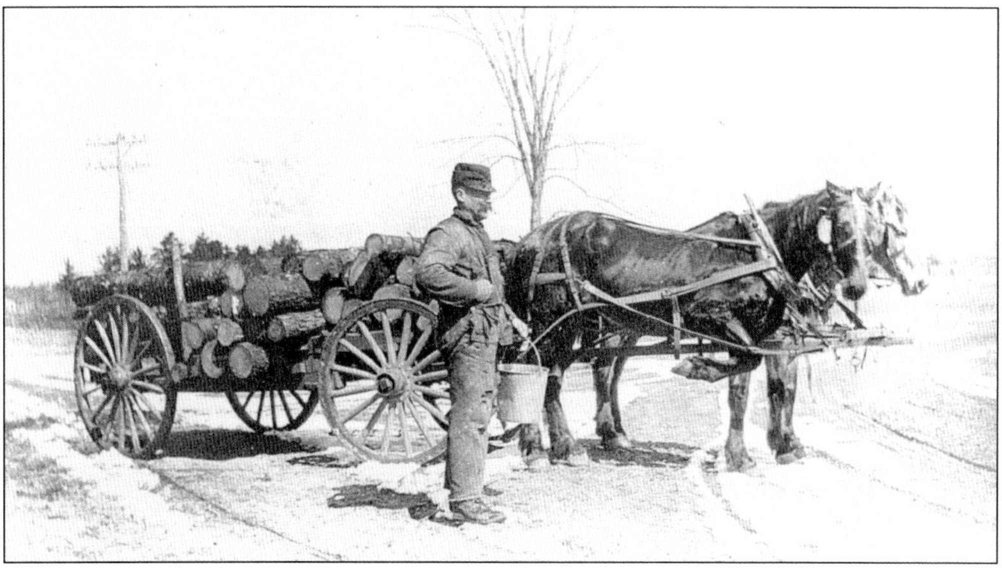

Alton Chandler hauls a wagonload of logs *c.* 1920. (Courtesy of Larry Cole.)

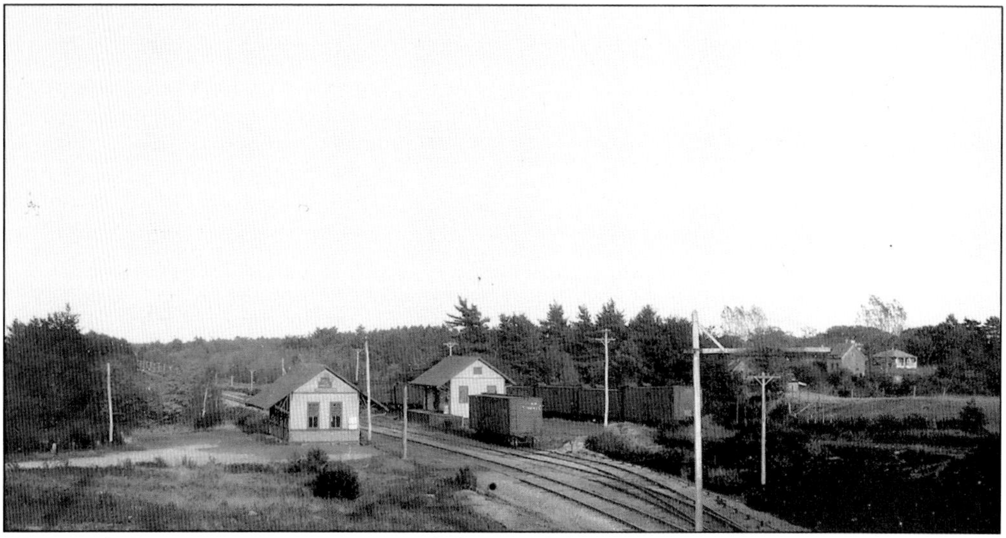

The North Carver Train Station serviced the Middleborough-Plymouth line of the New York, New Haven, & Hartford Railroad, which ran from 1891 to 1930. The freight trains, used to transport cranberries and products from the mills, stopped running in 1936. The station has been extensively remodeled and is now a private home. (Courtesy of Dana Ward.)

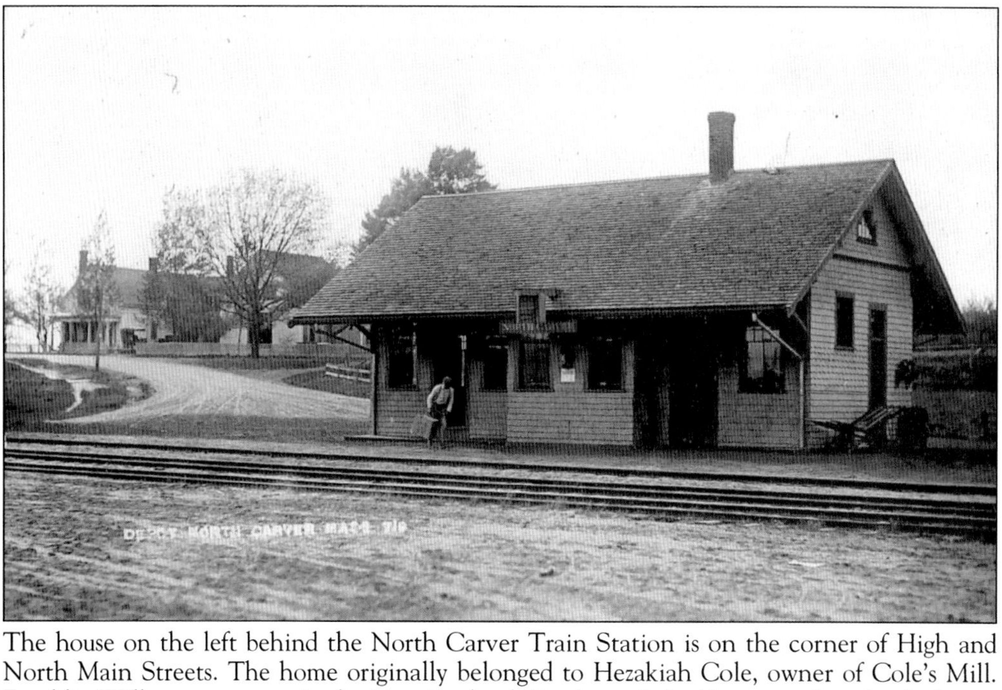

The house on the left behind the North Carver Train Station is on the corner of High and North Main Streets. The home originally belonged to Hezakiah Cole, owner of Cole's Mill. Franklin Wilbur, a manager in the New England Cranberry Sales Company, bought the home in 1893. (Courtesy of Bob Wilson.)

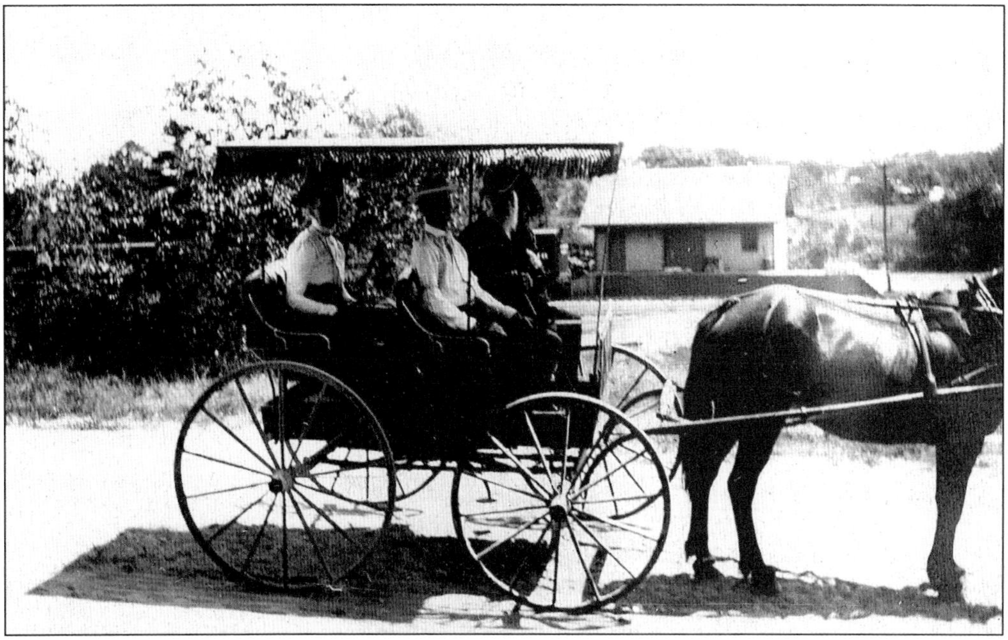

The North Carver Railroad Station is located behind the horse and family in the carriage. It took three years to build the train tracks between Plymouth and Middleborough. According to Ellsworth Braddock, a half-mile of track was completed in one day. The work involved the dynamiting of rocks and the creation of culverts. All passengers got a free round-trip ride on the first day of train service.

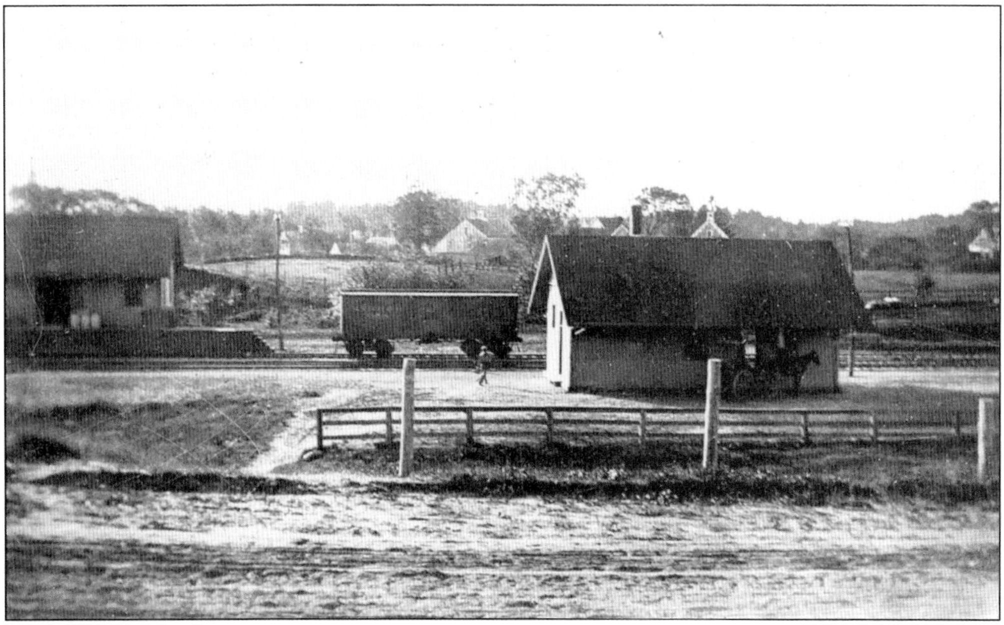

The North Carver Train Station had little activity between trains. All of the mail for the town was delivered on the morning train from Plymouth, and after the mail carrier delivered to the various parts of town, he would bring all of the outgoing mail back to the station to be sent on a train later in the day. (Courtesy of Dana Ward.)

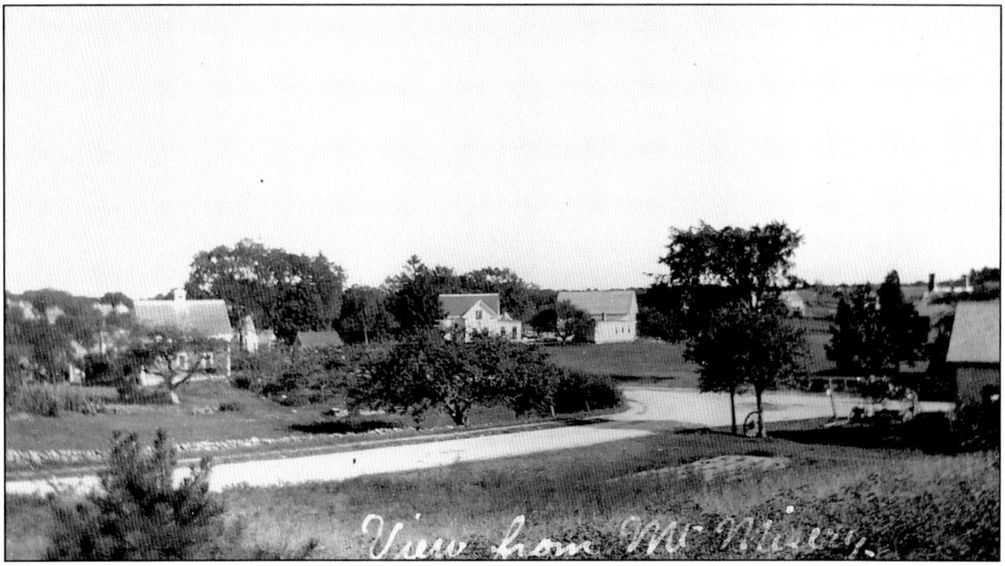

This photograph was taken from the top of "Mount Misery," once considered to be the highest point in Carver. The hill is located on the northwest corner of the Route 58 and Plymouth Street intersection, where the New England Cranberry Sales Company building was located. (Courtesy of Dana Ward.)

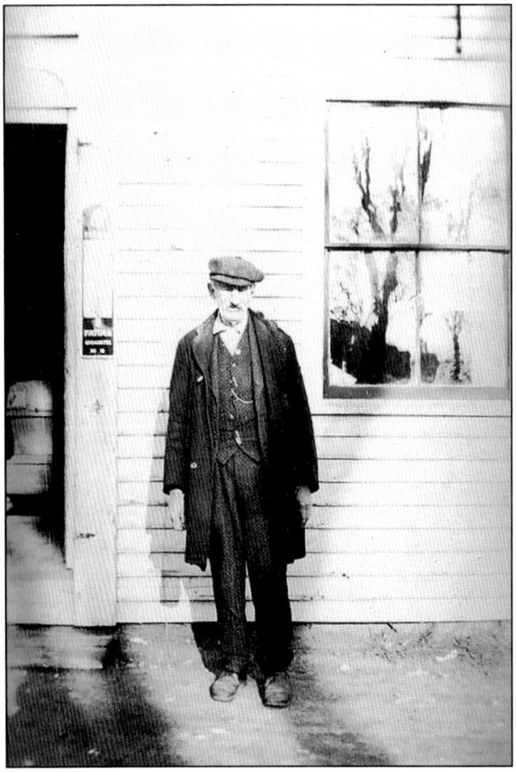

Edward Churchill was a regular at Pink's Store in the early 1920s. He worked at the North Carver Grammar School as the custodian for many years. (Courtesy of Dana Ward.)

Lydia Hammond Robbins, pictured here, was the mother of five children and the grandmother of Larry Cole of North Carver. Her daily diaries, which she kept faithfully, give an excellent description of the past. (Courtesy of Larry Cole.)

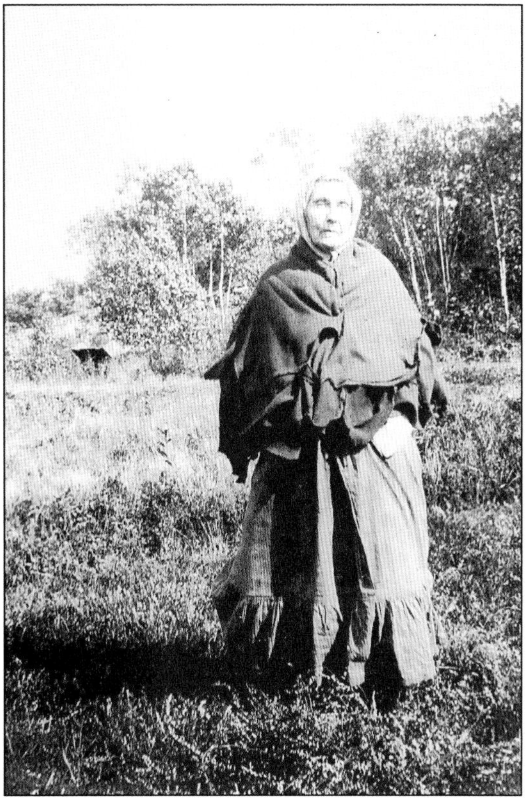

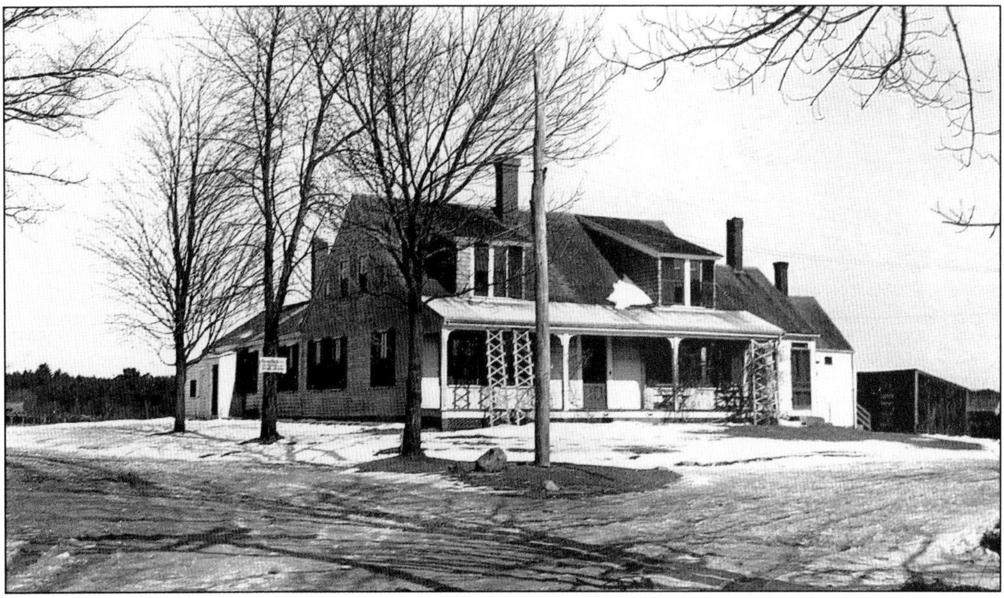

John Cole Jr. built this home in the early 1700s, and it served as the Cole homestead and farm for 250 years. It is the oldest Cole residence in the area. (Courtesy of Larry Cole.)

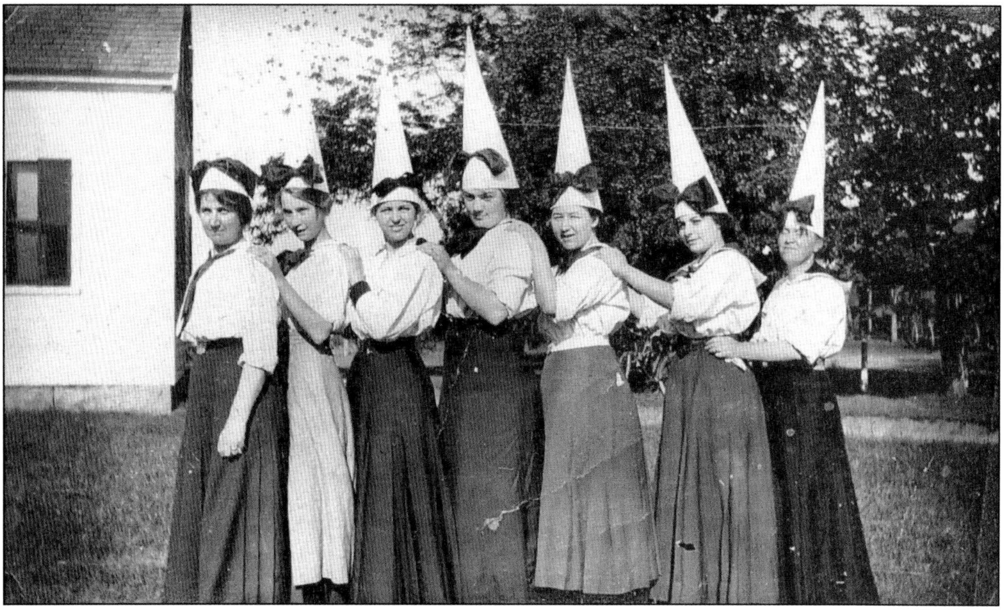

North Carver ladies participate in a social gathering wearing unique headpieces. From left to right are Emma Washburn, unidentified, Florence Washburn, Cordie Pink, Grace Gardner, Mrs. Ernest Gardner, and Grace Burgess. (Courtesy of Dana Ward.)

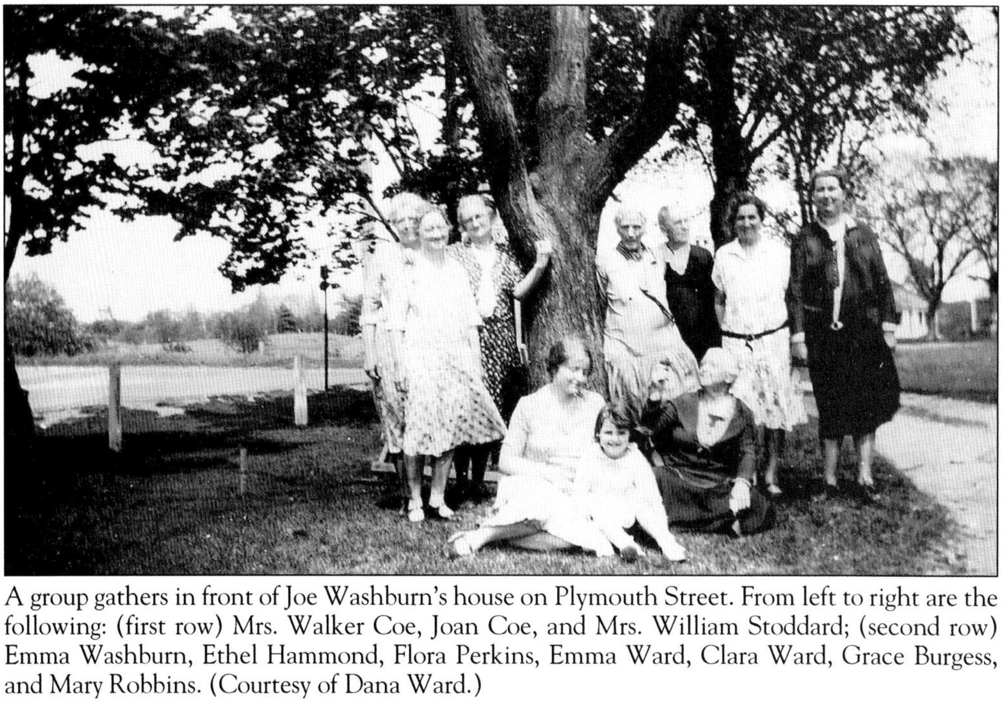

A group gathers in front of Joe Washburn's house on Plymouth Street. From left to right are the following: (first row) Mrs. Walker Coe, Joan Coe, and Mrs. William Stoddard; (second row) Emma Washburn, Ethel Hammond, Flora Perkins, Emma Ward, Clara Ward, Grace Burgess, and Mary Robbins. (Courtesy of Dana Ward.)

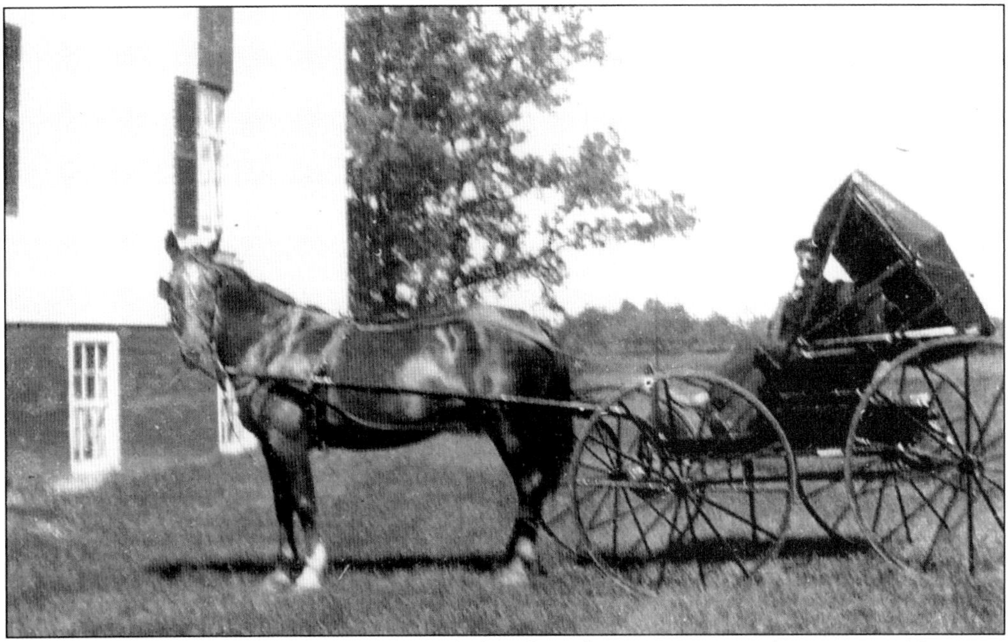

A horse stands next to the Congregational church with a passenger in the carriage. (Courtesy of Charles Bezanson.)

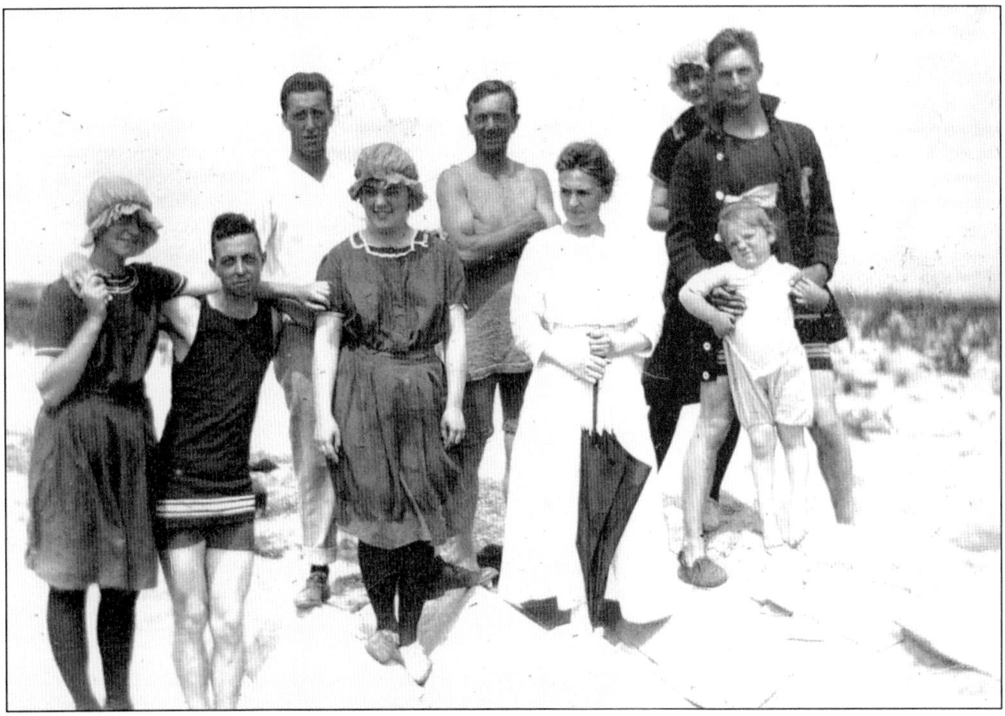

Local Carver residents enjoy an outing at Brant Rock *c.* 1918. From left to right are the following: (first row) Lucille Shaw, unidentified, Cordie Pink, Anna Shurtleff, and an unidentified child; (second row) unidentified, Ellsworth Shaw, Aravista Griffith, and Ken Shaw. (Courtesy of Dana Ward.)

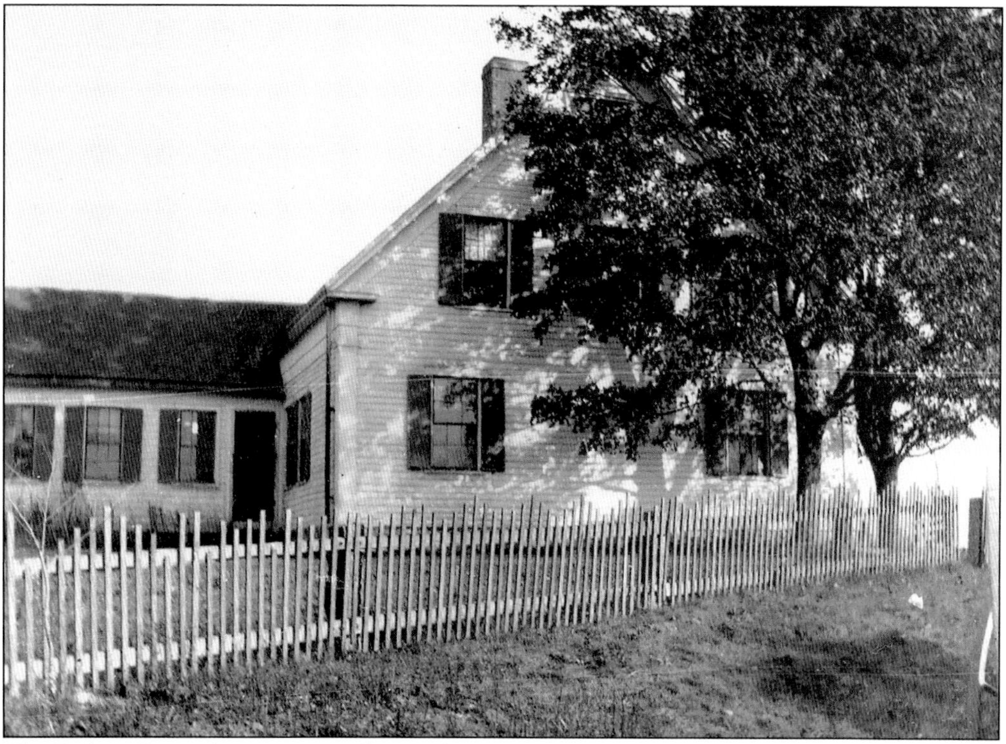

The Embert Eames home sits on the northeast side of the Route 44 and 58 interchange. The home was built in the early 1700s and is believed to have belonged to the Vaughan family, who built a number of other homes in Carver. Eames, a member of a prominent North Carver family, purchased the house in 1902.

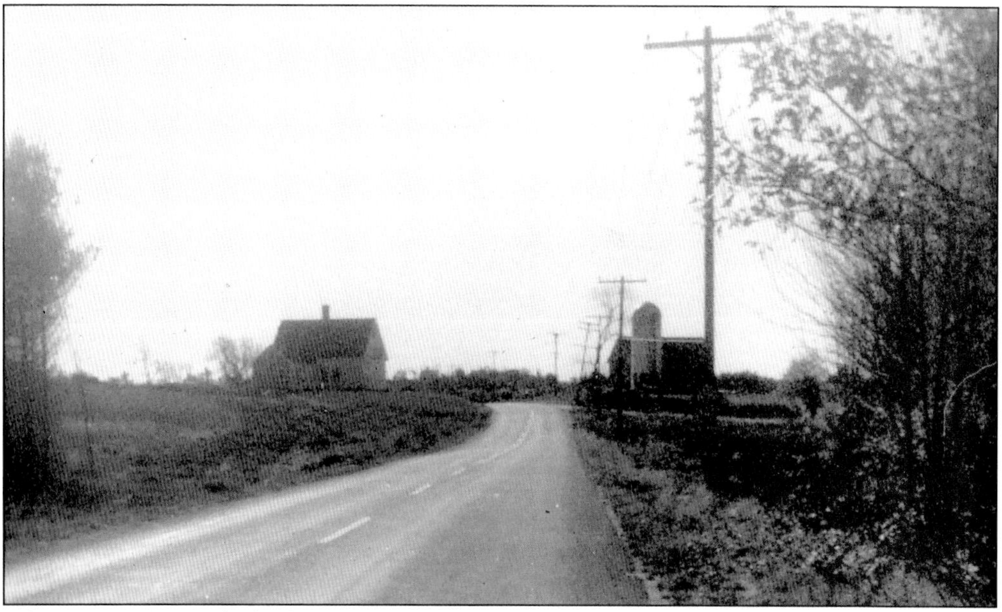

When Route 58 was built, the Eames property was divided. The home is on the east side of the street, whereas the white silo is on the west side.

Embert Eames sits on his truck with a load of hay in 1940. (Courtesy of Larry Cole.)

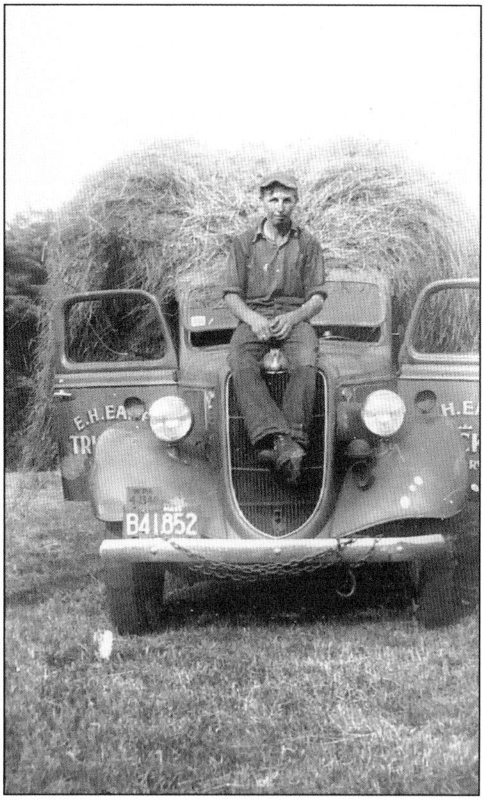

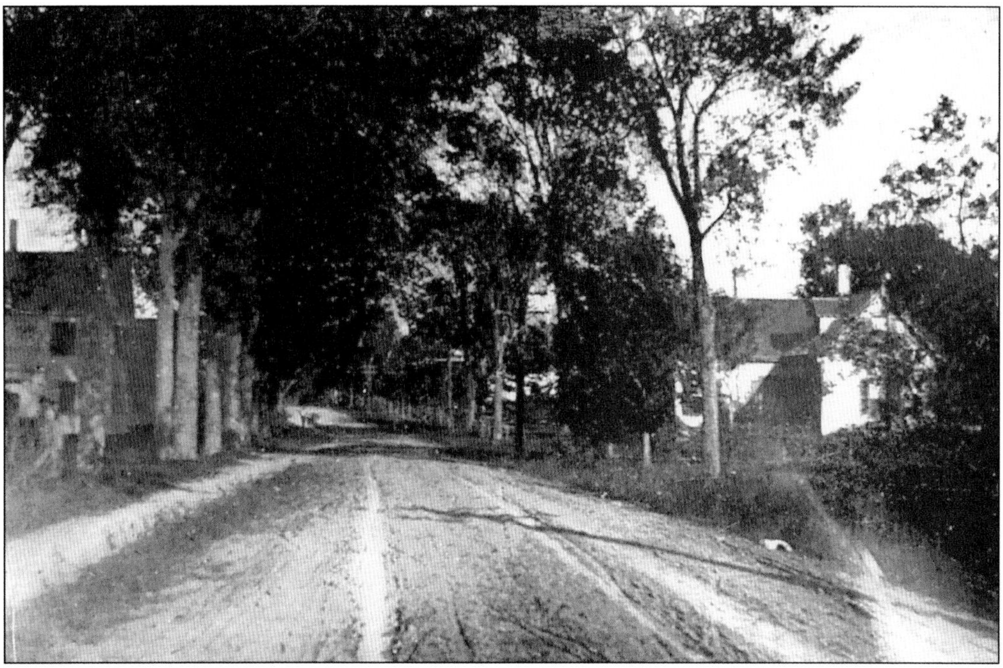

This view of Plymouth Street, taken before the road was paved, looks east.

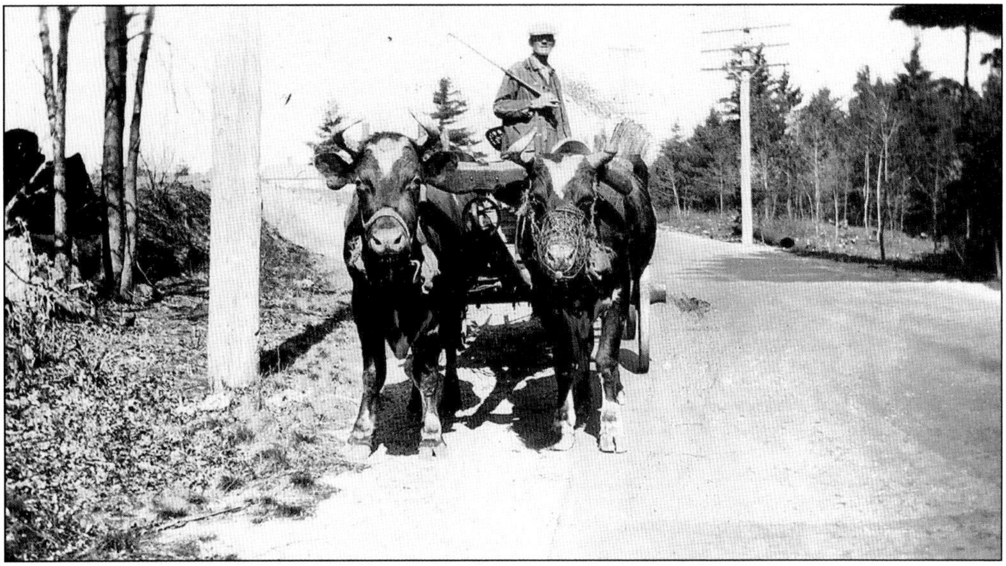

Morris Robbins drives his team of oxen. (Courtesy of Dana Ward.)

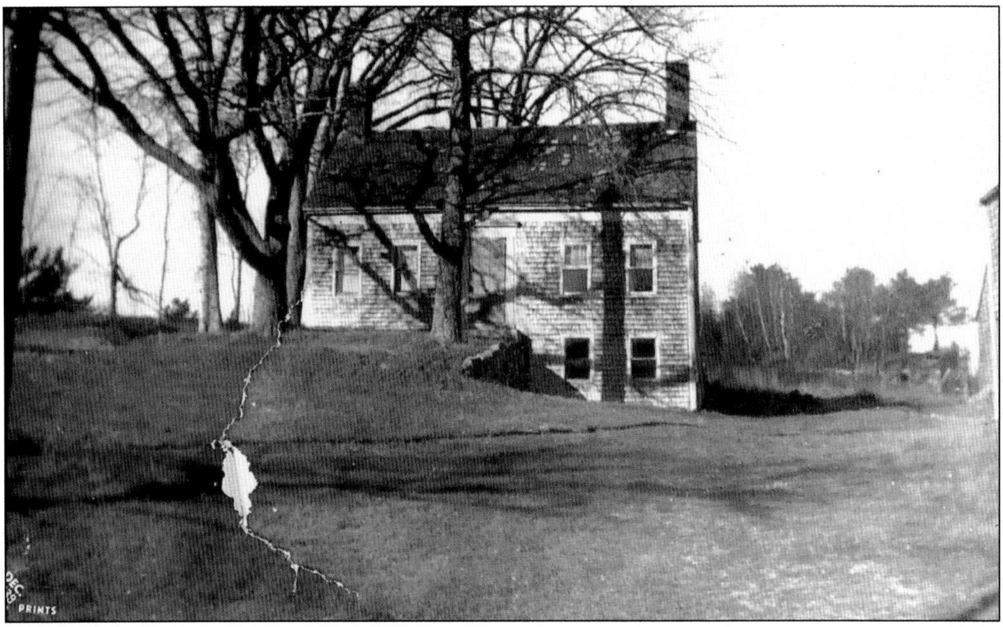

The Robbins house, located on the corner of Gate and High Streets, was owned by the Shaw family until Joseph Robbins bought it in 1855. The Robbins family worked the land, running one of the largest farms in the area. In the 1890s, cranberries were added as crops.

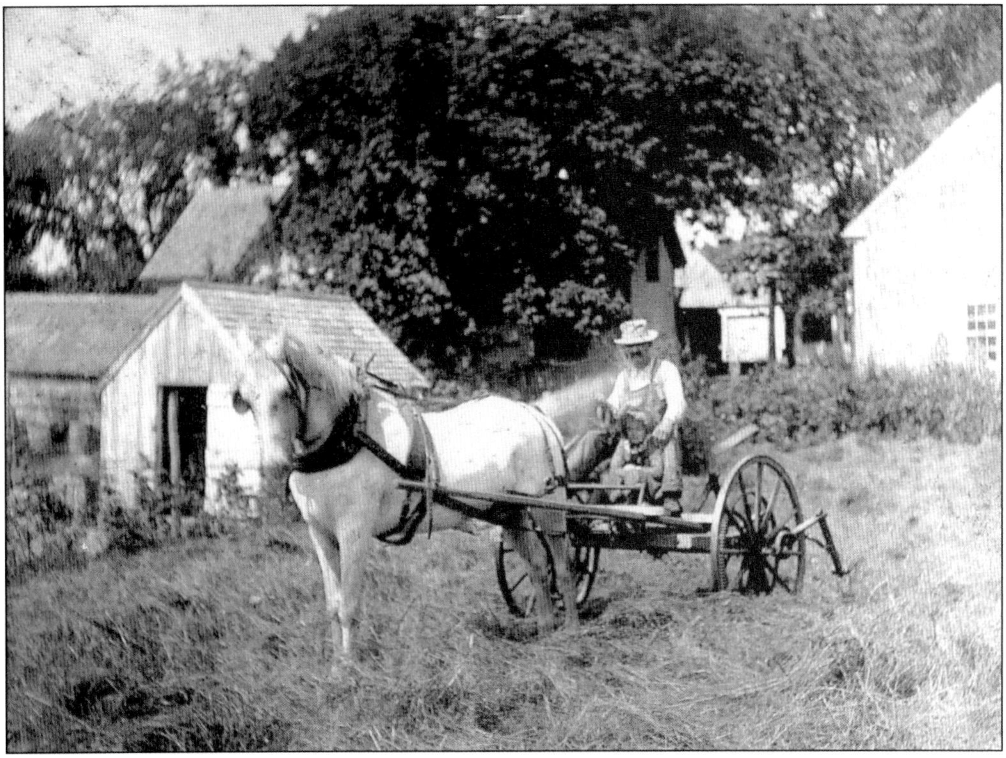

Helen Chandler goes along for a ride as Fred Ward works to pull a hay tedder, which turns the cut hay so it can dry. (Courtesy of Dana Ward.)

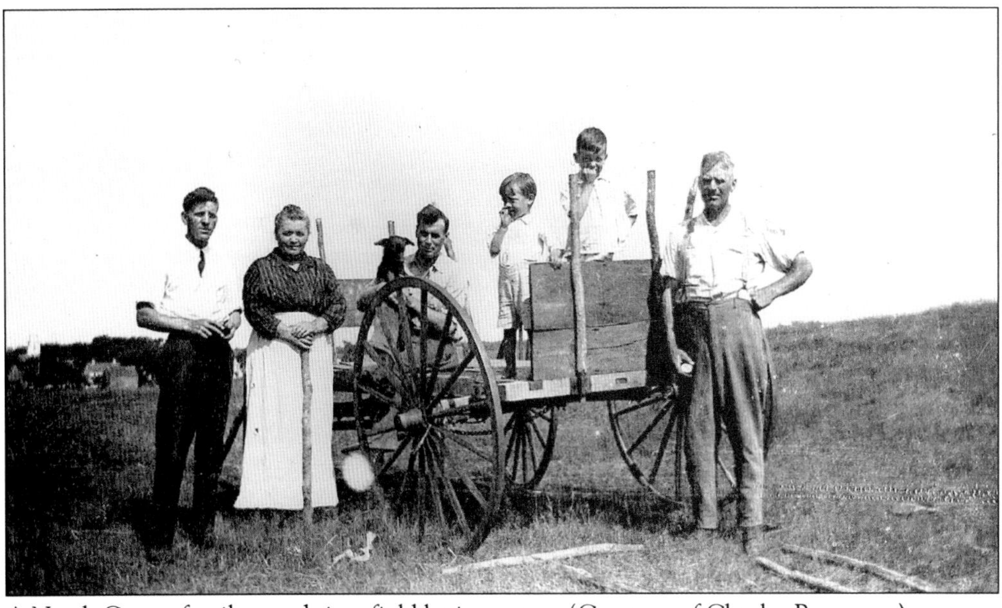

A North Carver family stands in a field by its wagon. (Courtesy of Charles Bezanson.)

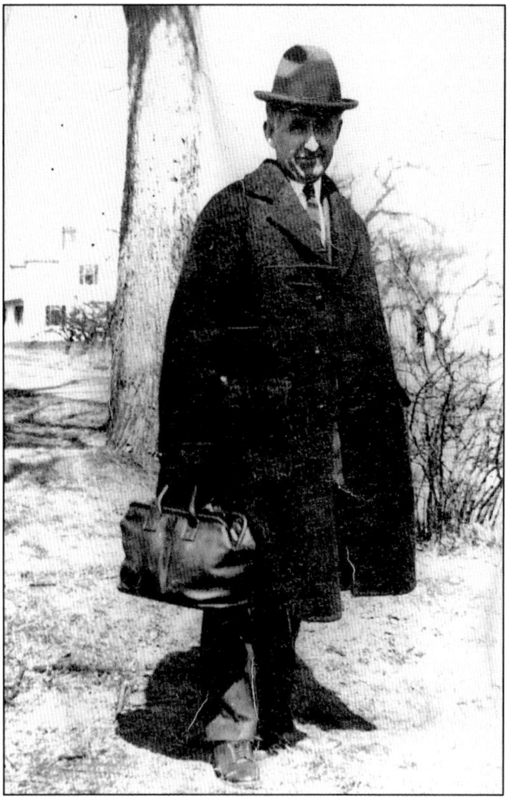

Dr. Laurence M. Chase practiced medicine in Carver in the early 1900s. He graduated from Tufts School of Medicine in 1904. Dr. Chase boarded with a family in North Carver where he had his office. He was also the school physician for several years. (Courtesy of William Holmes.)

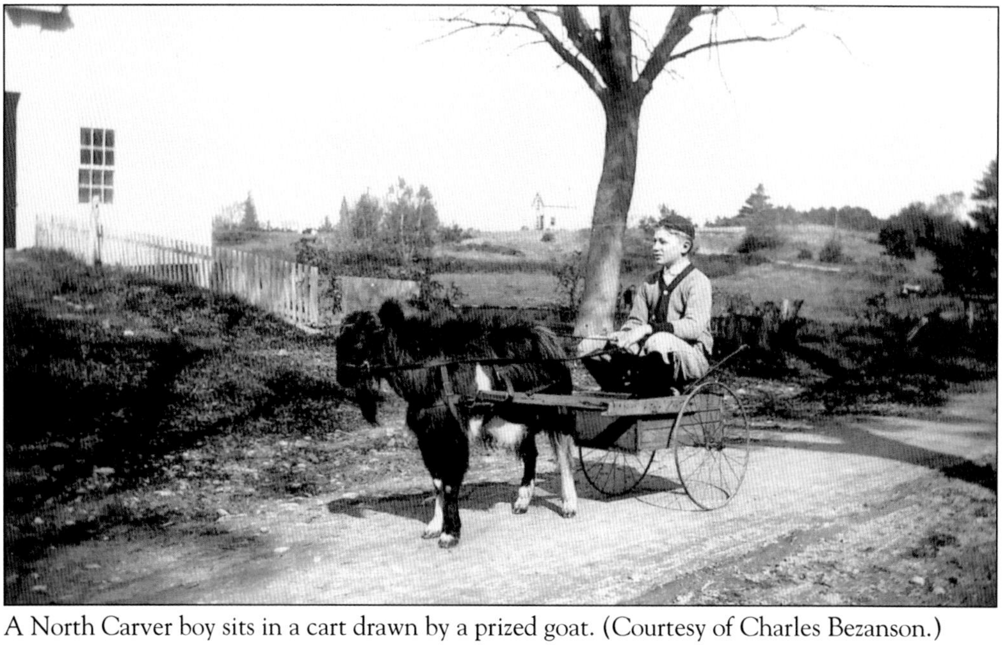

A North Carver boy sits in a cart drawn by a prized goat. (Courtesy of Charles Bezanson.)

Two

Carver: East and West

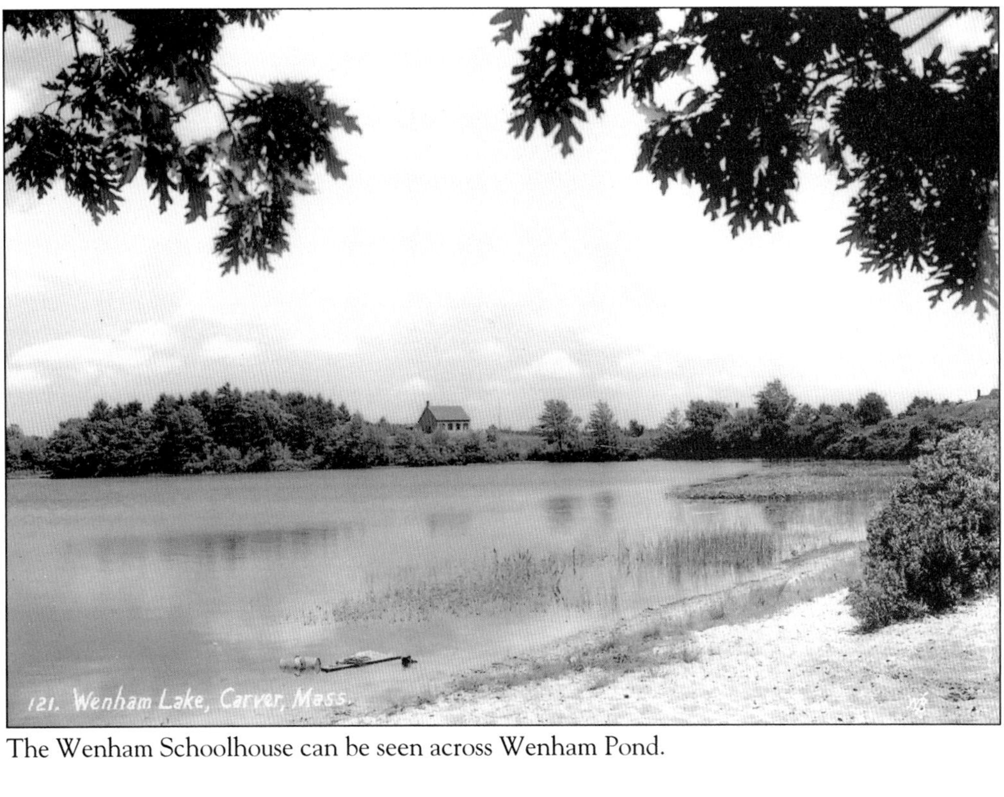

The Wenham Schoolhouse can be seen across Wenham Pond.

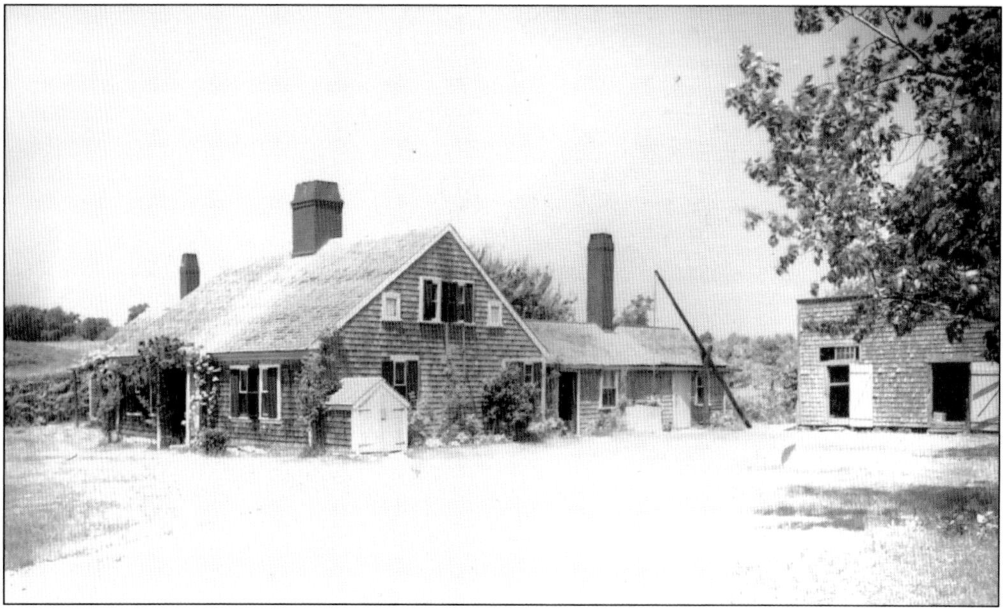

The Hammond homestead was built in the 1700s by John Doty. Owned by the Hammond family for many generations, the home was more recently occupied by Betsy Thankful Moore. She wrote the book *Well Sweep*, which details the house and grounds.

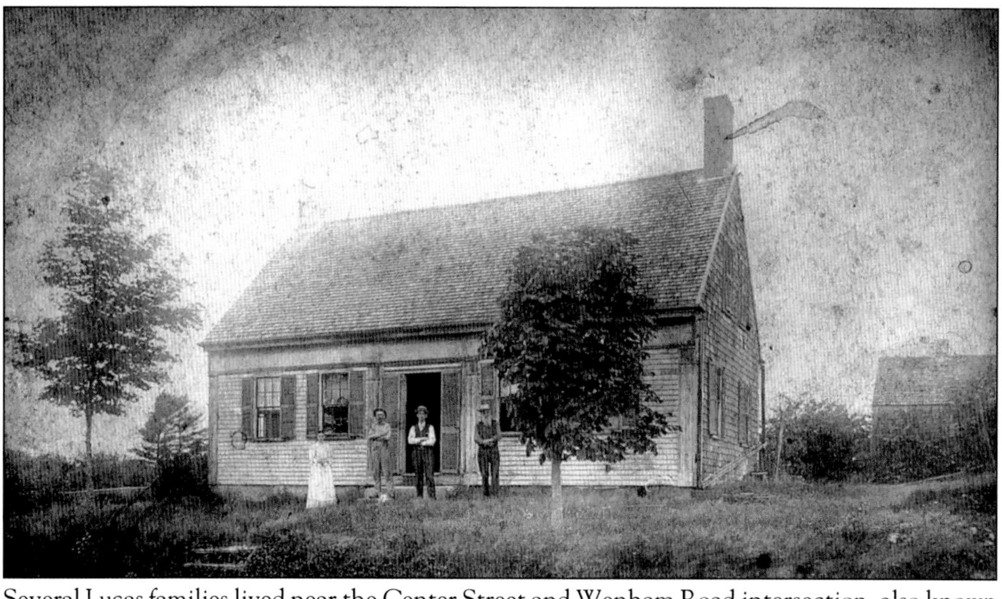

Several Lucas families lived near the Center Street and Wenham Road intersection, also known as Story's Corner.

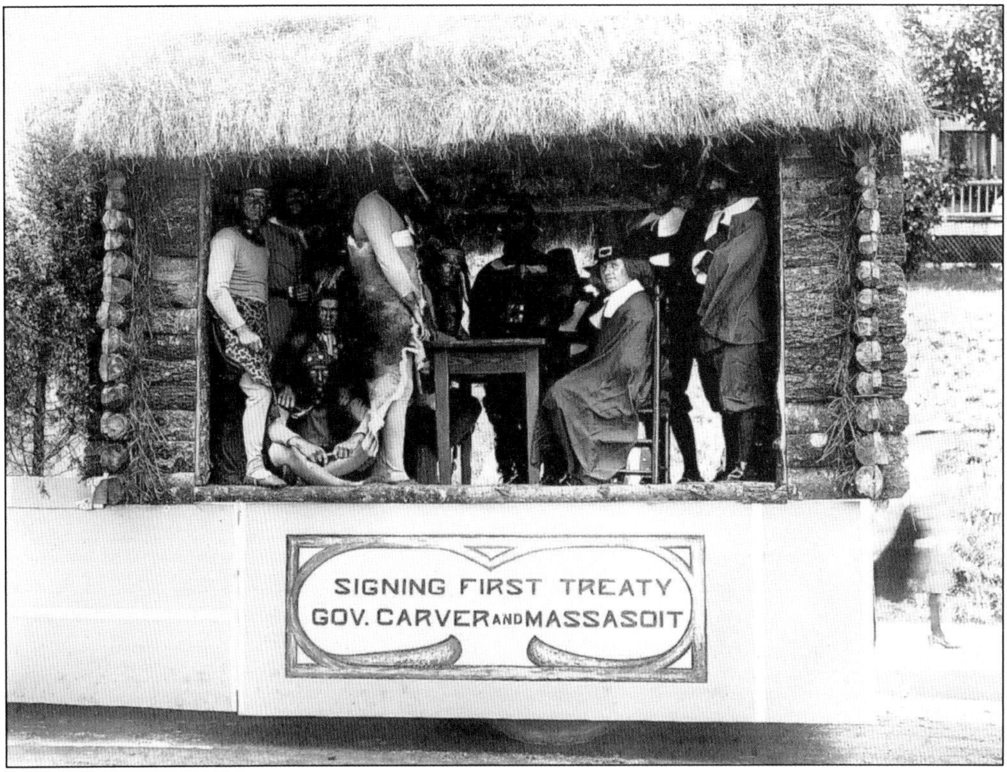

These Carver men take part in a parade at the 1920 tercentennial celebration in Plymouth. Rodney Griffith appears on the left dressed as an American Indian. Other "American Indians" are Kenneth Shaw, Ruel Gibbs, Francis Merritt, and Ted Vaughan. The "Pilgrims" are Herbert Vaughan, Ernest Gardner, Maynard Peterson, Ellis Atwood, John Shaw, Andrew Griffith, Howard Gardner, and Homer Gibbs.

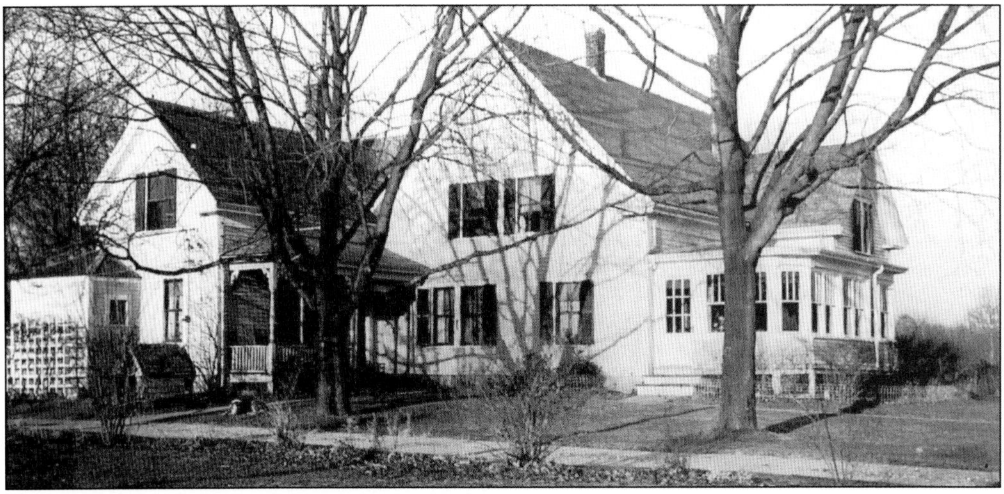

Jesse Holmes and his wife, Blanche, a Carver schoolteacher, lived in this home on Holmes Street. It was originally owned by Jesse's father, Philander J. Holmes. Jesse was active in town government and owned the Jesse Holmes Box Mill, which was known as Old Center Mill and was located in the center of town. (Courtesy of William Holmes.)

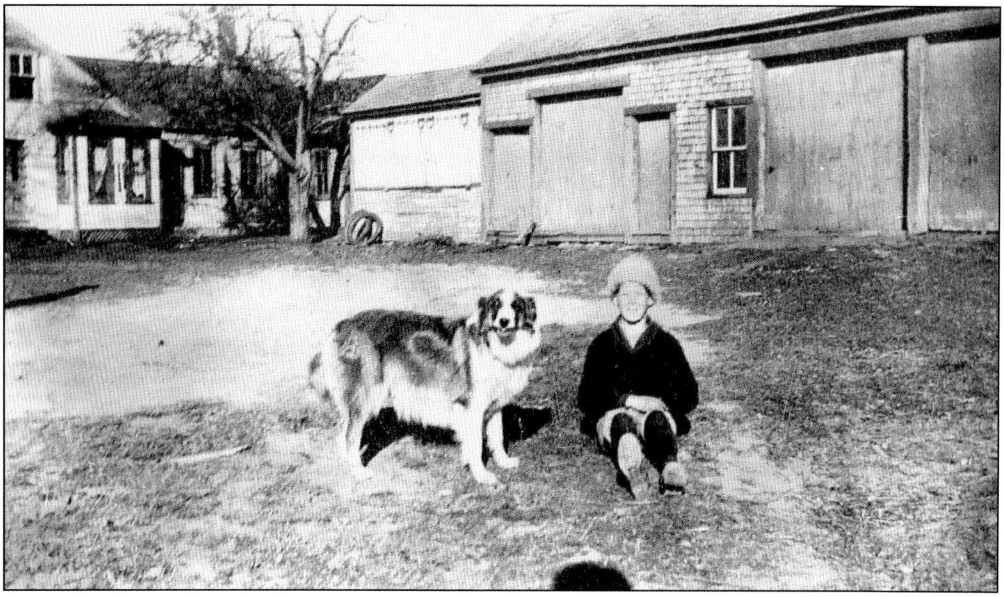

Stuart Fowler and his dog Peggy are pictured in front of the John Bent farmhouse in 1923. This home on Pope's Point Road is believed to have been built in the late 1700s. Bent, active in town affairs, worked in the foundry business. (Courtesy of Patricia Miller.)

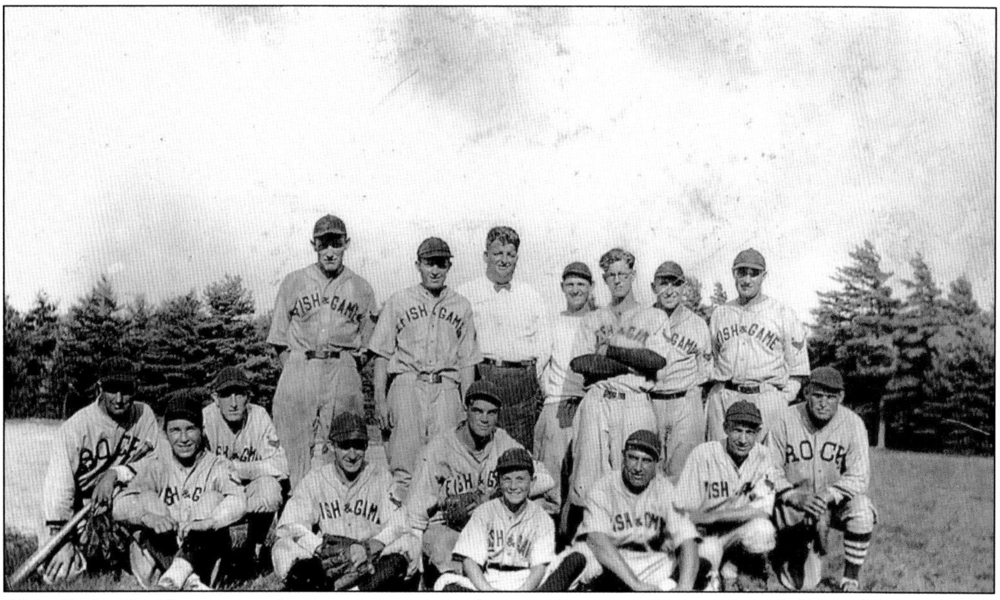

The Fish & Game baseball team poses for a photograph in the 1930s. (Courtesy of Christine Demers.)

Fiilus and Lempi Harju arrived in the United States c. 1903 and moved to Carver in 1910, where they raised a family of four boys and two girls. They acquired cranberry bogs, and the family remains in the cranberry business and owns extensive acreage. (Courtesy of Wilho Harju.)

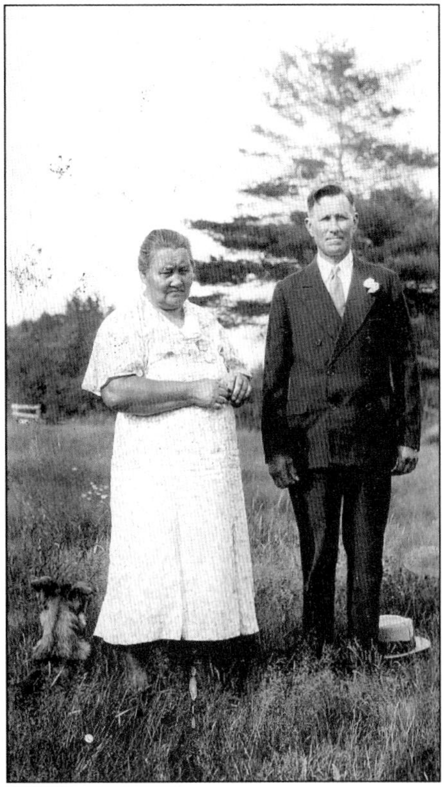

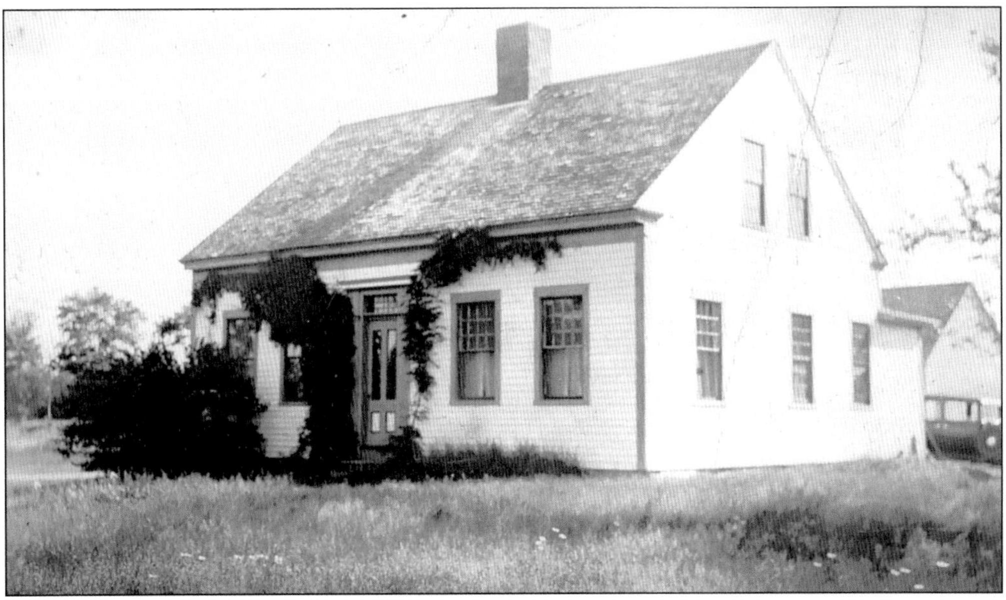

The Harju home, located on Meadow Street in West Carver, was built in 1848 by Atwood Shaw. Fiilus and Lempi Harju purchased the home in 1910 from Clark Finney. The home, which is still owned by the Harjus, has two fireplaces and a beehive oven. (Courtesy of Wilho Harju.)

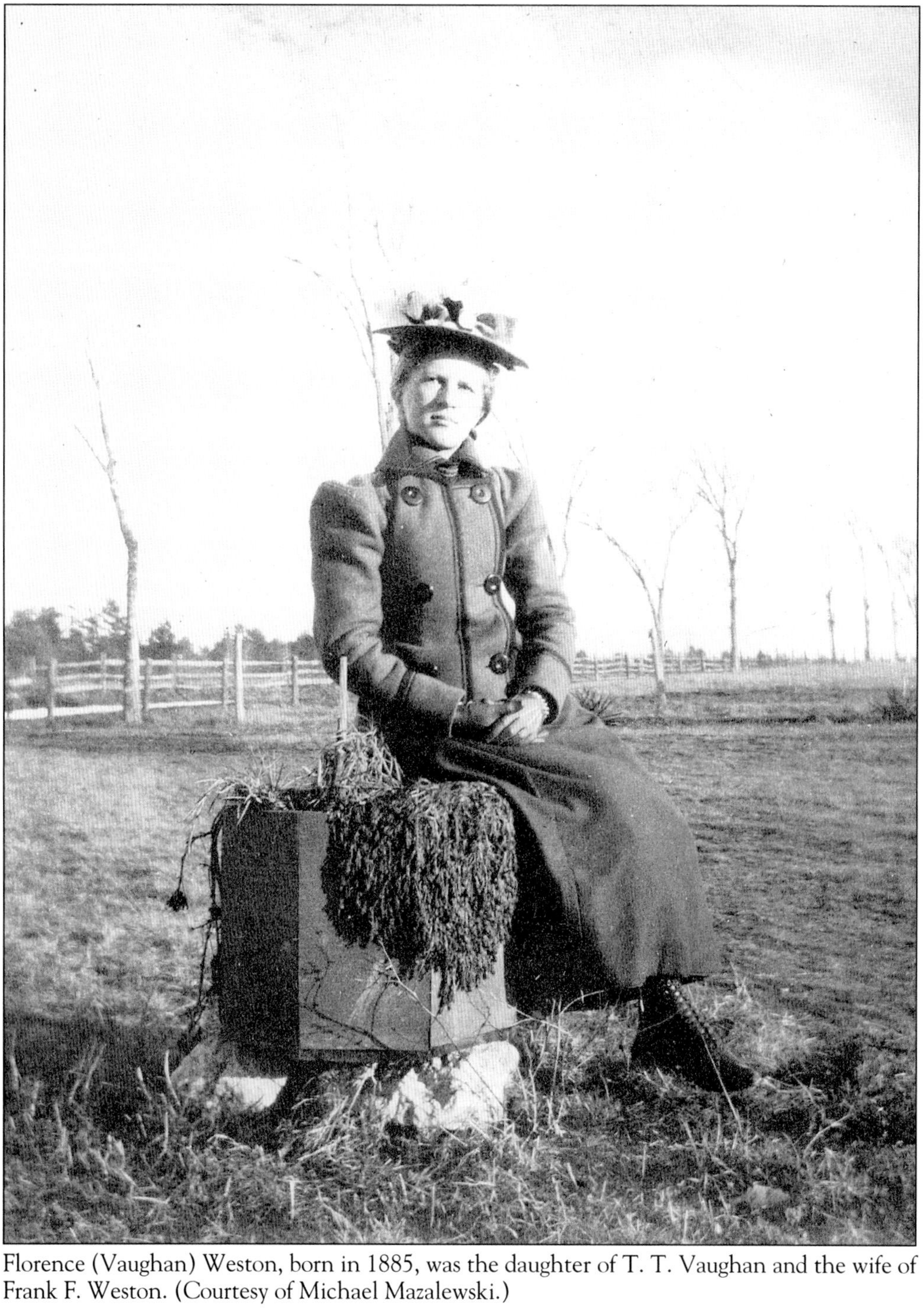

Florence (Vaughan) Weston, born in 1885, was the daughter of T. T. Vaughan and the wife of Frank F. Weston. (Courtesy of Michael Mazalewski.)

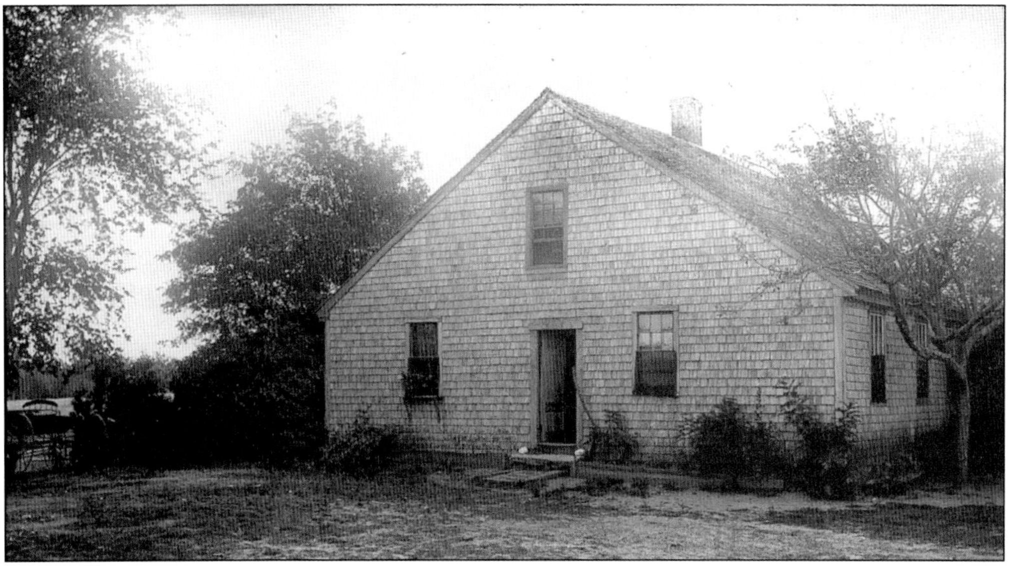

This was originally the home of Nathaniel Shaw, proprietor of the Pope's Point Furnace in the 1730s. A relative, E. Watson Shaw, was the last resident of the West Street house before it was razed.

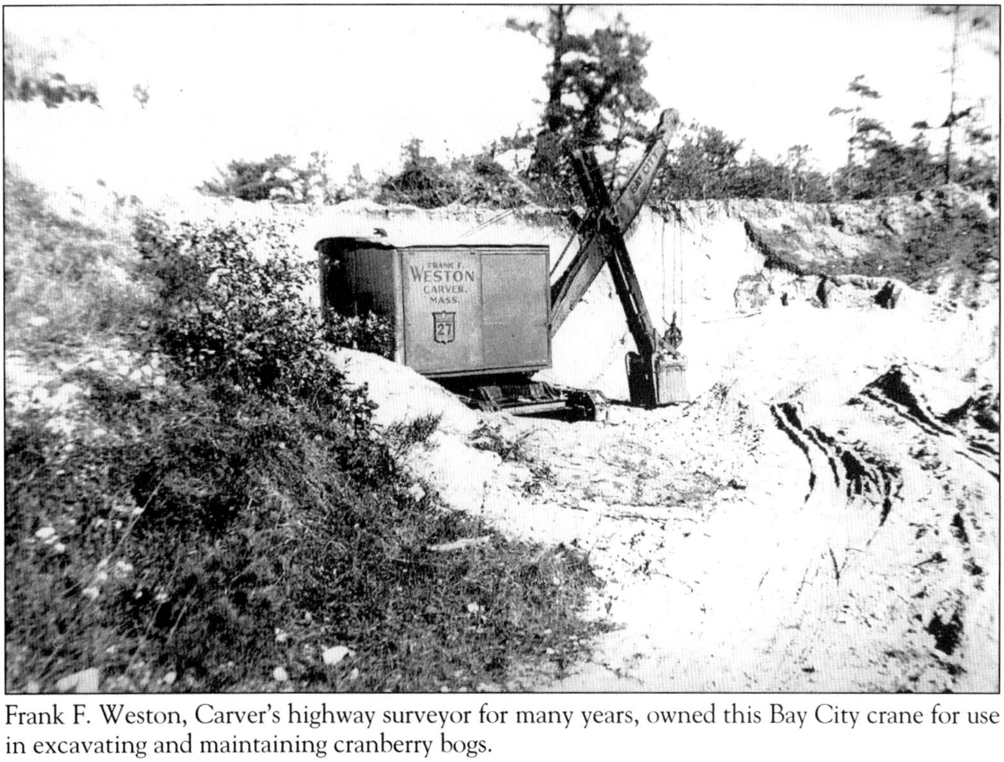

Frank F. Weston, Carver's highway surveyor for many years, owned this Bay City crane for use in excavating and maintaining cranberry bogs.

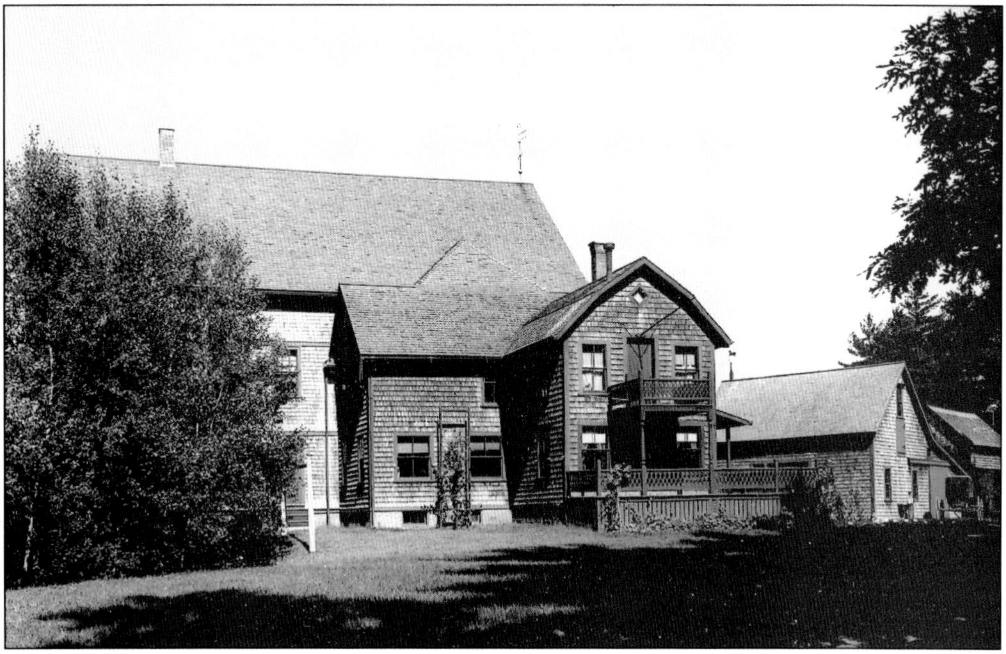

Lucian Fosdick, a Boston businessman, built an elaborate house on Fosdick Road that was primarily used as a summer residence. Each fall, Fosdick held large parties to bring his friends together, and the guests harvested the cranberries on his many acres of bogs. When this home burned, Fosdick built another one for his daughter Laura Thomas in the early 1900s.

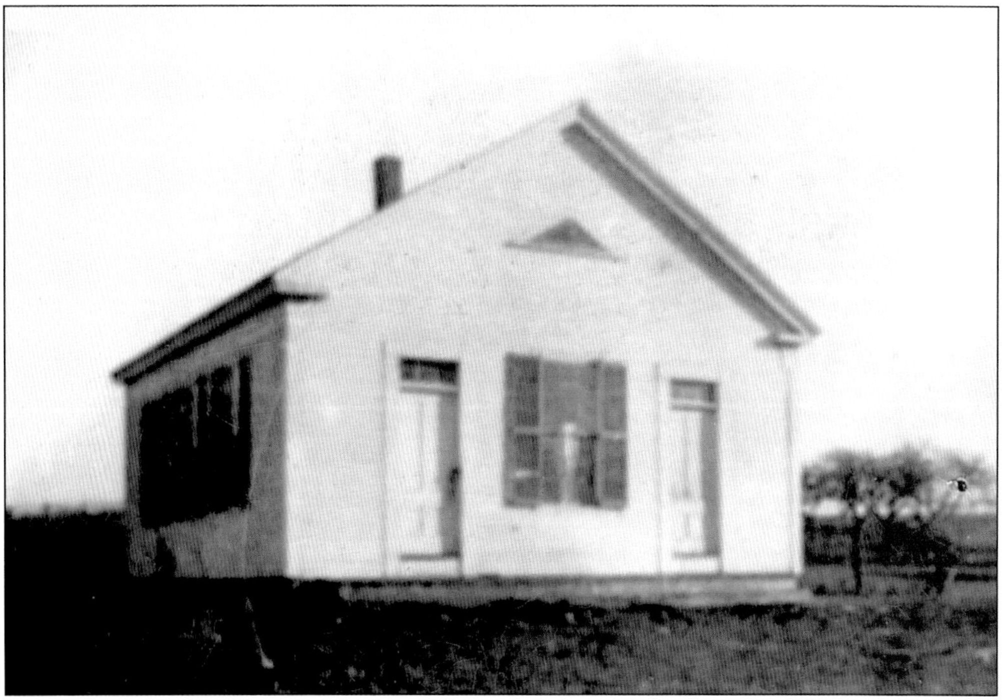

A typical 1800s schoolhouse in Carver consisted of one room with a wood stove in the corner and an outhouse.

Three

Industry

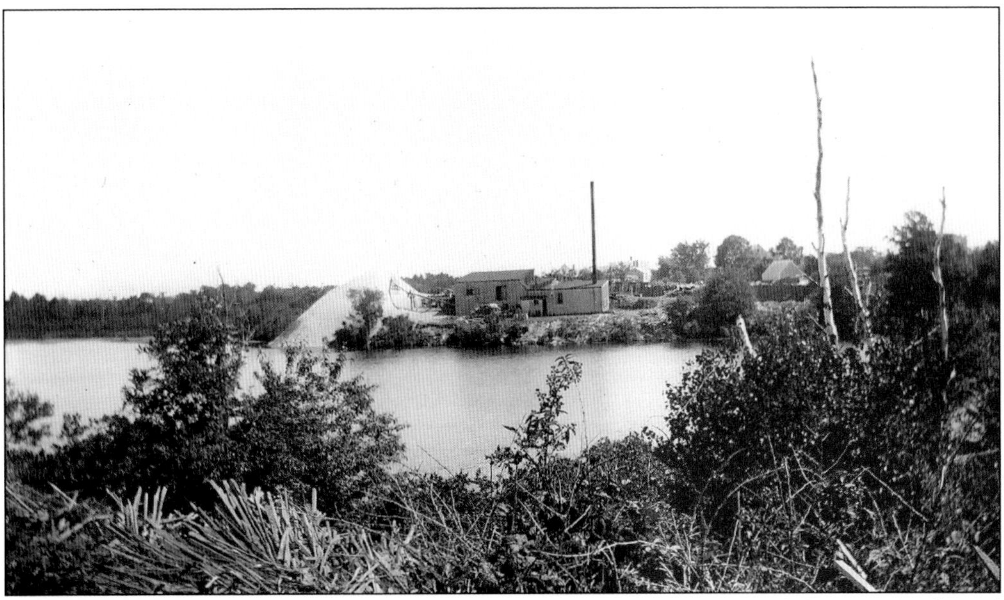

The Cole family established several mills, one of which was an up-and-down sawmill, and produced tacks, barrels, and boxes. The up-and-down sawmill was later replaced by steam power. The cranberry-box mill burned in 1947 in what was described as a "roaring inferno." Following the fire, a smaller cement-block building was built. Wooden cranberry boxes continued to be manufactured there until the arrival of cellophane packaging. (Courtesy of Larry Cole.)

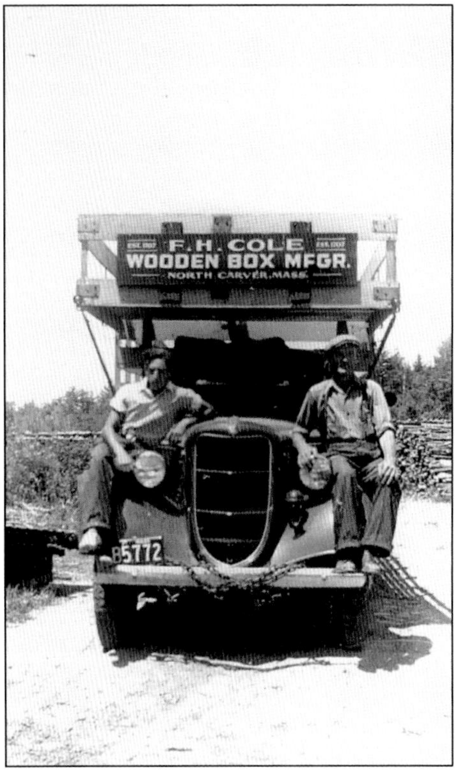

Victor (left) and Everett (right) Collins sit on the Cole's Mill V-8 truck in 1937. (Courtesy of Larry Cole.)

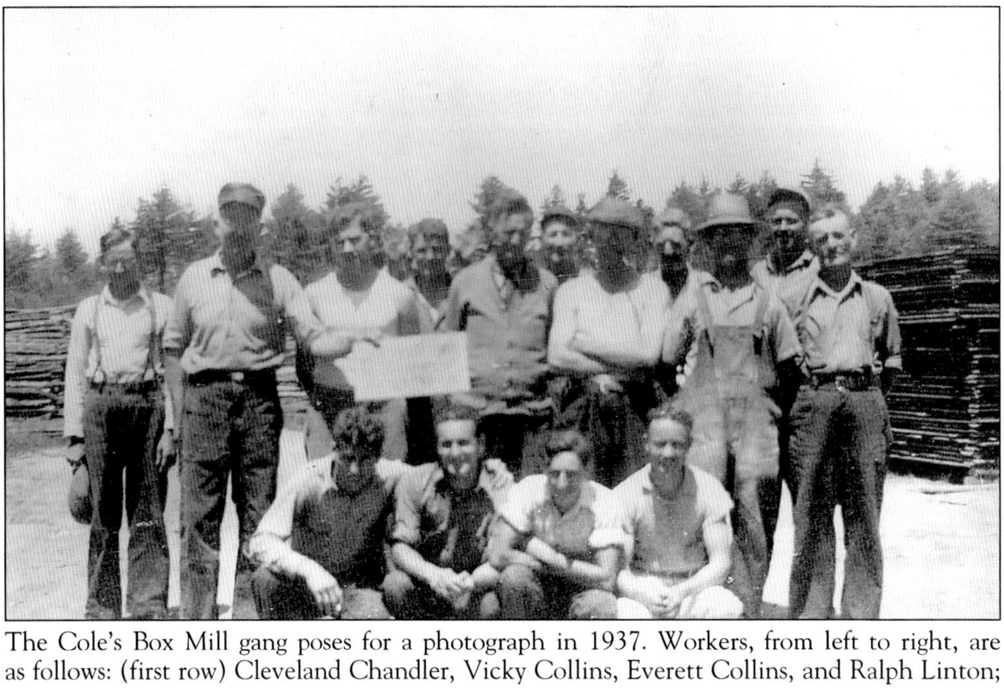

The Cole's Box Mill gang poses for a photograph in 1937. Workers, from left to right, are as follows: (first row) Cleveland Chandler, Vicky Collins, Everett Collins, and Ralph Linton; (second row) Elsworth Braddock, Wilfred Loring, Gordon Garnett, Emerson Chandler, Frank Cole, Charles Miller, Melvin Garnett, Birt Chandler, Gene April with his nephew Gene April, and Victor Collins. (Courtesy of Larry Cole.)

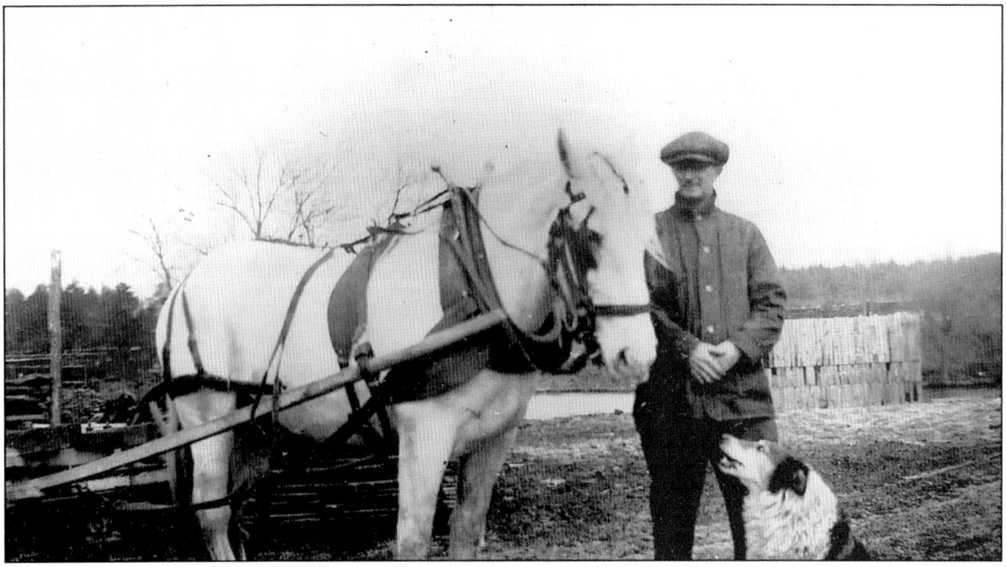

Frank Cole stands with his horse Madam Queen and his dog Beauty in 1937. (Courtesy of Larry Cole.)

T. M. COLE,

Manufacturer of

Boxes, Barrels, Cranberry Crates, etc.

High Street, NO. CARVER, MASS.

An advertisement for T. M. Cole, manufacturer, appears in *The 1902–1903 Resident and Business Directory of Carver, Halifax, Hanson, and Plympton*.

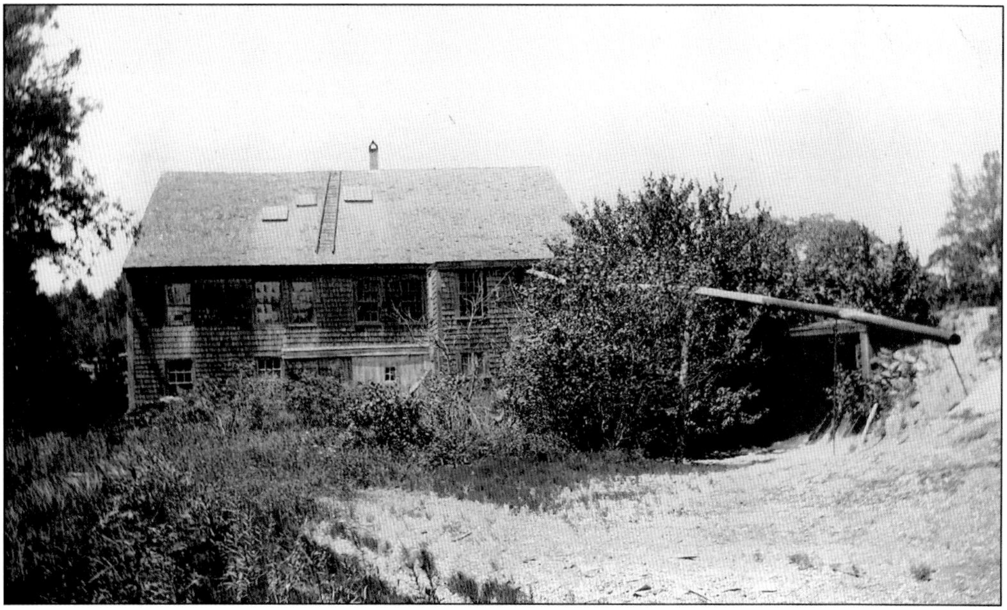

Cole's Mill in North Carver was located on Cole's Mill Pond. The original mill, believed to have been built in 1706 by John Cole, was a gristmill where neighbors of the Coles brought their annual harvests to be ground into meal and flour. As the years went by, the Cole family provided the community with products and services, as well as jobs, all of which contributed to the local economy. (Courtesy of Larry Cole.)

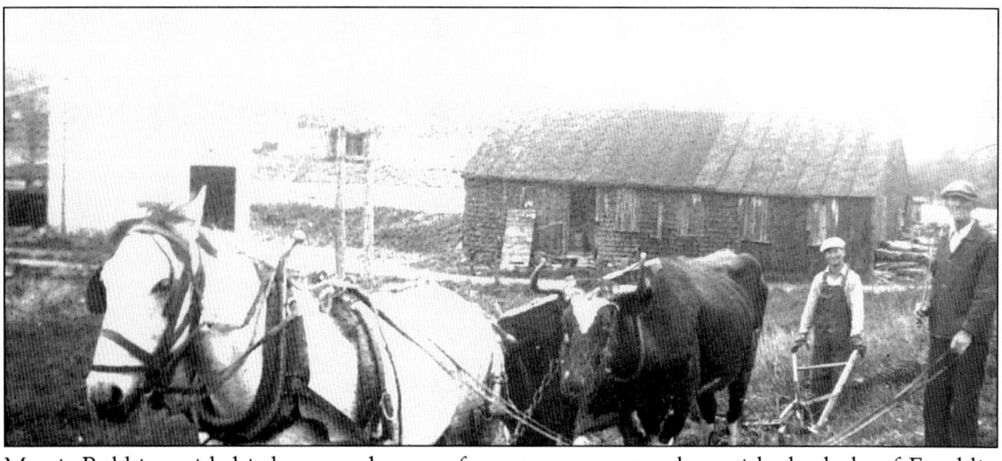

Morris Robbins with his horse and team of oxen prepares to plow with the help of Franklin Wilbur *c*. 1920. (Courtesy of Larry Cole.)

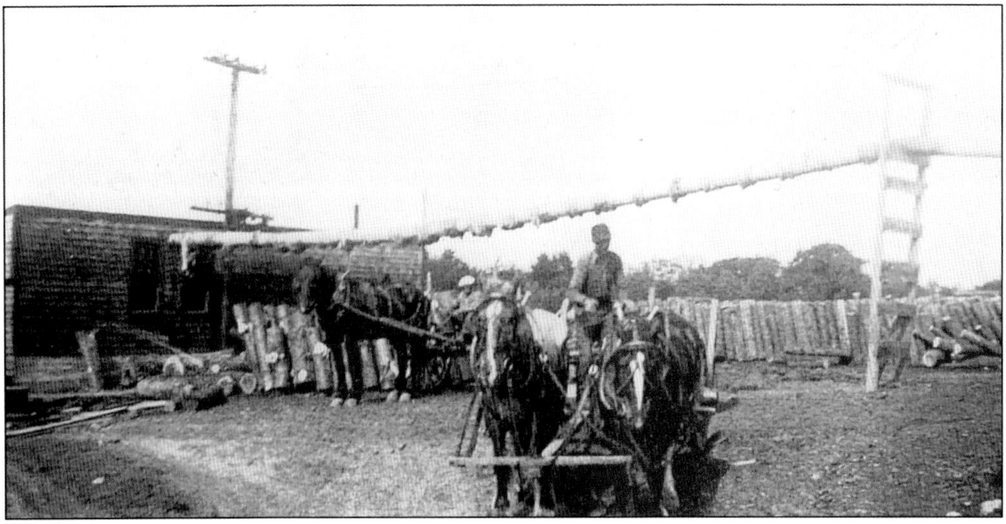

Embert Eames and his father haul logs at Cole's Mill in 1937. (Courtesy of Larry Cole.)

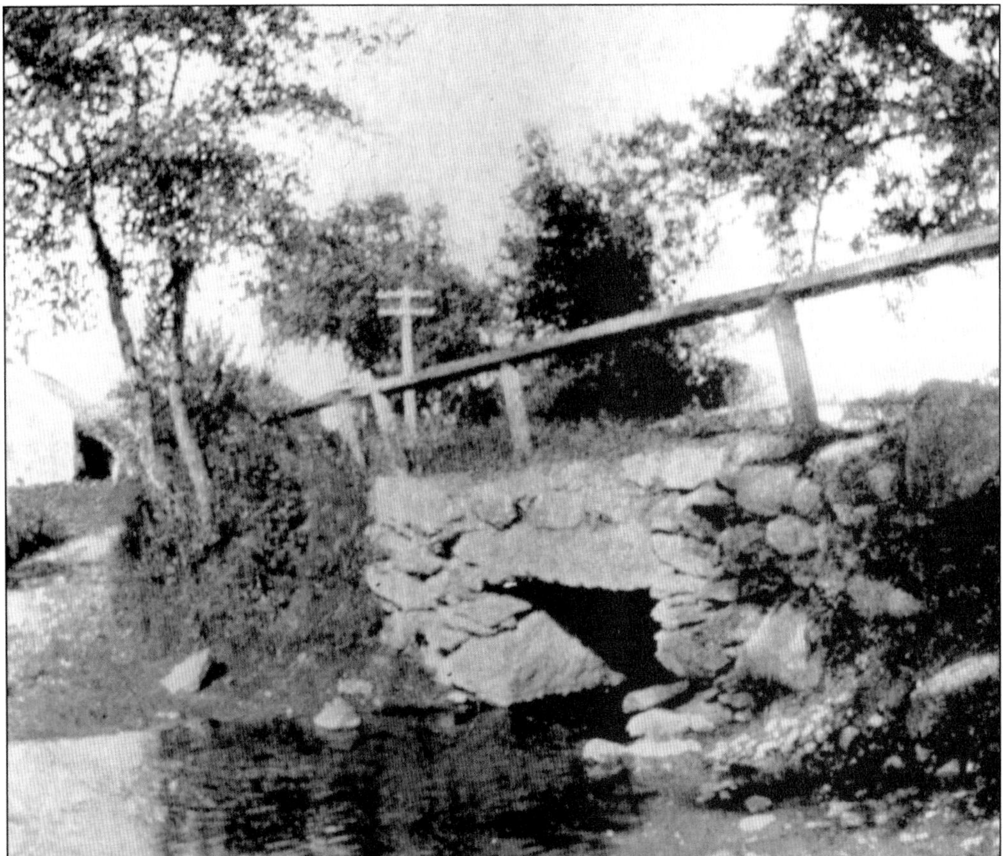

The original Cole gristmill stood beside the mill pond into which the Winatuxet River and Lakenham Brook flowed, less than a mile from this location on Plymouth Street near the Congregational Church.

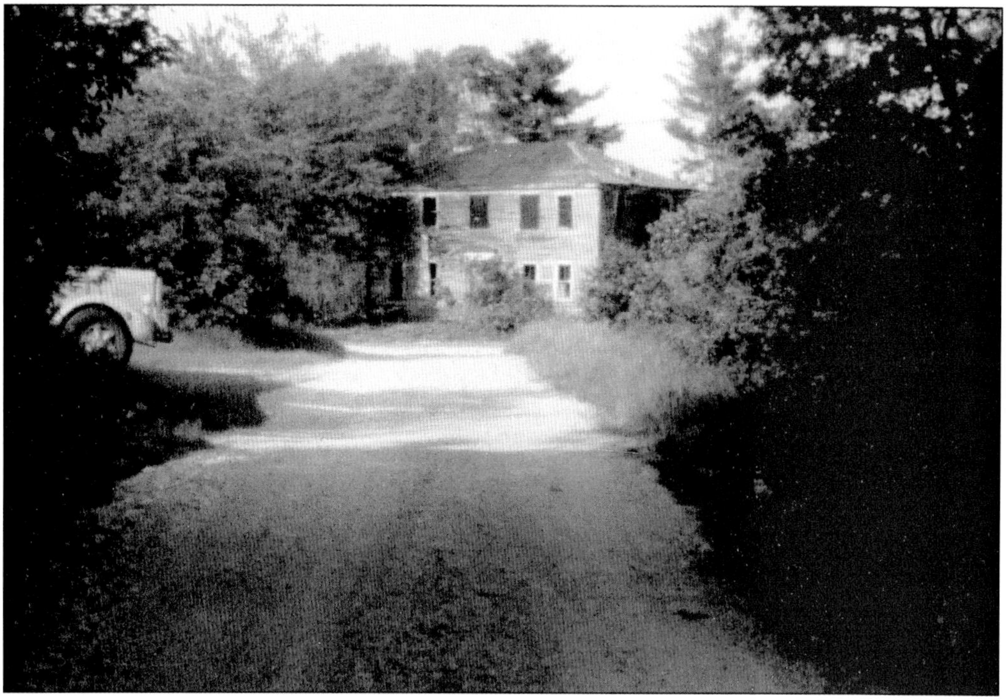

Located on France Street, the boardinghouse for Pope's Point Foundry can be traced back to the mid-1800s but was probably built some time before that since the last blast at Pope's Point Furnace was in 1837. The building was later owned by the Weston family until it was torn down in 1983. (Courtesy of Sandra McDonald.)

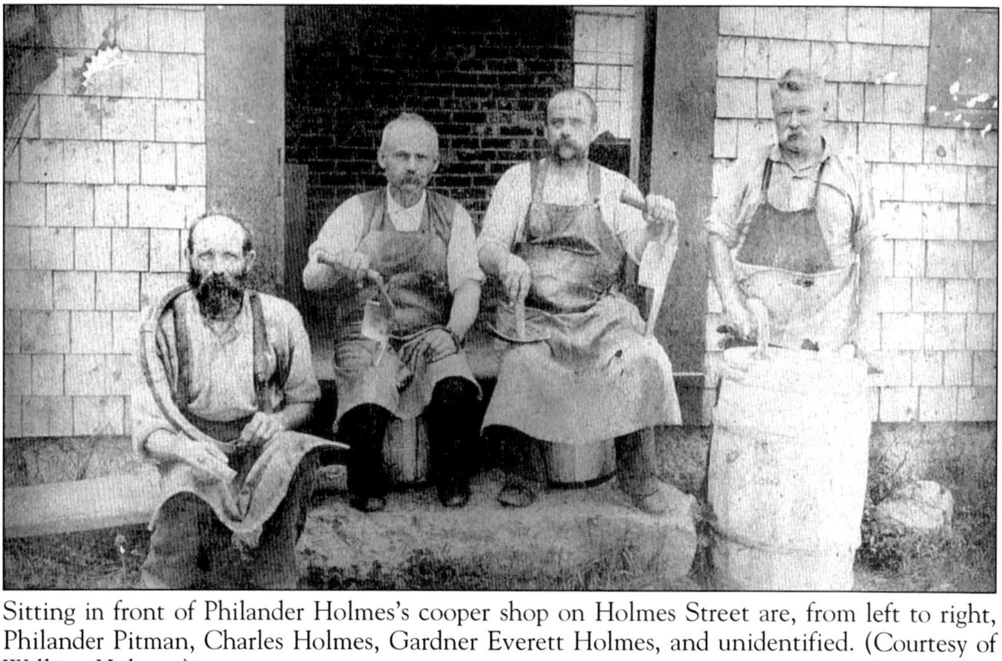

Sitting in front of Philander Holmes's cooper shop on Holmes Street are, from left to right, Philander Pitman, Charles Holmes, Gardner Everett Holmes, and unidentified. (Courtesy of William Holmes.)

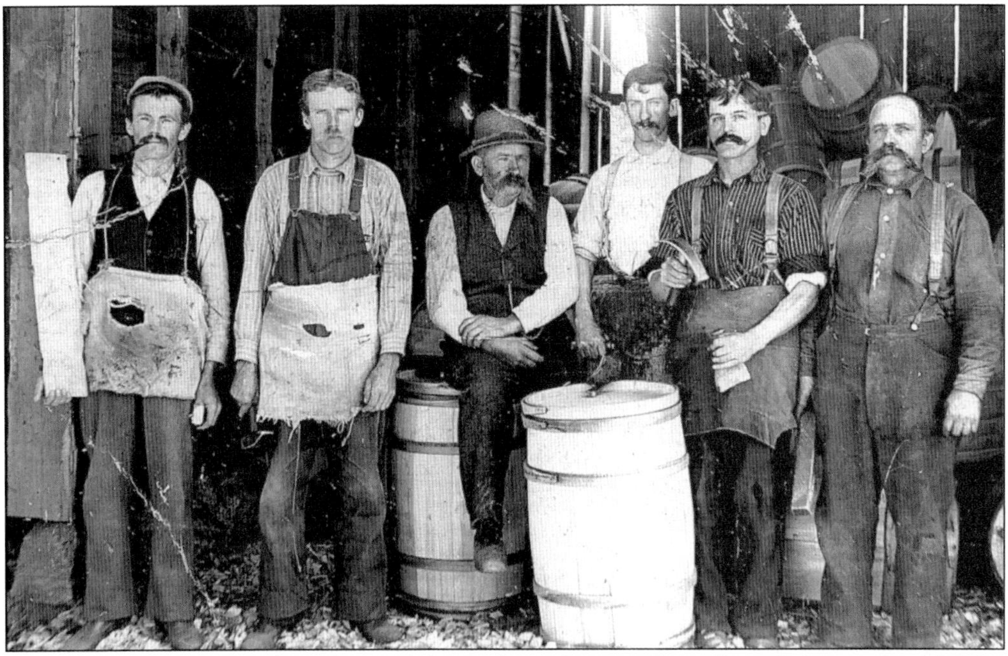

A group of workers stands in front of the Holmes Cooper Shop. From left to right are John Garnier, Madison Jefferson, owner Philander Holmes, Oliver Wood, Cyrus Doty, and Gardner Holmes. (Courtesy of William Holmes.)

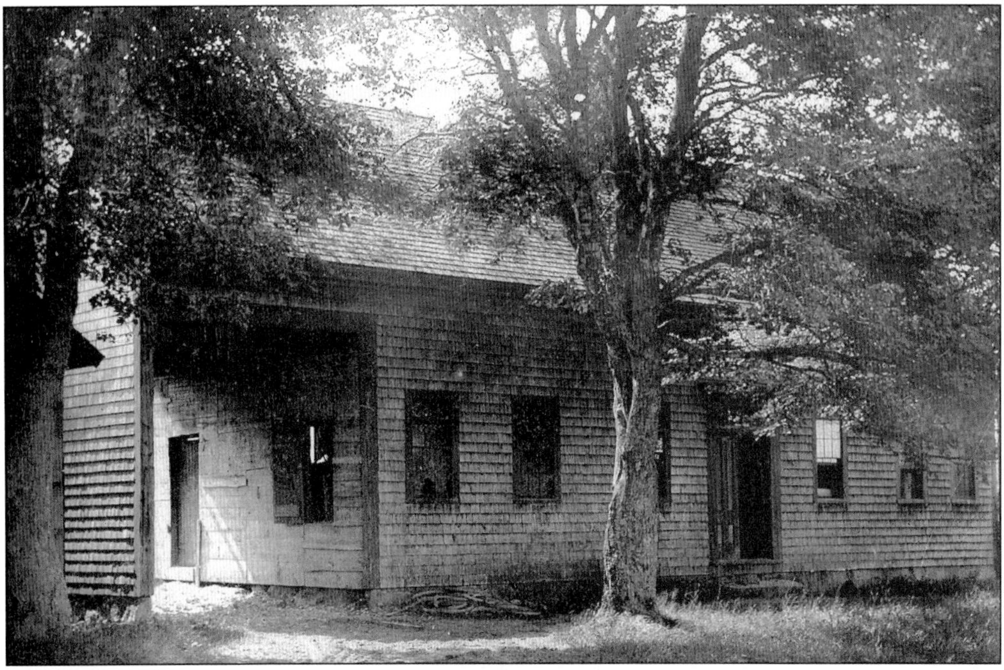

The Holmes Cooper Shop was owned by Philander Holmes, great-uncle to William R. Holmes. Philander was a millwright at the Quitticus Sawmill. Later, he established this shop where barrels were made. Strips of Maine birch trees were bent to make the barrel staves. (Courtesy of William Holmes.)

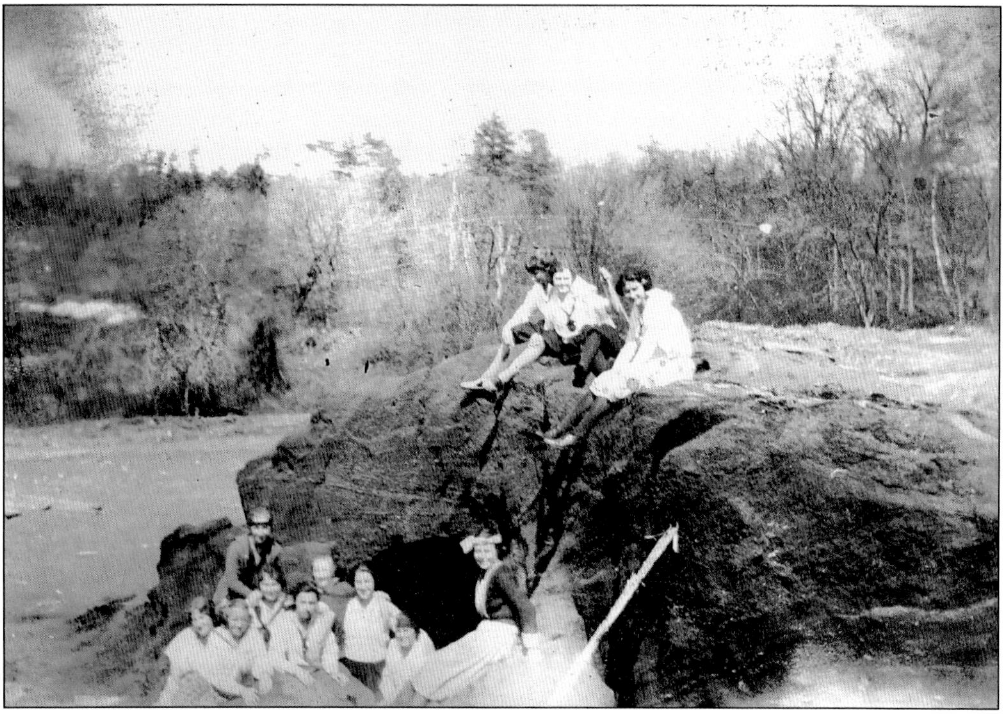

Carver High School girls sit atop a pile of wood shavings behind the Old Center Mill in the early 1920s. The mill was located in the center of town on the site of the present playground. (Courtesy of William Holmes.)

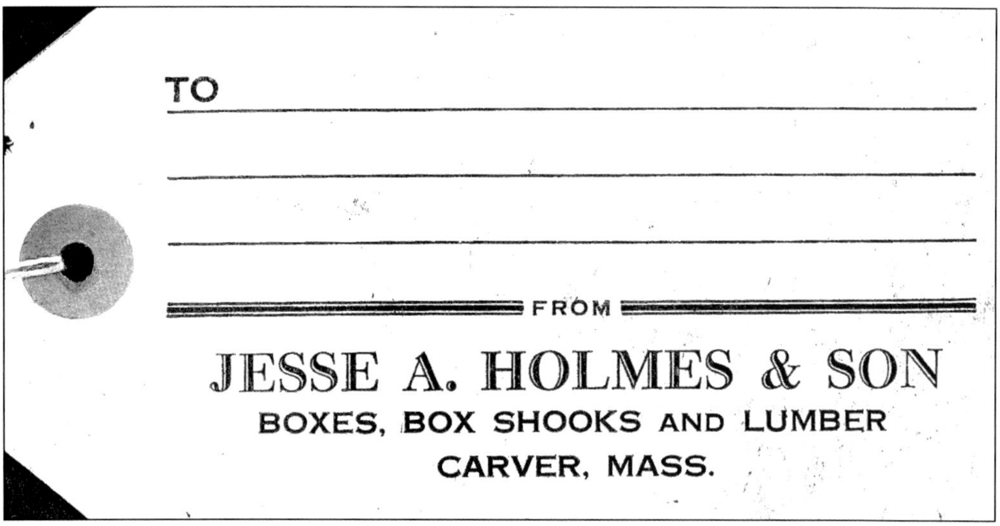

In 1914, Jesse Holmes relocated his business from Holmes Street to the T. T. Vaughan's mill in Center Carver where the town playground is now situated. (Courtesy of Marjorie Mosher.)

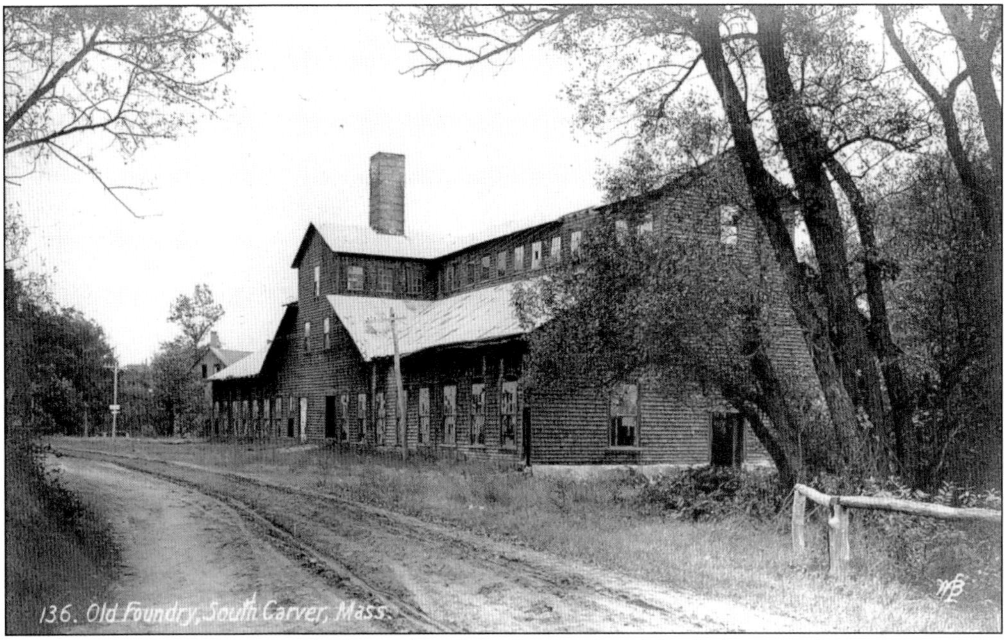

The Charlotte Furnace was built in the 1760s by Bartlett Murdock and other partners. The furnace was located on the southeast side of Tremont Street across from Furnace Pond. Hollowware, which included long-legged kettles, spiders, andirons, and tea kettles, was made at the furnace. During the 1800s, the furnace produced aluminum and iron hollowware, grates, sinks, stable fixtures, and boilers.

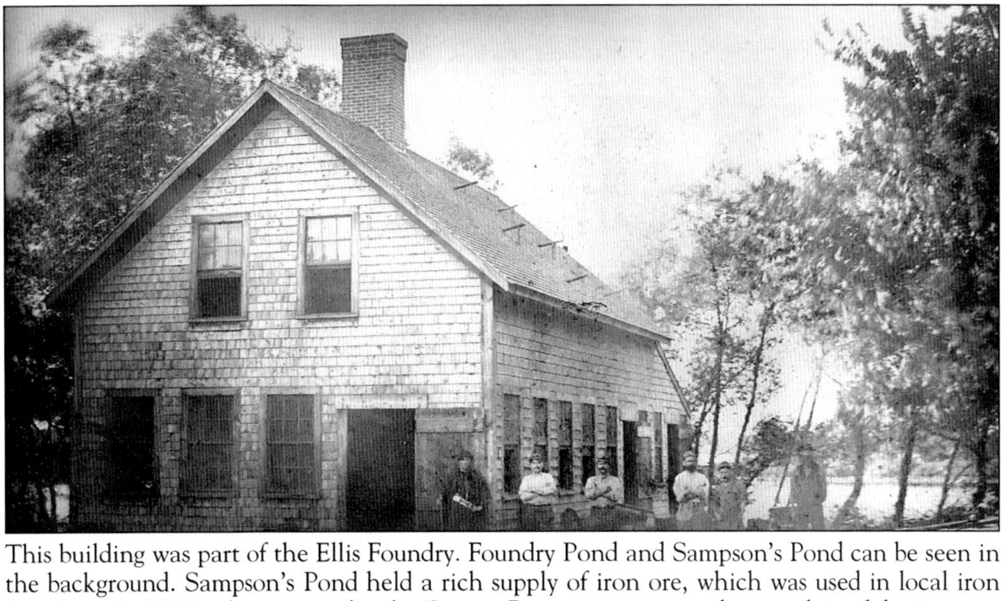

This building was part of the Ellis Foundry. Foundry Pond and Sampson's Pond can be seen in the background. Sampson's Pond held a rich supply of iron ore, which was used in local iron foundries. In 1758, after a court battle, George Barrows was granted ownership of the iron ore on the east side of Sampson's Pond, and Bartlett Murdock was granted ownership of the iron ore on the west side of the pond.

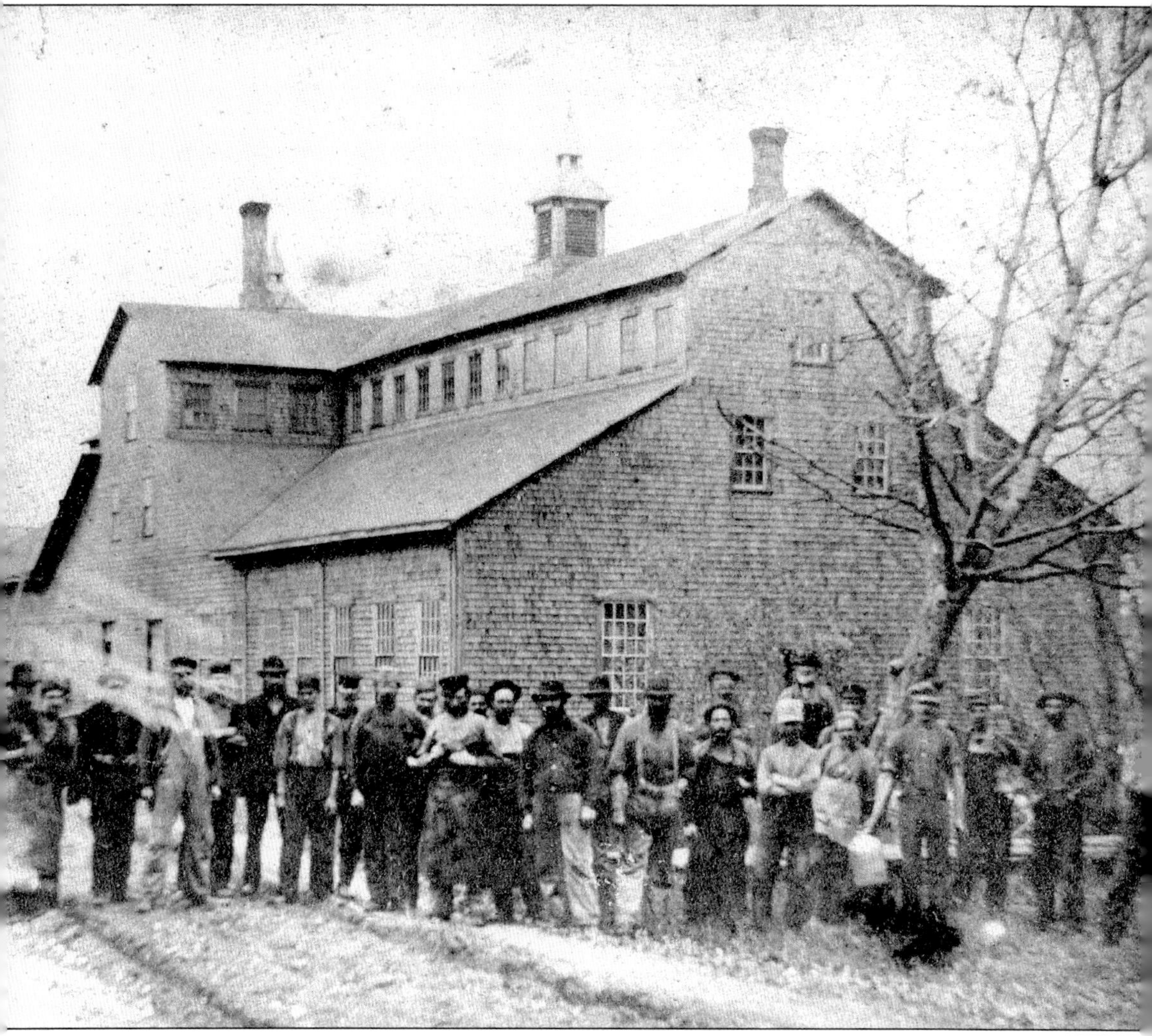

Ellis Foundry workers gather for a photograph in front of the foundry in the 1870s. The Charlotte Furnace had several different owners over the years. Benjamin Ellis, a worker at the Charlotte Furnace, became the owner in 1810. He made his fortune through government ammunition contracts for the War of 1812. Investing wisely, he became even more prosperous by involving sailing vessels in his business, whereby he was able to ship his hollowware products. Active in both town and state government, he was nicknamed "the Cast Iron Senator" because he produced cannonballs for the War of 1812. Jesse Murdock, Benjamin Ellis's son-in-law, was a later owner and prompted the name change to Ellis Foundry. This furnace was the longest running in Carver. The building burned twice, once in 1808 and again in 1872. (Courtesy of Michael Mazalewski.)

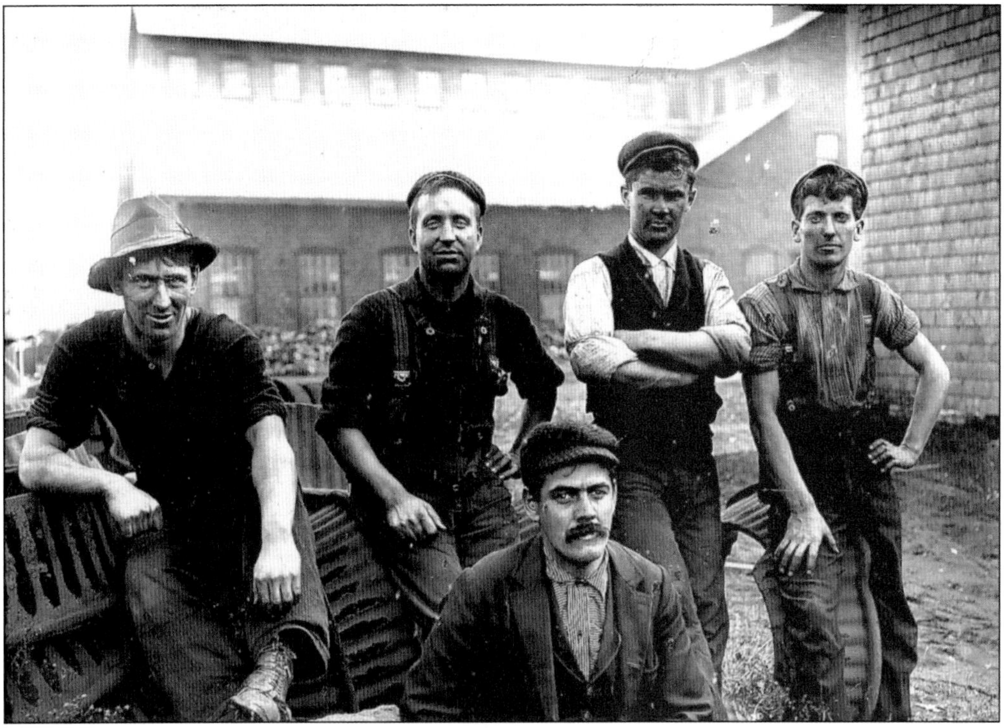

The workers pictured in front of the Ellis Foundry are, from left to right, as follows: (first row) John Andrews; (second row) Bill Hart, J. Lees, Al Bailey, and Frank Harp.

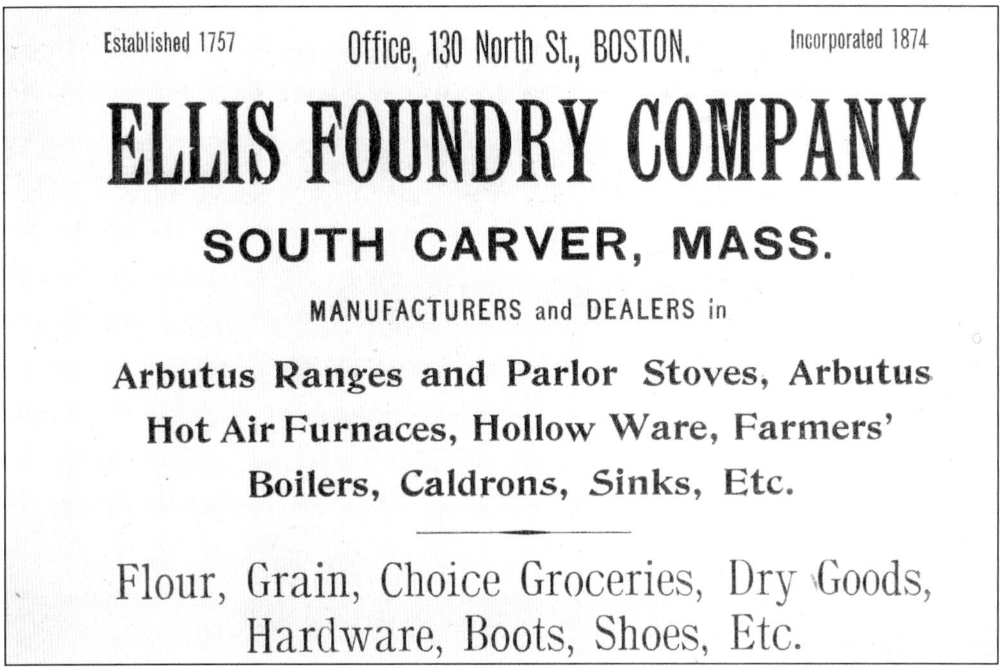

An advertisement for the Ellis Foundry Company appeared in *The 1902–1903 Resident and Business Directory of Carver, Halifax, Hanson, and Plympton*.

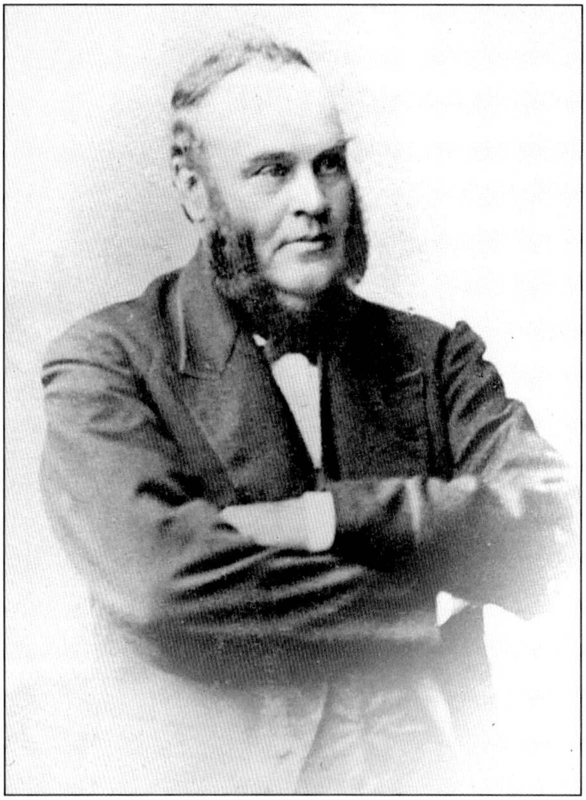

Jesse Murdock was born in Carver in 1806. He was involved in the iron foundry at an early age, becoming a partner of Benjamin Ellis in 1827. He married Ellis's daughter in 1840 and retired from the foundry business in 1863. Active in town and state affairs, he also had an interest in the Murdock Parlor and Grate Company, which he held until his death in 1875.

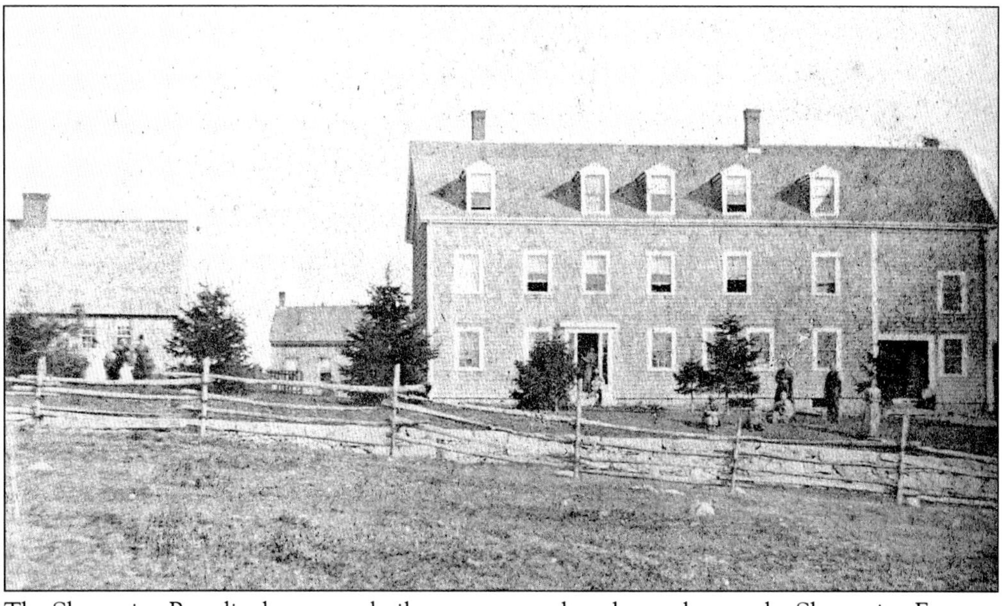

The Shoestring Boardinghouse was built to accommodate the workers at the Shoestring Factory. The boarders came from southeastern Massachusetts and Nova Scotia. Many of the girls married local men. The boardinghouse was remodeled and used for cranberry workers after the factory burned down in 1880. The boardinghouse burned in the mid-1930s, when a boarder accidentally knocked over an oil lamp.

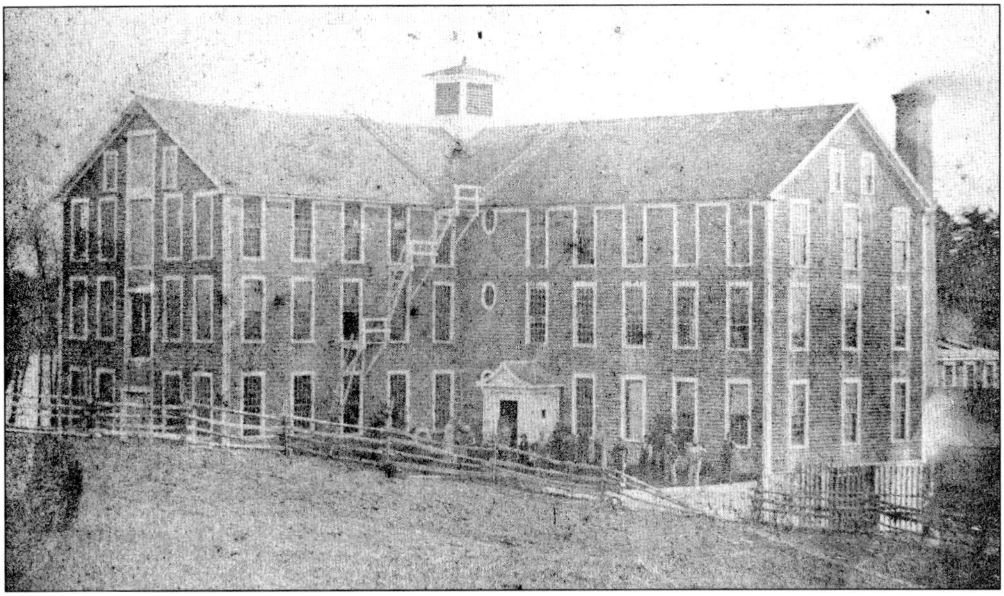

The William F. Jenkins & Company Shoestring Factory, established in 1852, manufactured cotton goods, including shoestrings, cord, braid, and the material that covered whalebone and steel-hooped skirts. The factory was located off Tremont Street opposite Mayflower Road and burned in 1880.

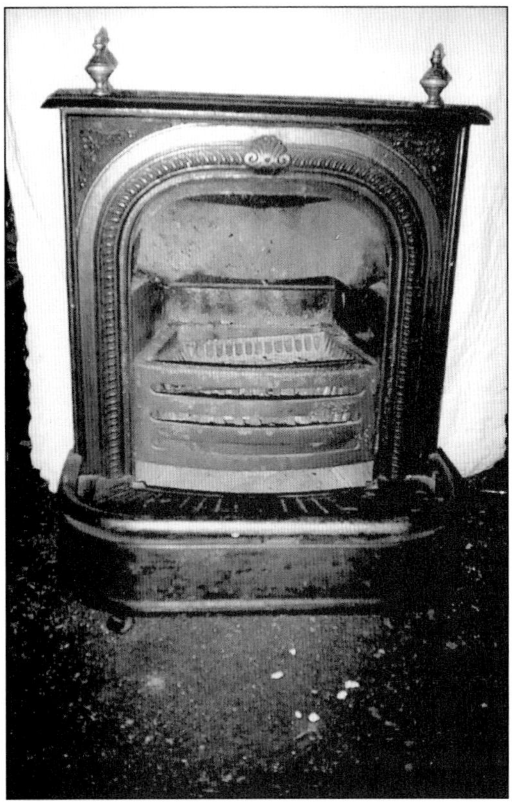

This stove bears the name of the Murdock Parlor and Grate Company, which began in South Carver in 1853. Thomas Griffith, Jesse Murdock, and George Bent were partners in the original grate manufacturing company named Bent, Griffith & Company. The business grew after the Civil War, and in 1877, the company was incorporated as the Murdock Parlor and Grate Company. A fire destroyed the plant in 1885, and the business was moved to Middleborough. (Courtesy of Carol L. Bostock.)

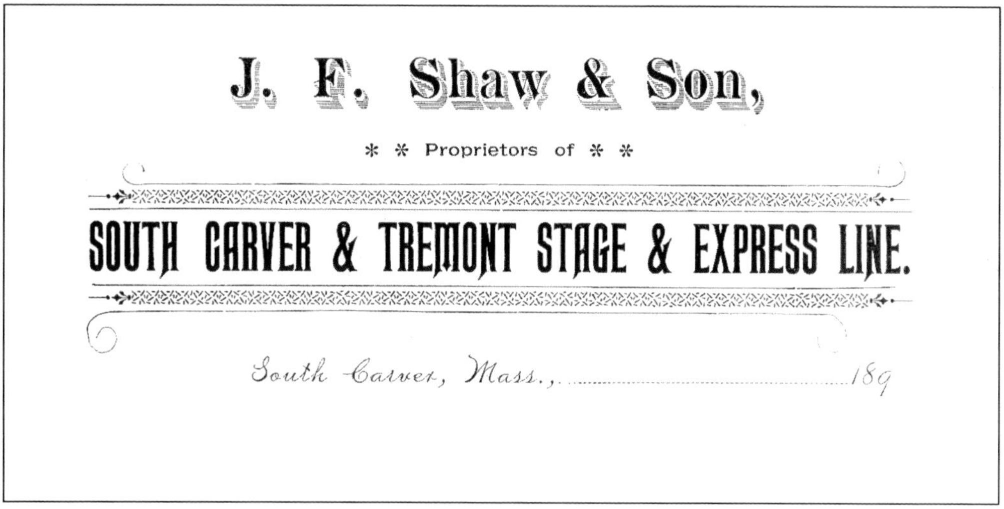

J. F. Shaw & Son,

* * Proprietors of * *

SOUTH CARVER & TREMONT STAGE & EXPRESS LINE.

South Carver, Mass., ...189

Shown here is a letterhead from the J. F. Shaw teaming business.

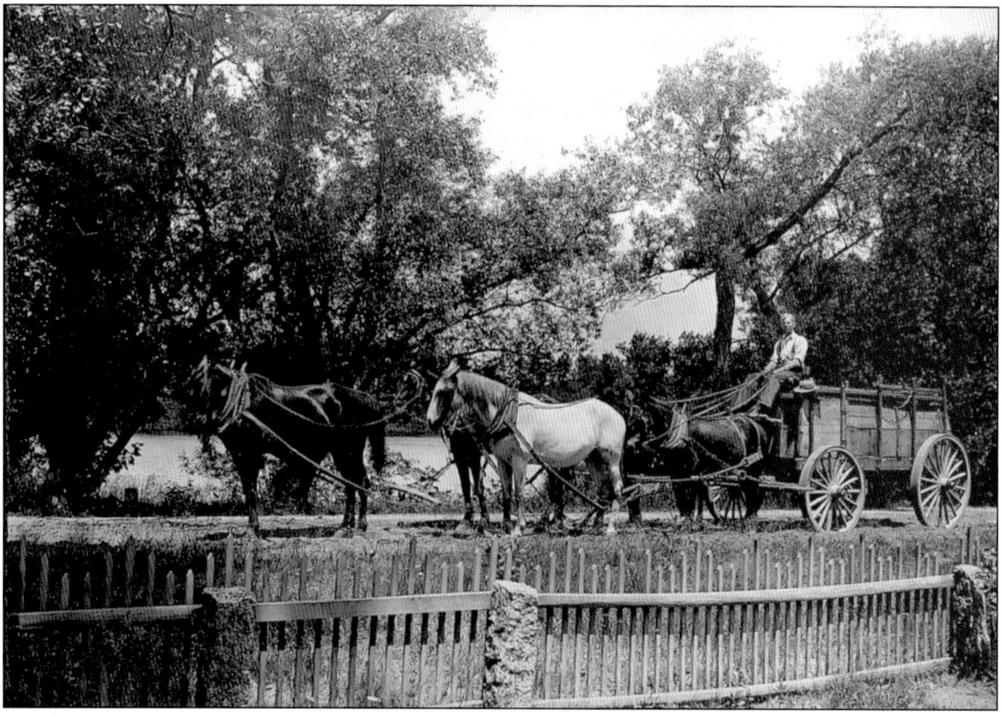

Employing wagon-and-horse teams, the J. F. Shaw & Son Trucking Company moved manufactured goods from the Ellis Foundry to the Tremont Train Depot in West Wareham.

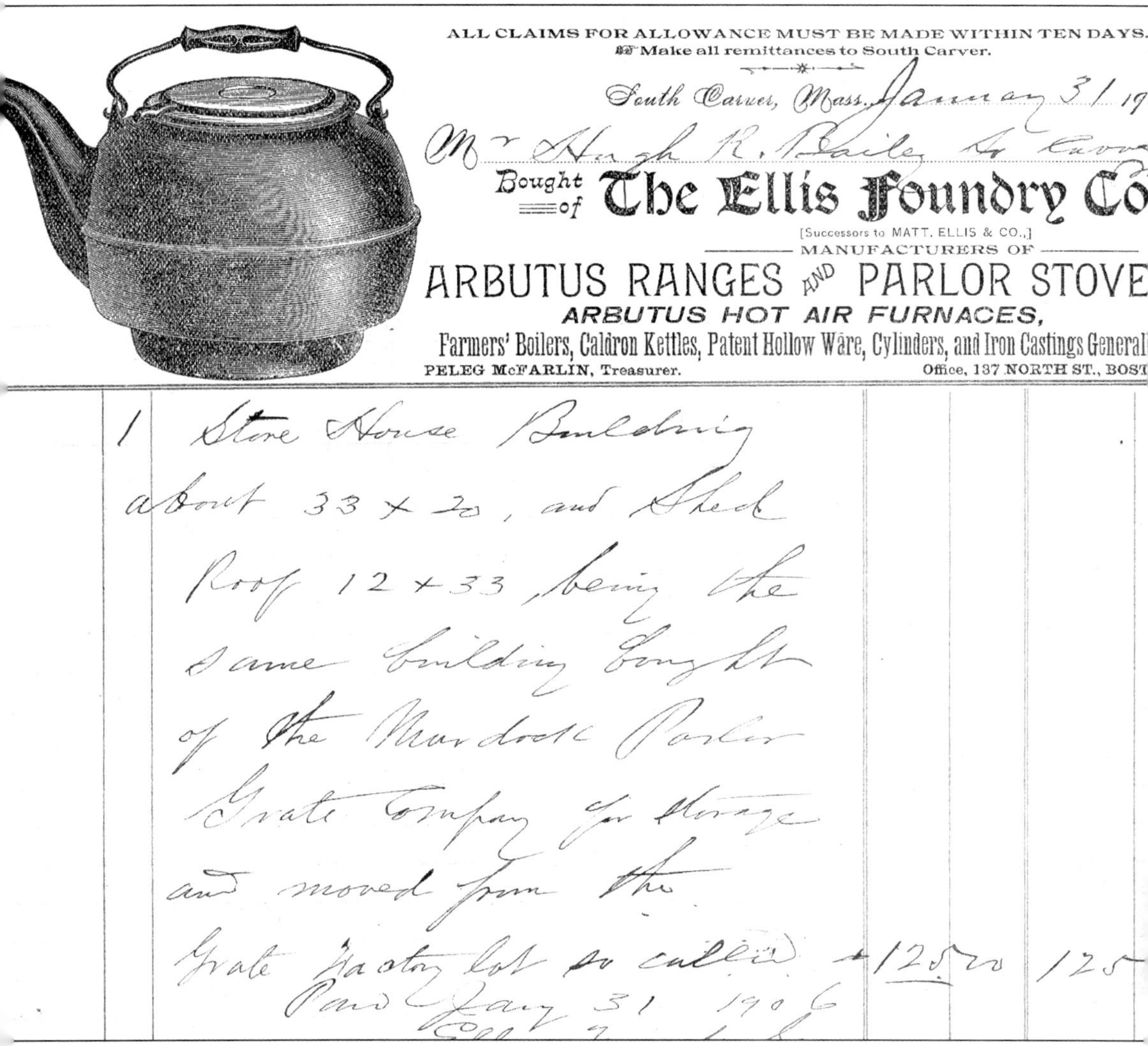

ALL CLAIMS FOR ALLOWANCE MUST BE MADE WITHIN TEN DAYS.
Make all remittances to South Carver.

South Carver, Mass., January 31 19

Mr Hugh R. Bailey So Carver

Bought of The Ellis Foundry Co

[Successors to MATT. ELLIS & CO.,]
MANUFACTURERS OF
ARBUTUS RANGES AND PARLOR STOVE
ARBUTUS HOT AIR FURNACES,
Farmers' Boilers, Caldron Kettles, Patent Hollow Ware, Cylinders, and Iron Castings General
PELEG McFARLIN, Treasurer. Office, 137 NORTH ST., BOST

1	Store House Building about 33 x 20, and Shed Roof 12 x 33, being the same building bought of the Murdock Parlor Grate Company for storage and moved from the Grate Factory lot so called	125.00	125
	Paid Jany 31 1906		

The Ellis Foundry Company issued a bill of sale on January 31, 1906, to H. R. Bailey for a stone house building in the amount of $125. The bill states that the structure is "the same building bought of the Murdock Parlor Grate Co. for storage and moved from the Grate Factory lot so called." This building became H. R. Bailey's blacksmith shop.

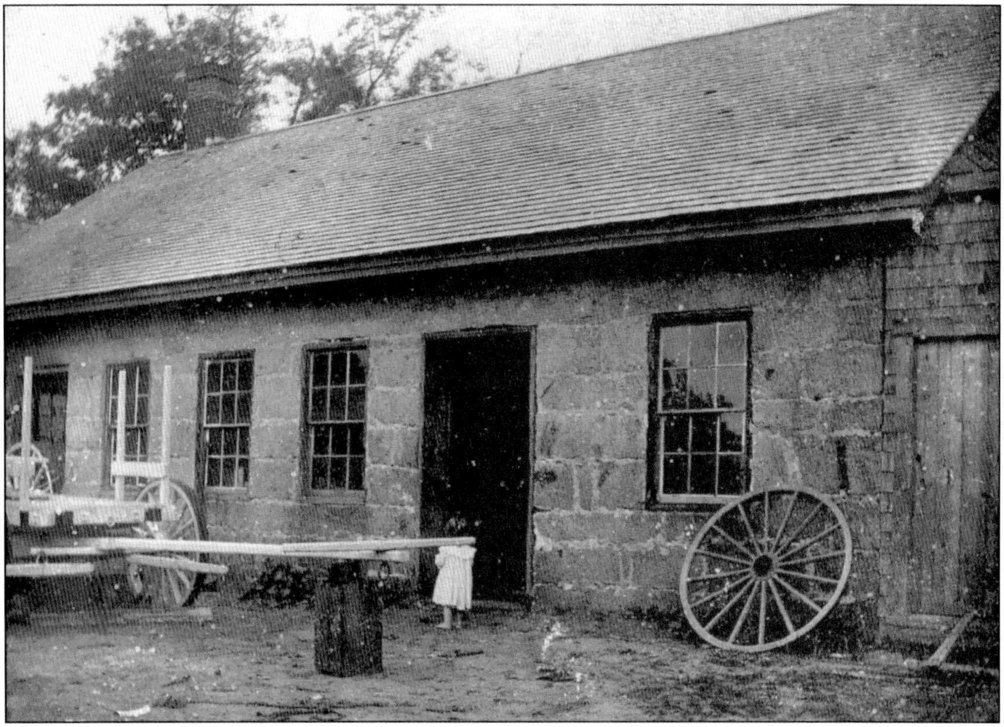

H. R. Bailey's blacksmith shop was made from stone that originally came from the Charlotte Furnace. The Murdock Parlor & Grate Company used this building before it was forced to relocate to Middleborough when the other buildings in the plant were destroyed by fire.

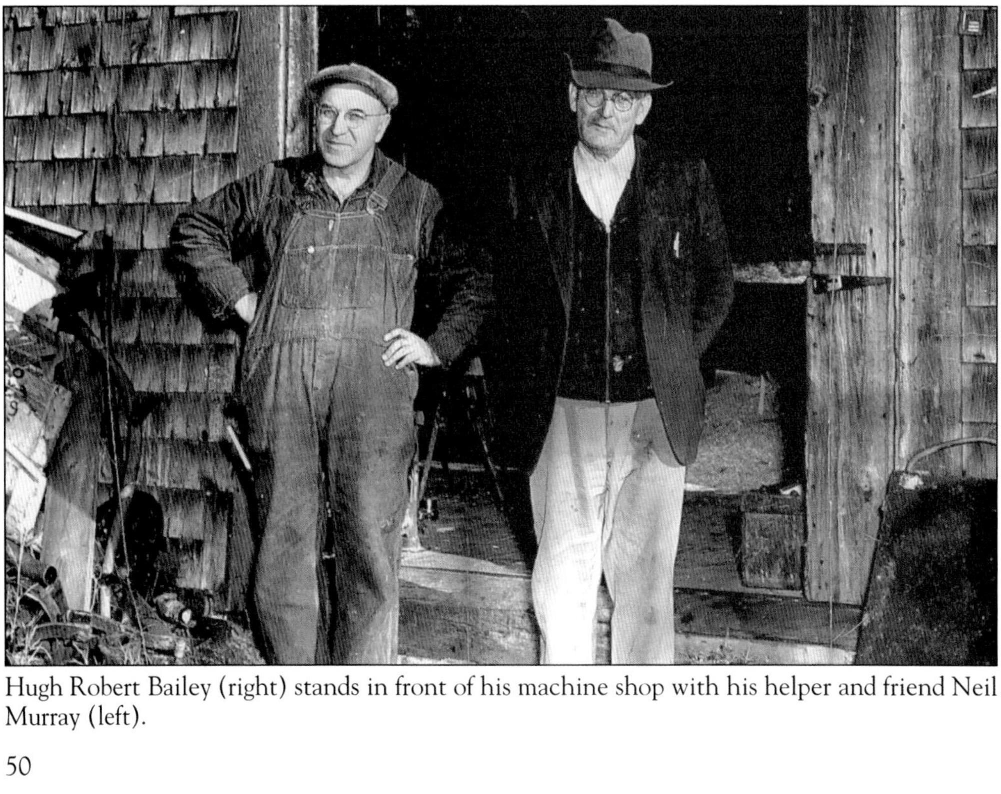

Hugh Robert Bailey (right) stands in front of his machine shop with his helper and friend Neil Murray (left).

Four

Center Carver

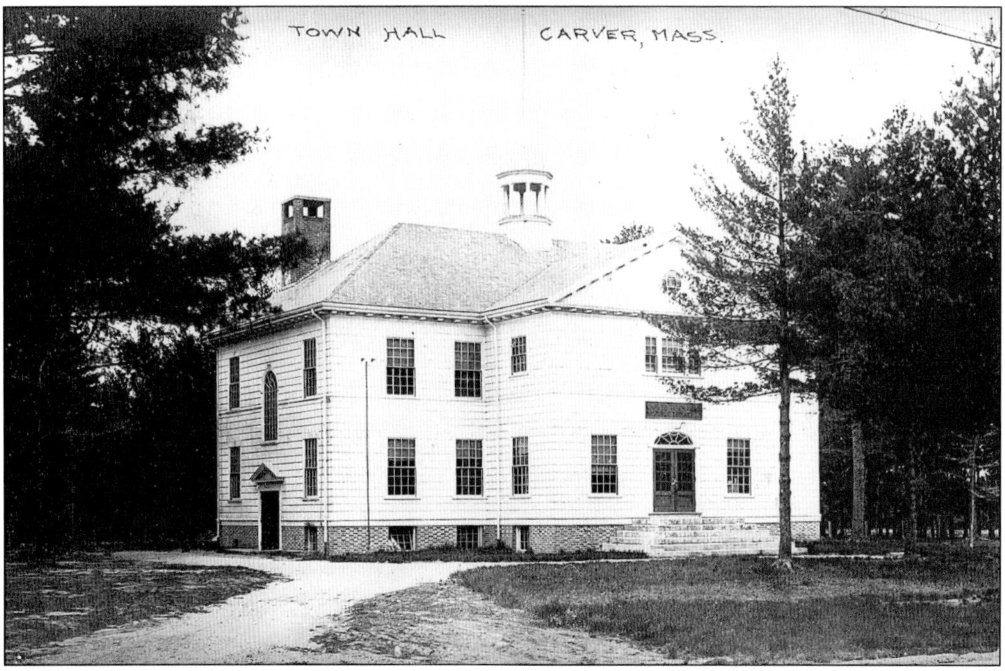

The Carver Town Hall was completed when the cupola was added in 1915. Offices and the public library occupied the first floor; a large hall with a stage on the second floor was used for public gatherings, including school graduations and public dances. The library remained in the town hall until the early 1970s, when a library building was constructed.

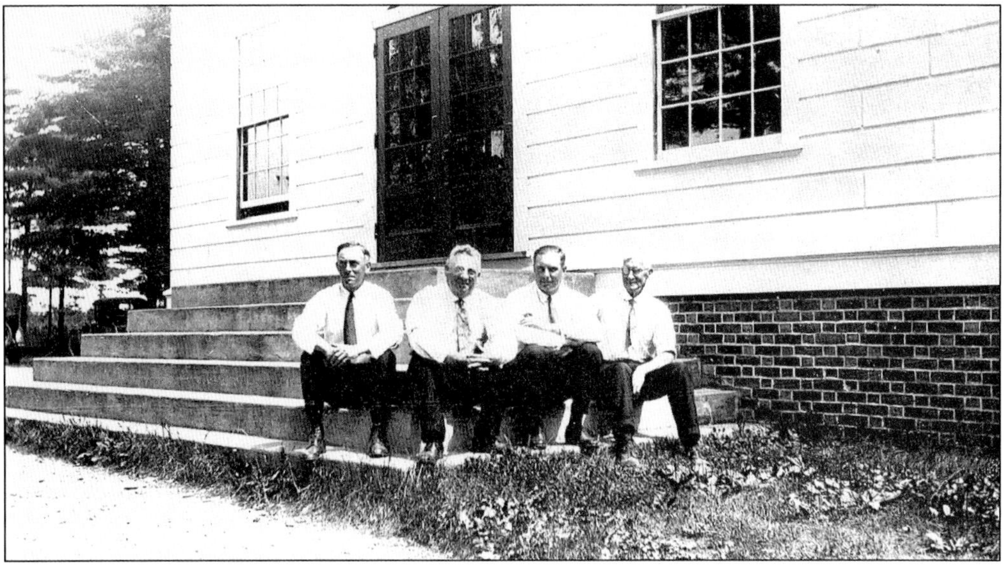

This photograph was taken on the steps of the town hall in 1924. From left to right are Bernard Shaw, Kenneth Shaw, Charles Taylor, and Henry Griffith, who was both town clerk and town treasurer.

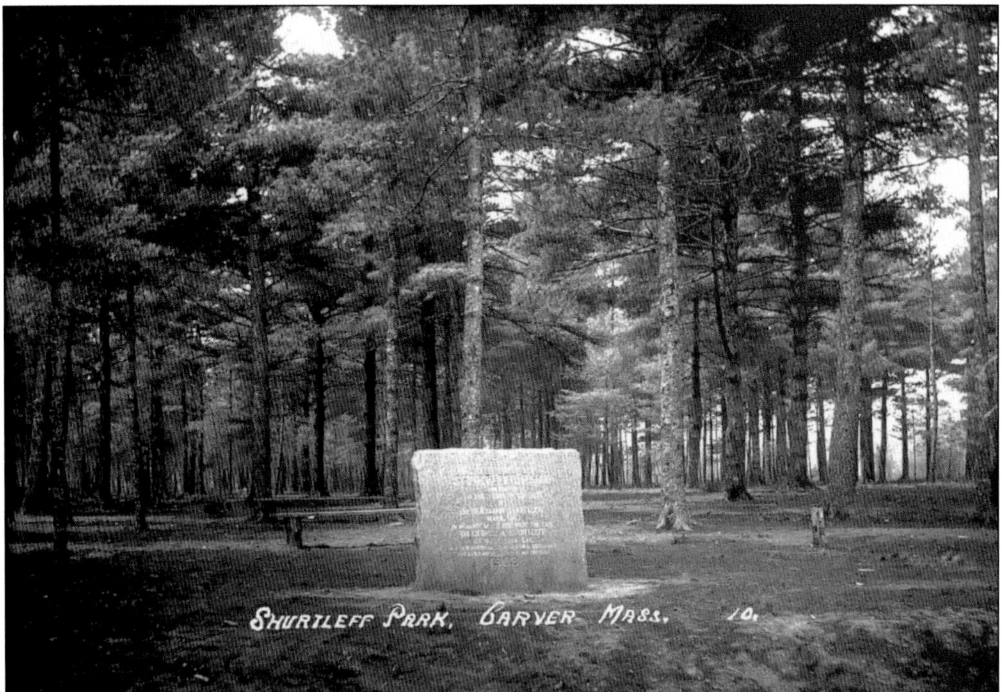

In 1908, Dr. Benjamin Shurtleff donated the land that is now Shurtleff Park to the town. The land originally belonged to the Shurtleff family estate. Shurtleff Park is used as a public park and is also the site for the annual Old Home Day celebrations.

The Soldiers Monument was dedicated in 1910 in memory of the Carver men who fought in the Revolutionary War, the Civil War, the War of 1812, and the Spanish War. Capt. William McFarlin presided at the unveiling of the statue. The monument was funded through the efforts of the Carver Women's Relief Organization led by Jane Barrows.

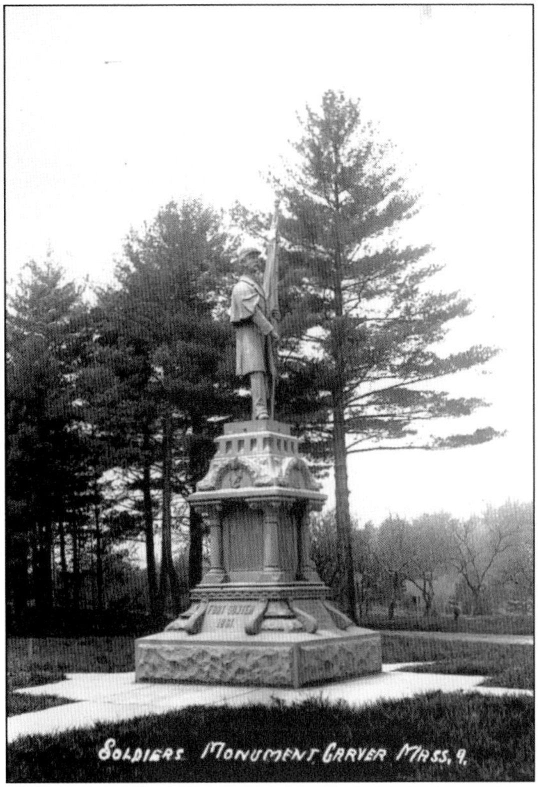

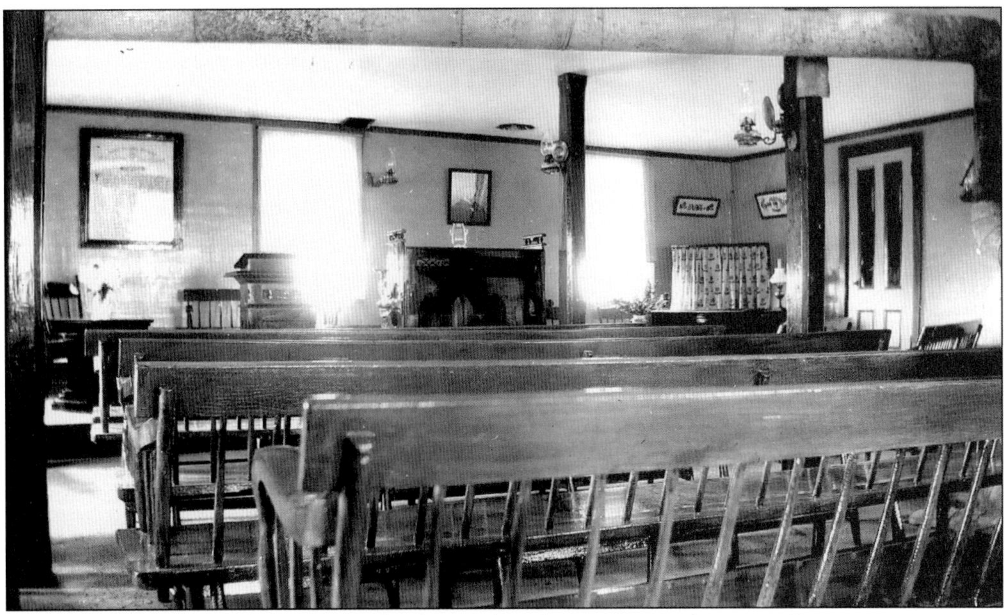

This is believed to be the interior of either a church or a meetinghouse in Carver.

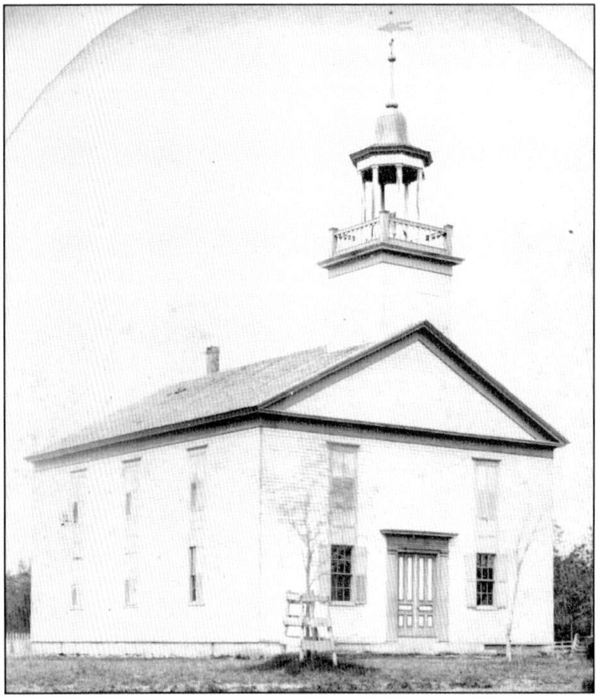

The Baptist church of Carver was built in 1824 although the Baptist Society was founded in 1791. Baptists used the South Meeting House and the Spruce Street Meeting House in South Middleborough before the church in Center Carver was built. The church has had several additions, and in 1970, it became the United Parish of Carver. (Courtesy of Marjorie Mosher.)

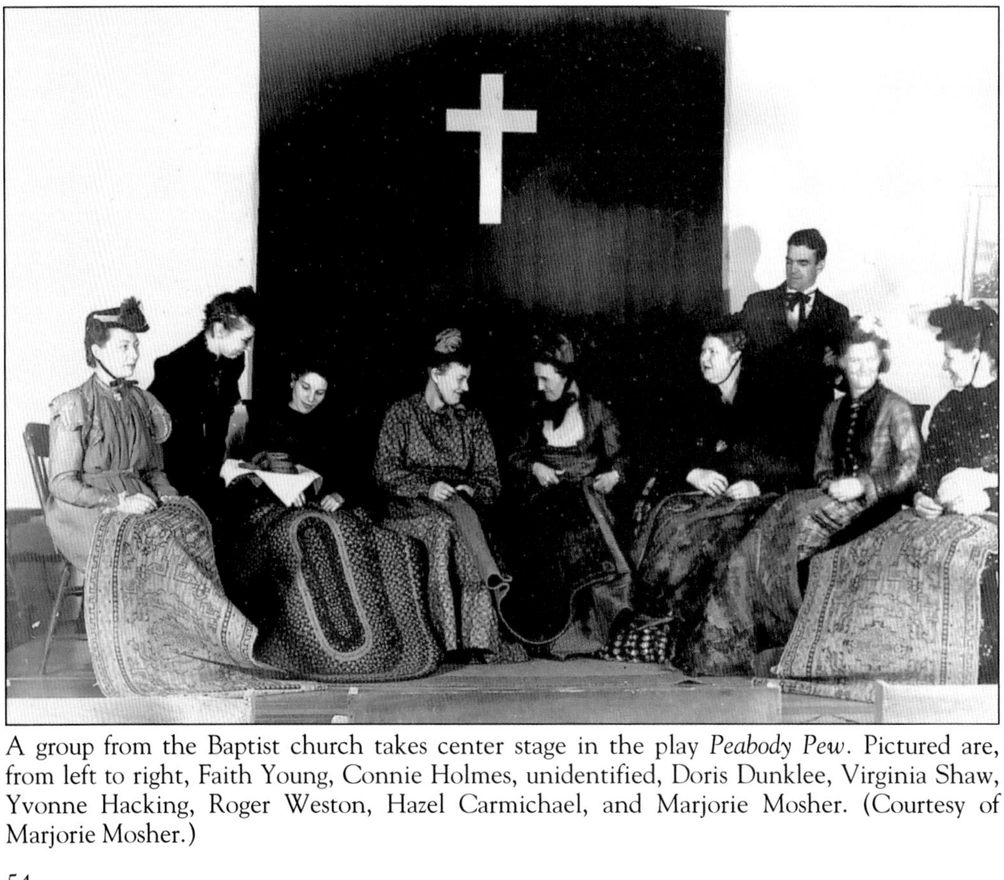

A group from the Baptist church takes center stage in the play *Peabody Pew*. Pictured are, from left to right, Faith Young, Connie Holmes, unidentified, Doris Dunklee, Virginia Shaw, Yvonne Hacking, Roger Weston, Hazel Carmichael, and Marjorie Mosher. (Courtesy of Marjorie Mosher.)

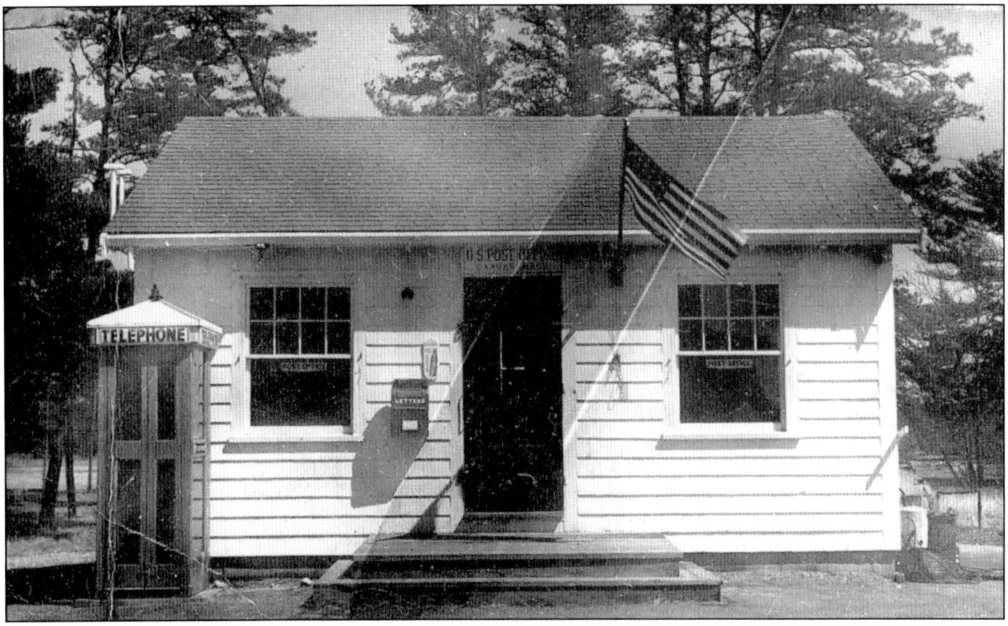

The Center Carver Post Office on Main Street was located across from the Baptist church on a piece of property that was just north of the parsonage. Orrie Dempsey, who lived next-door in the former parsonage was the postmistress for 23 years. (Courtesy of Marjorie Mosher.)

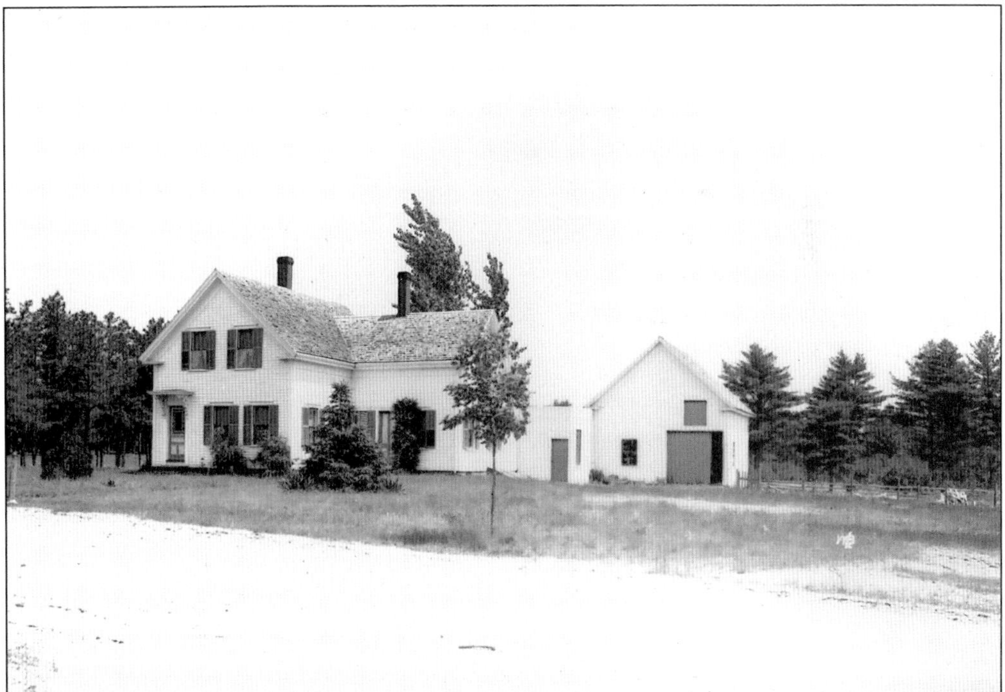

The Baptist parsonage, built in 1906, replaced an earlier structure that had burned. The home served as a parsonage for the Baptist church across the street until 1932, when it was sold to the Dempsey family.

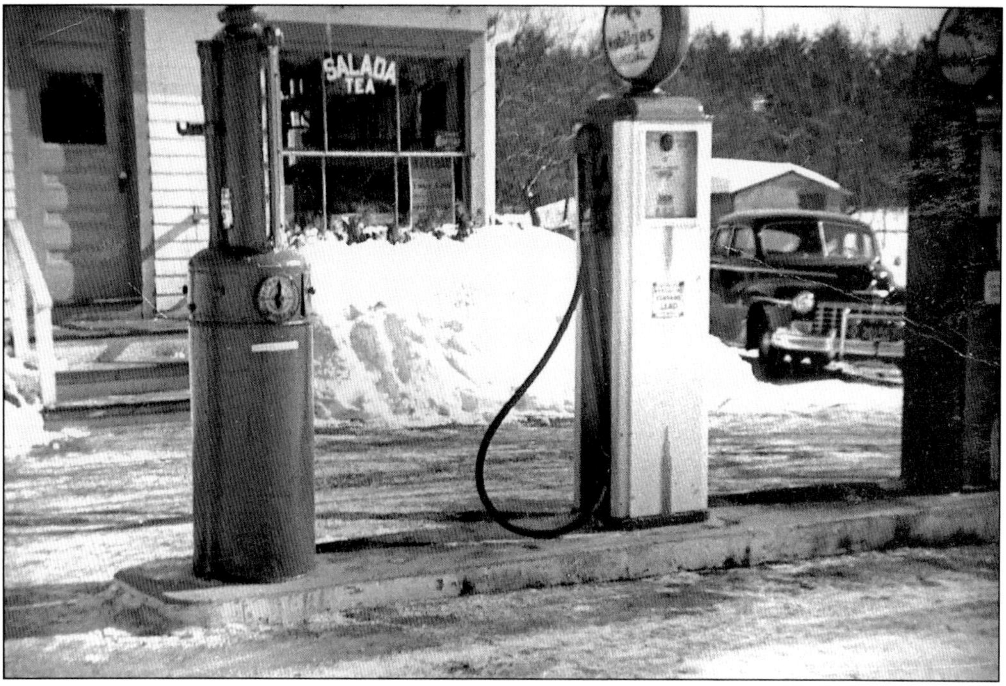

Carmichael's Store in Center Carver was opened in 1929 by Walter Carmichael. He and his wife, Thalia, ran the business and served the community well until the business was sold in 1988. The building has since been removed and replaced by a chain gas station. This photograph was taken in 1947. (Courtesy of Thalia Carmichael.)

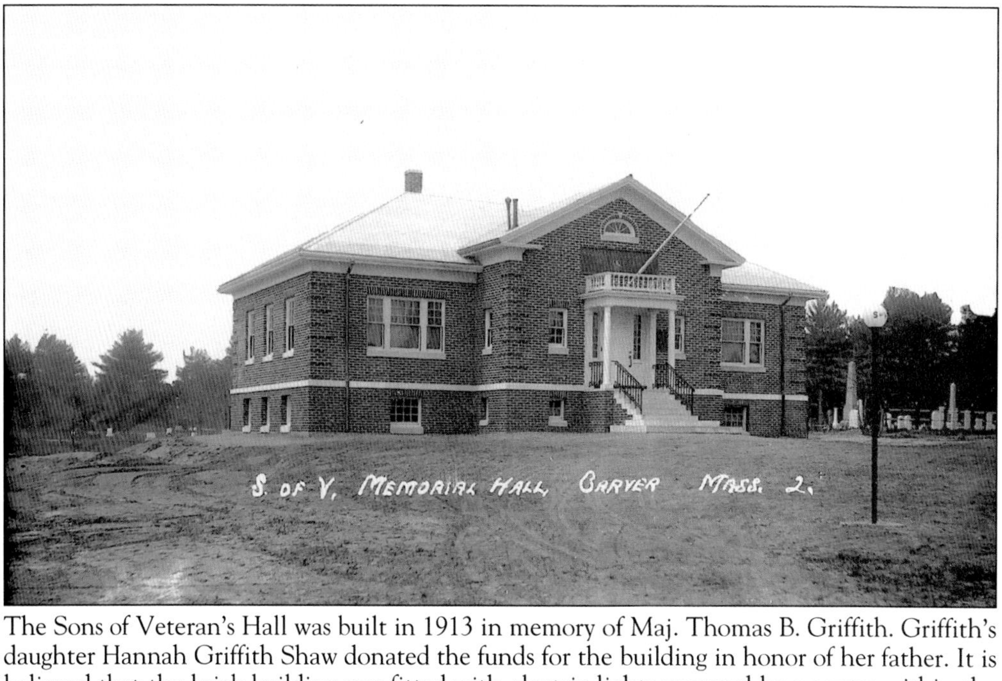

The Sons of Veteran's Hall was built in 1913 in memory of Maj. Thomas B. Griffith. Griffith's daughter Hannah Griffith Shaw donated the funds for the building in honor of her father. It is believed that the brick building was fitted with electric lights powered by a source within the structure before electricity was generally available in Carver.

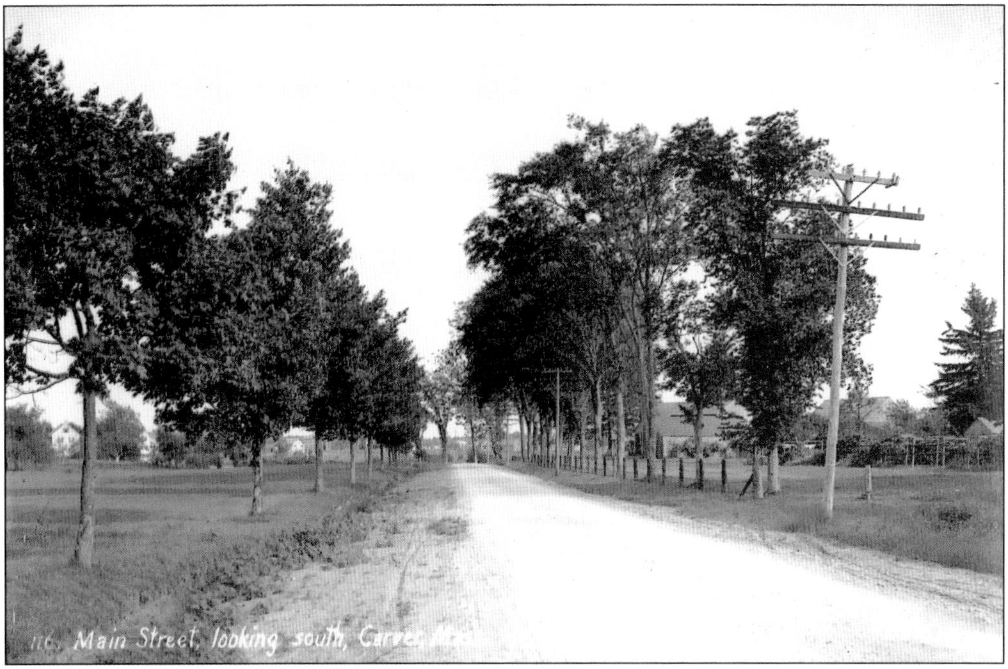

This view, taken near the Sons of Veteran's Hall, looks south on Main Street.

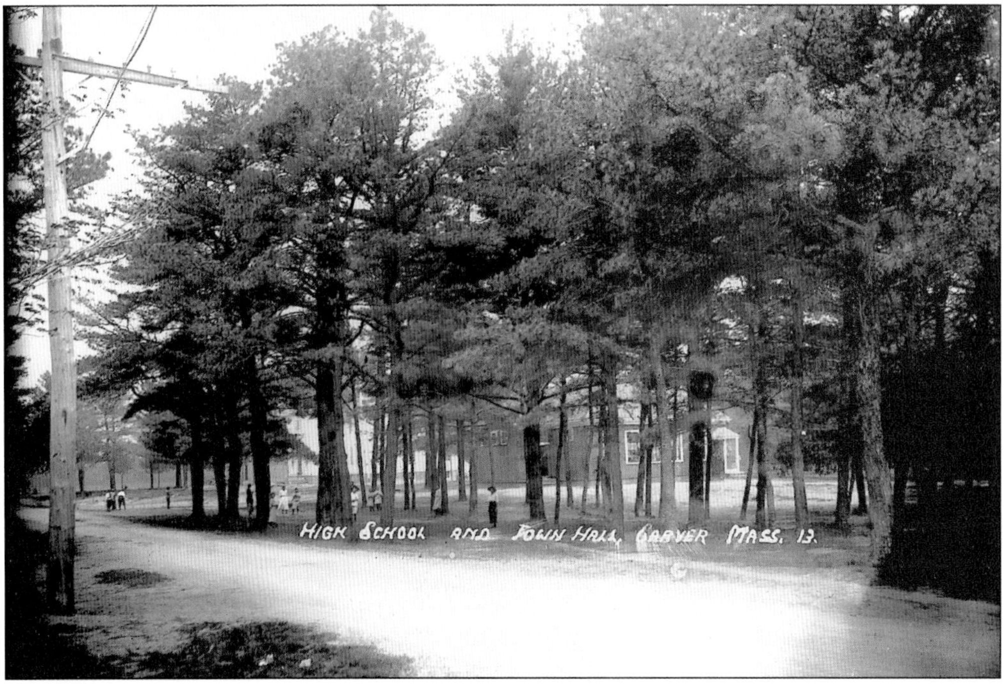

The Carver High School was built in 1899. For a brief period before the high school was constructed, students were housed in the first town hall on Main Street, now Crescent Street. In 1925, high school students were sent out of town, and the school was used for elementary children from all sections of town. The new town hall can be seen through the trees, to the left of the high school.

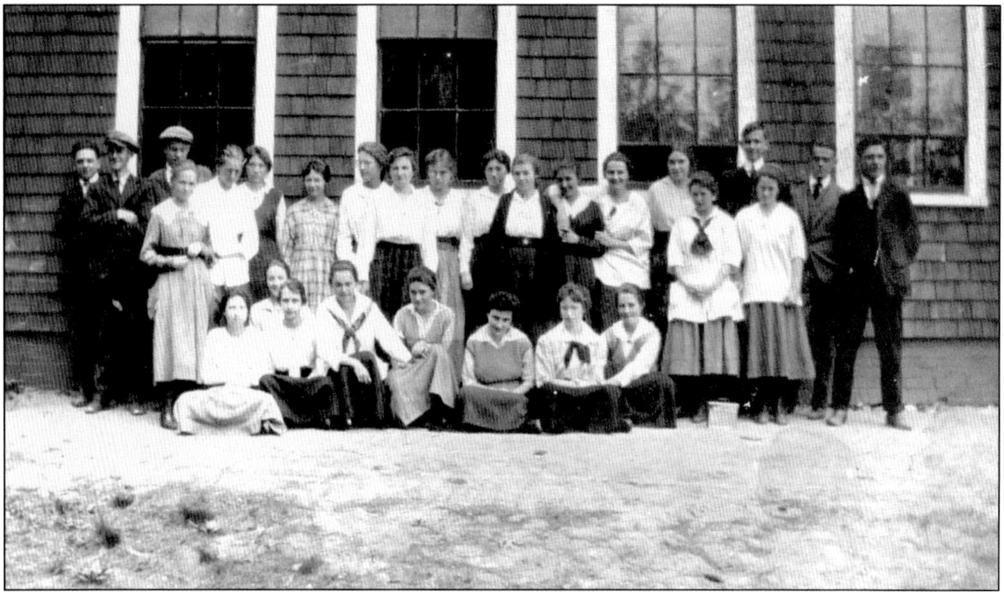

Among the Carver High School students including the class of 1915 are Cubby Perkins, Lyman Douglas, Harold Robbins, Eunice Atwood, Marjorie Griffith, Ida Mae Atwood, Avis Shurtleff, Ella Peckham, Myrtle Perkins, Grace Gardner, Gertrude Robbins, Lillian Robbins, Orrie Shurtleff, Elizabeth Atwood, Dorothy Loring, John Peckham, Bernard Tillson, Leonard Shurtleff, and Dorothy Linton. (Courtesy of Michael Mazalewski.)

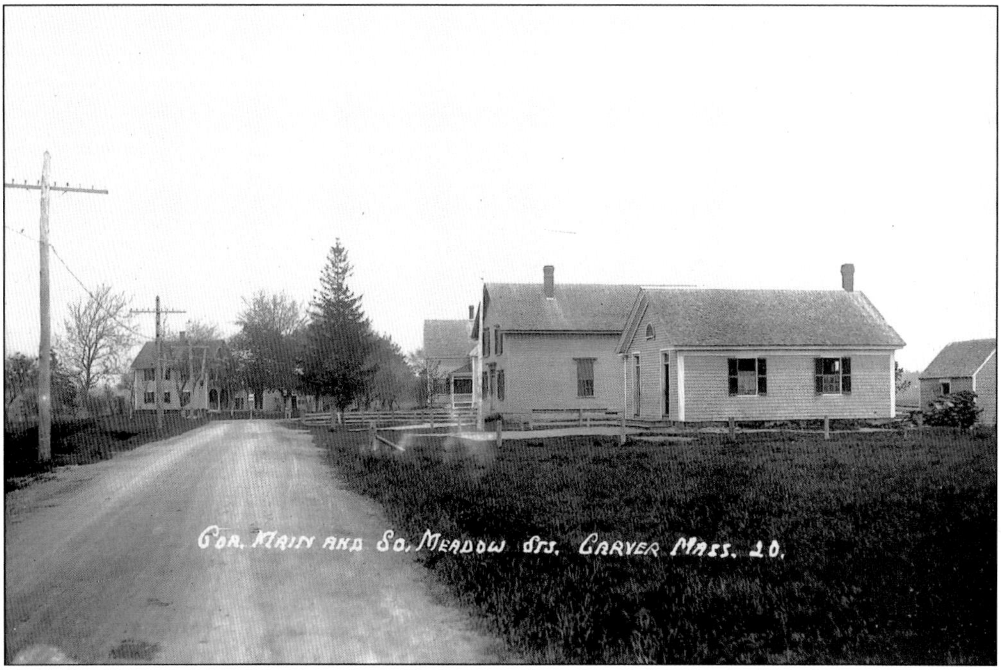

This view of Main Street, now known as Crescent Street, in Center Carver faces north toward South Meadow Road *c.* 1920. The building on the far left, the Shurtleff House, held the Center post office. The first small building on the right was the primary school, and the larger building beyond was the first town hall.

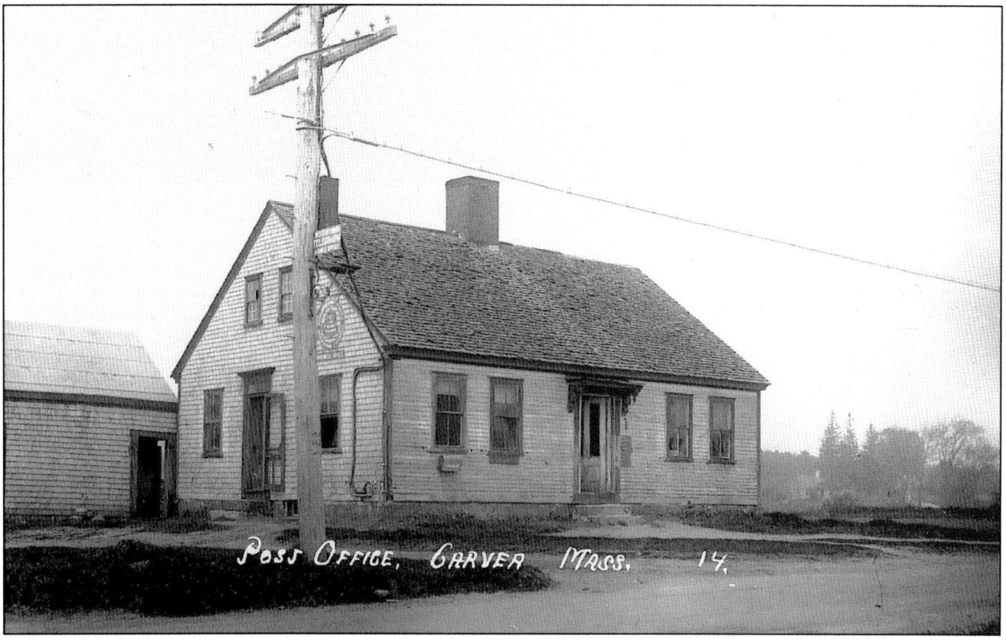

The Eliab Ward house is a pre-Revolutionary home. Eliab Ward Jr. was one of the first postmasters in Carver. An addition on the south side at one time housed a tailor's shop, a barber shop, and a store. Carver's telephone exchange was managed at this location by Frank Barrows. Later, Arthur Peterson and his wife, Lucy, owned the home. Lucy Peterson was the last telephone operator to work at the exchange.

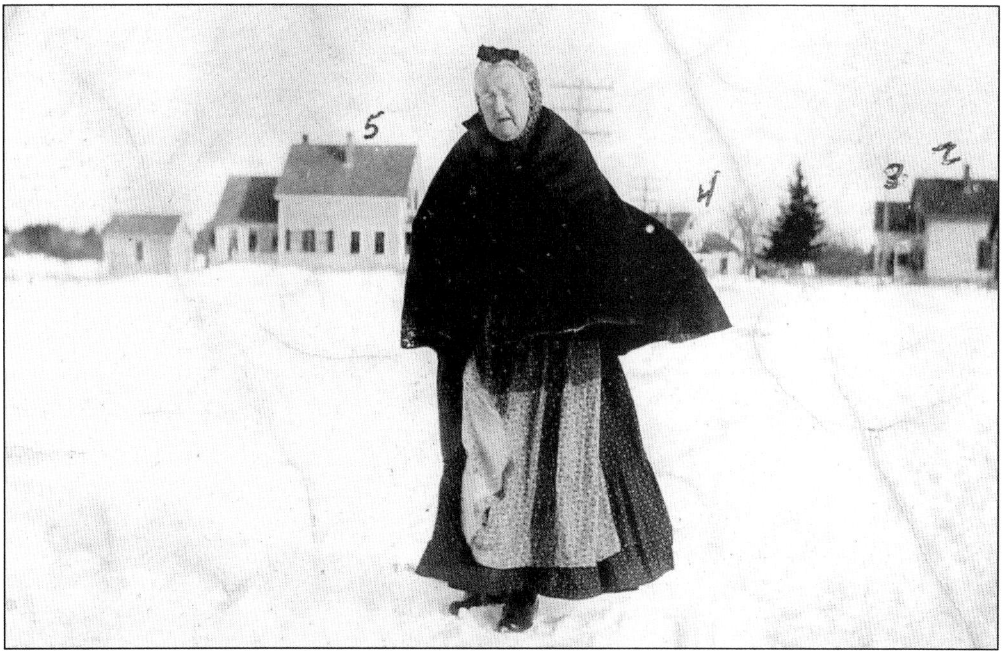

Jane Barrows is shown on Main Street, which is now Crescent Street. Seen behind her, from left to right, are the Hannah Shaw house, the home of Herbert Atwood, the town hall, and the old primary school.

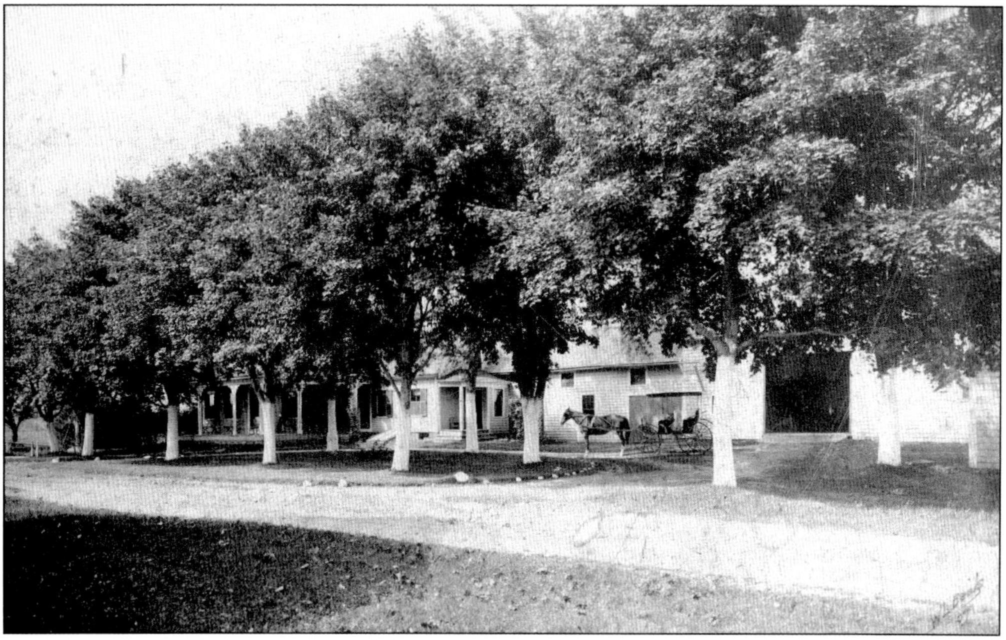

Albert T. Shurtleff lived in this home on South Meadow Road across from Crescent Street. It is not known when this house was built. but the original, probably a Cape, was built *c.* 1800. Shurtleff was the first Carver man to enlist in the Civil War. His right arm was amputated during the Battle of Bull Run, but this did not prevent Shurtleff from serving as town clerk from 1879 to 1892 and town selectman from 1882 to 1890. (Courtesy of James E. Weston.)

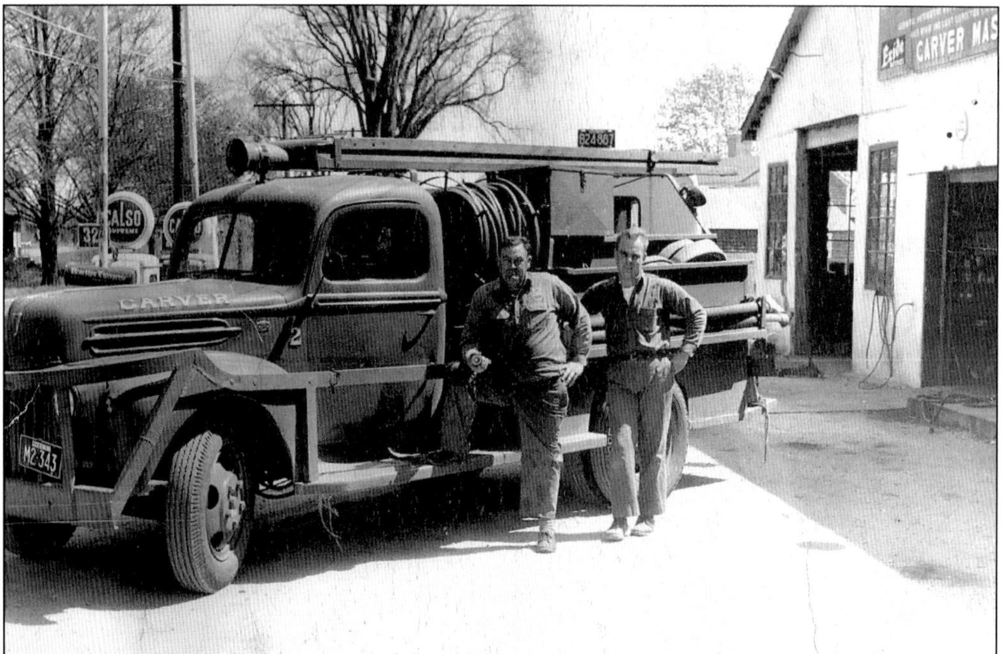

Bill Holmes (left) and Waldo Roby (right) stand beside a 1942 Ford fire truck equipped by the Maxim Company. (Courtesy of Bill Holmes.)

T. T. VAUGHAN,

Box Board Manufacturer.

DEALER IN

WOOD, CEDAR POSTS, SHINGLES, ETC.

MAIN ST., CARVER, MASS.

LOUIS RONDELLE,

WINE MANUFACTURER.

Wine for sale in large or small quantities.

FACTORY AND VINEYARD,

WARD STREET, NEAR SOUTH MEADOW,

CARVER, MASS.

Advertisements for T. T. Vaughan, box board manufacturer, and Louis Rondelle, wine manufacturer, appeared in *The 1902–1903 Resident and Business Directory of Carver, Halifax, Hanson, and Plympton*. Louis Rondelle was a later owner of the Ward House, built in 1773 on the corner of South Meadow Road and Ward Street. Capt. Benjamin Ward, the first owner of the house, fought in the Revolutionary War, and he and his son Col. Benjamin Ward were both active in town affairs.

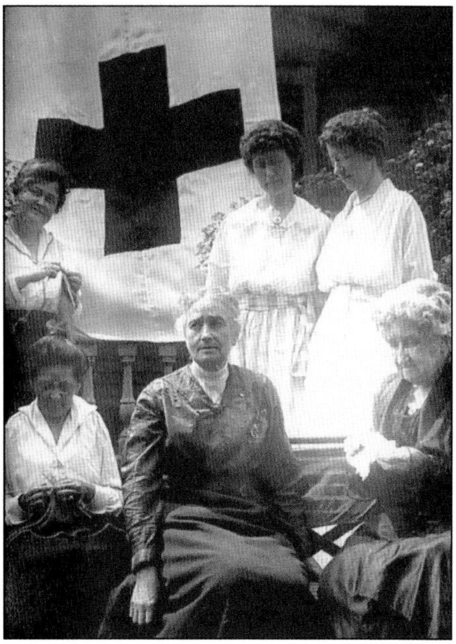

These ladies belonged to the local Carver Red Cross during World War I. They are, from left to right, Helena McFarlin, Ethel Savery, Anna Savery, Catherine Costello, Elderetta McFarlin, and Sarah Louise Savery (Ethel and Anna's mother).

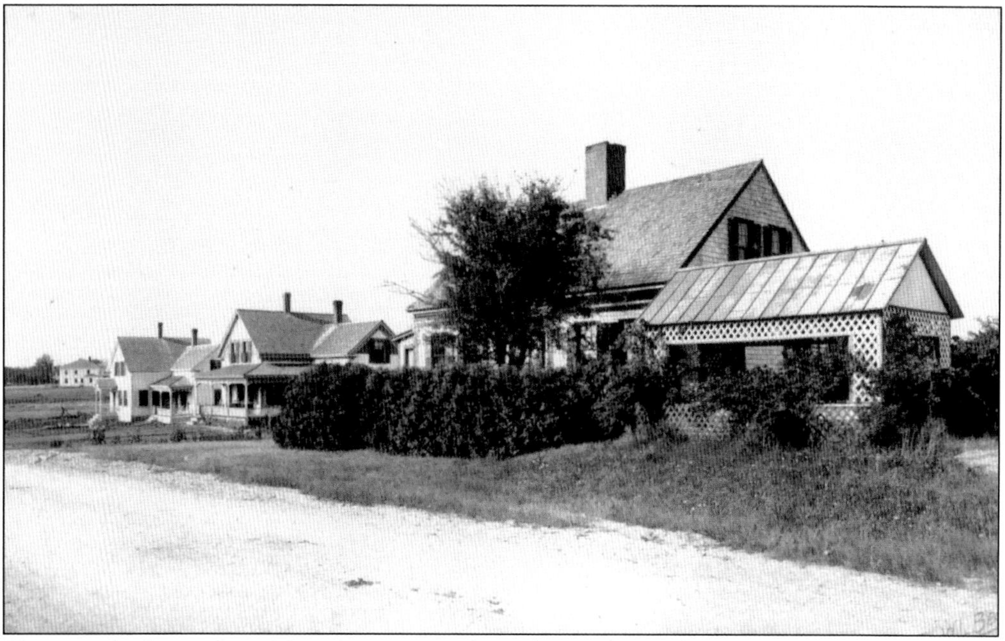

This view looks north on Main Street toward South Meadows. The first home on the right was built in 1840 and was owned by Shaws and Atwoods and later by Winfield Pratt. Pratt built the two houses to the north with identical floor plans. The building on the far left was Harry Jordan's store on Main Street, now Crescent Street. (Courtesy of James E. Weston.)

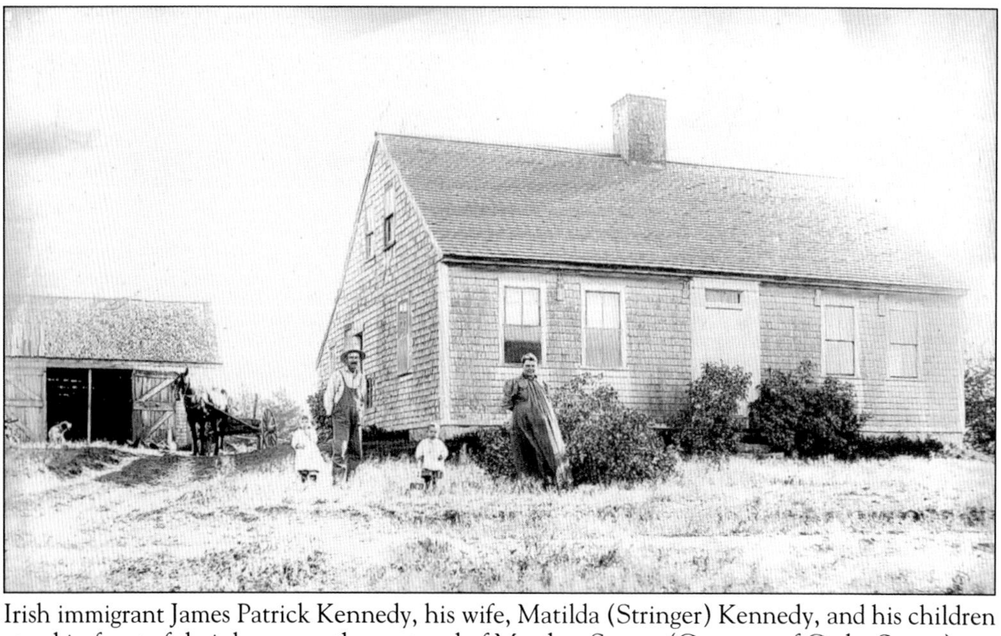

Irish immigrant James Patrick Kennedy, his wife, Matilda (Stringer) Kennedy, and his children stand in front of their house on the east end of Meadow Street. (Courtesy of Cathy Snow.)

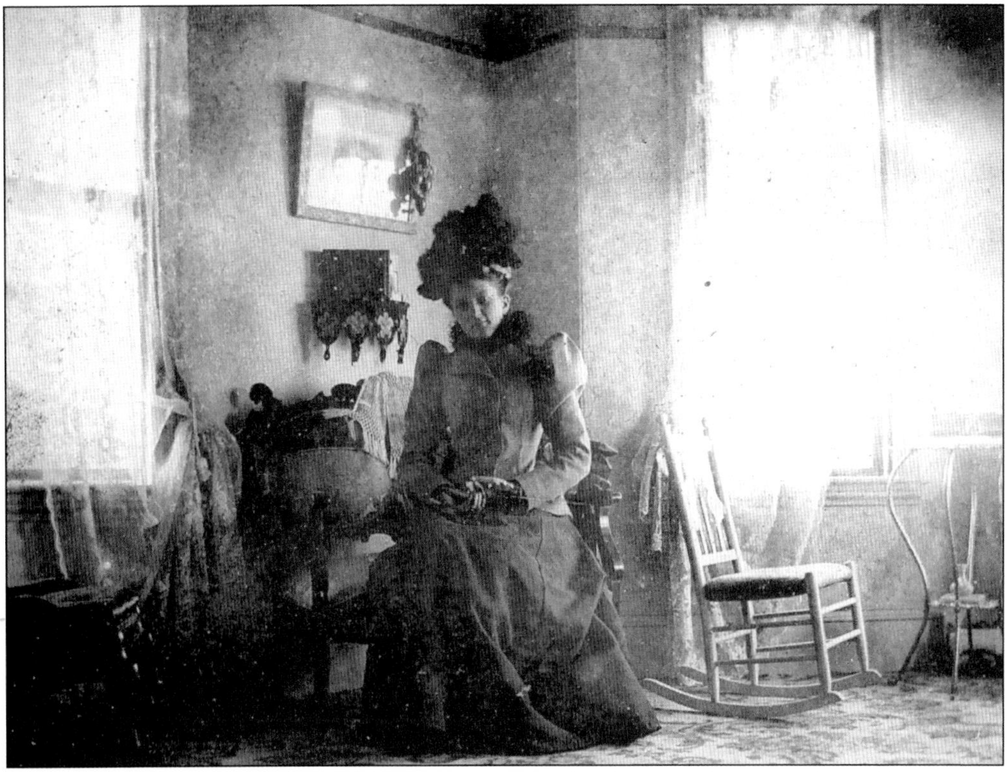

Lillian (Vaughan) Atwood, born in 1879, was the daughter of T. T. Vaughan. (Courtesy of Michael Mazalewski.)

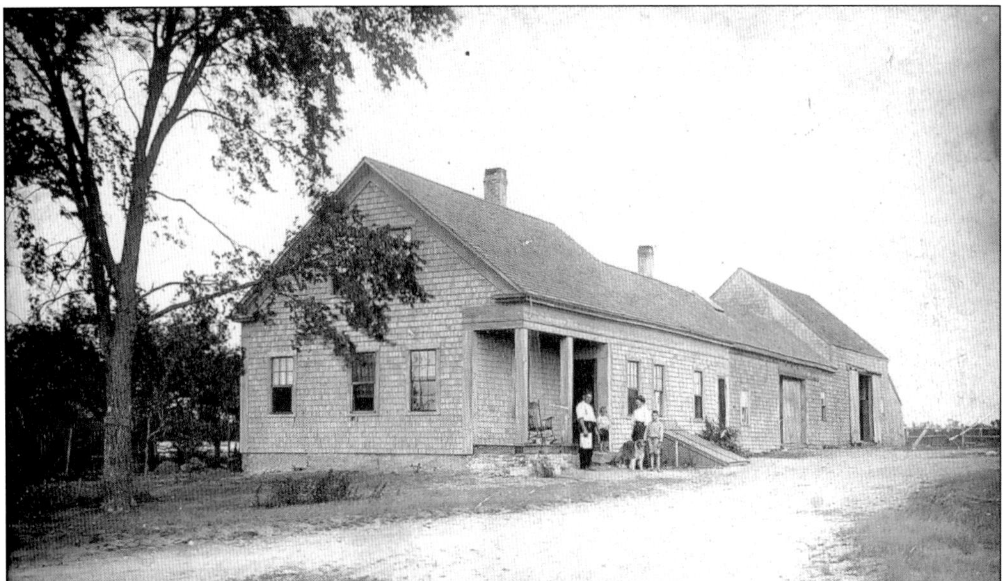

John E. Atwood, his wife, Lillian, and their two children stand in front of their home on Main Street *c.* 1905. The home is located north of Meadow Street on the opposite side of Main Street. (Courtesy of Michael Mazalewski.)

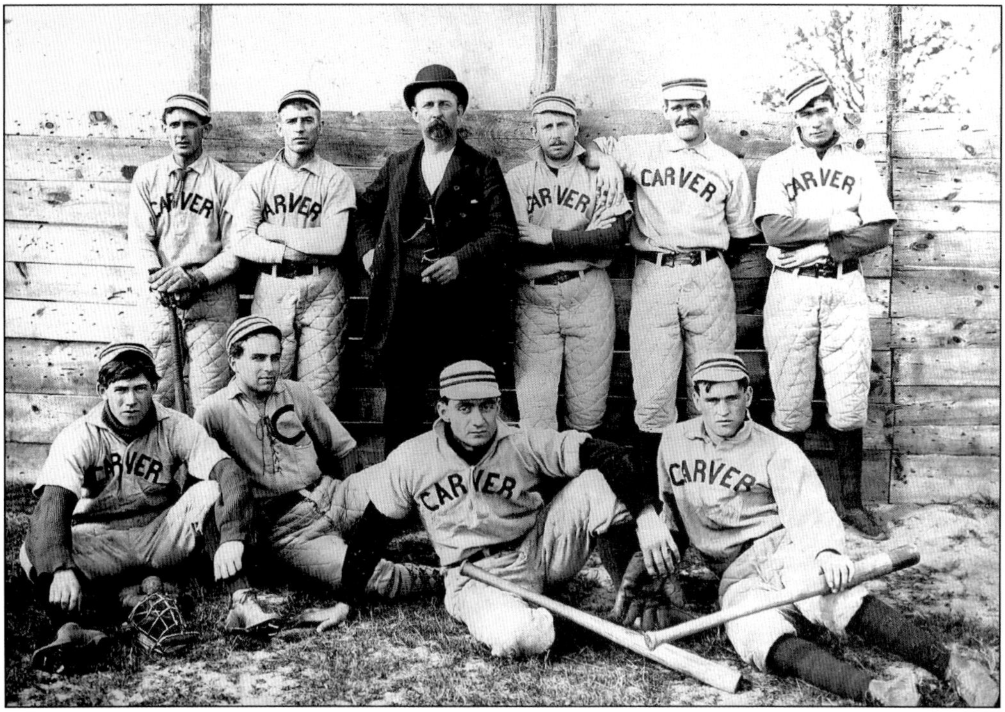

This photograph was taken in 1904 before a game between this Carver team and a Sandwich team. The men who are named—Philander Southworth, Harry Washburn, William Nickerson, Lloyd Griffith, and Frank Hudson—were almost all foundry managers and workers. Three of the players are referred to as simply "hired." (Courtesy of Charles Bezanson.)

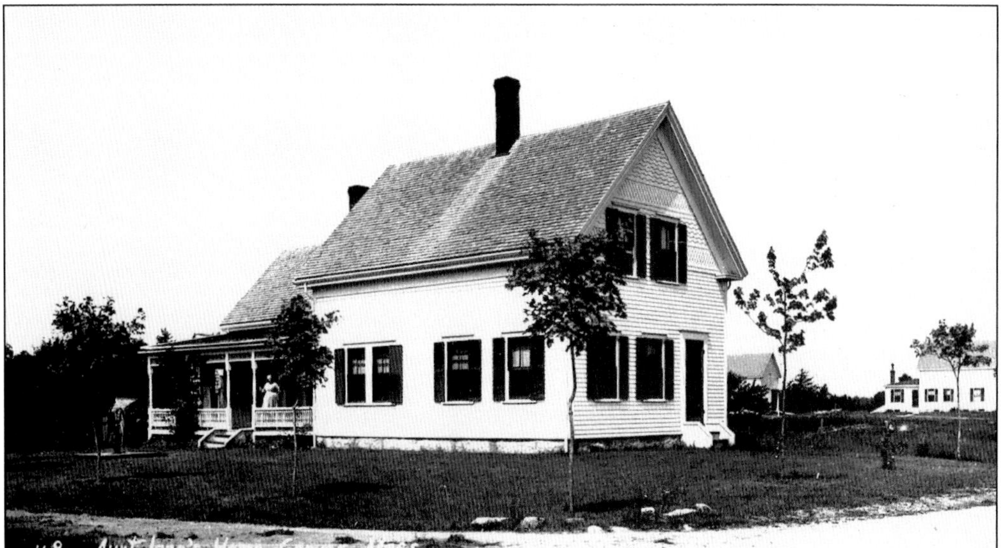

Jane Barrows stands on the porch of the home that she and her husband, Pelham, owned. The structure stood on the corner of Main and West Streets until it was replaced by a commercial plaza. Jane was affectionately known in the community as "Aunt Jane" because of her amiable ways. As a leader, she was active in church and community affairs.

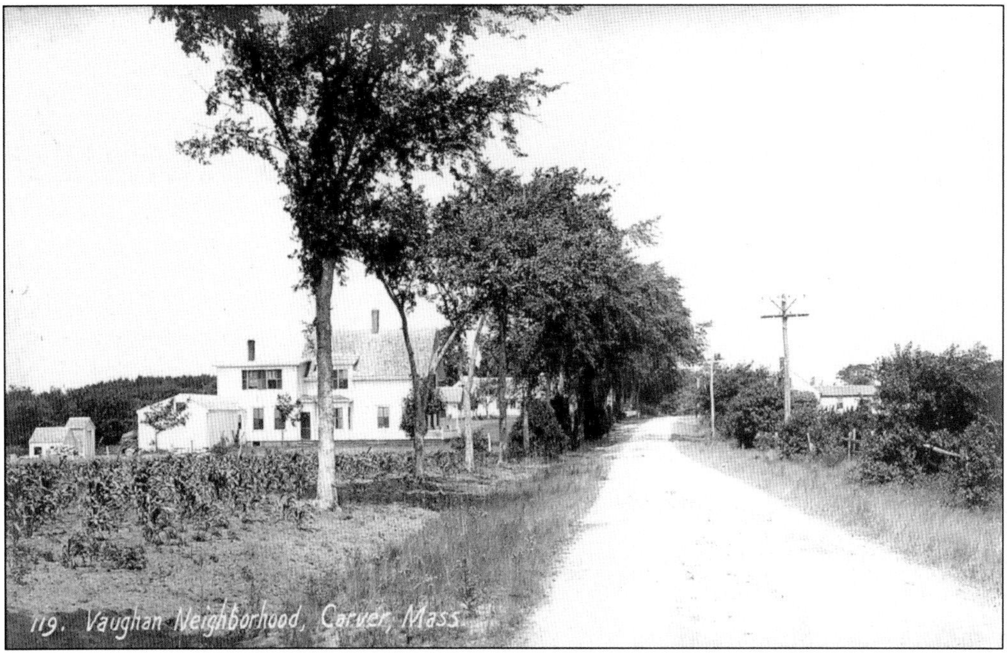

The Vaughan family had extensive holdings on this part of Main Street. Many of the Vaughans held town offices, beginning with Daniel in 1770. From the 1850s through the early 1900s, Theodore T. (T. T.) and Thomas both held various positions and were very popular citizens. T. T. operated a lumber mill in the center of town where the playground is currently located.

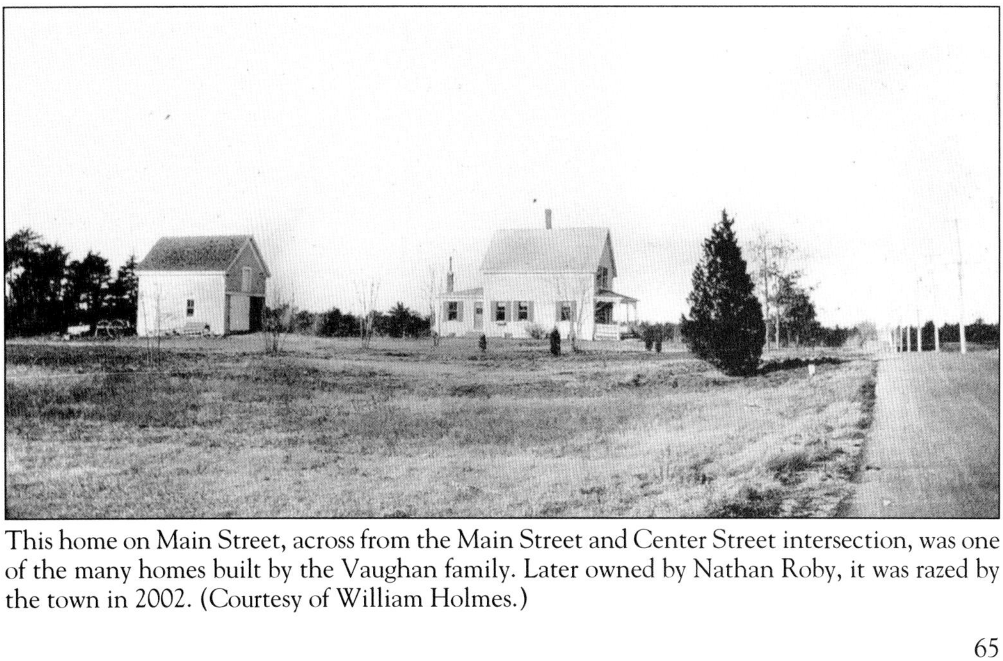

This home on Main Street, across from the Main Street and Center Street intersection, was one of the many homes built by the Vaughan family. Later owned by Nathan Roby, it was razed by the town in 2002. (Courtesy of William Holmes.)

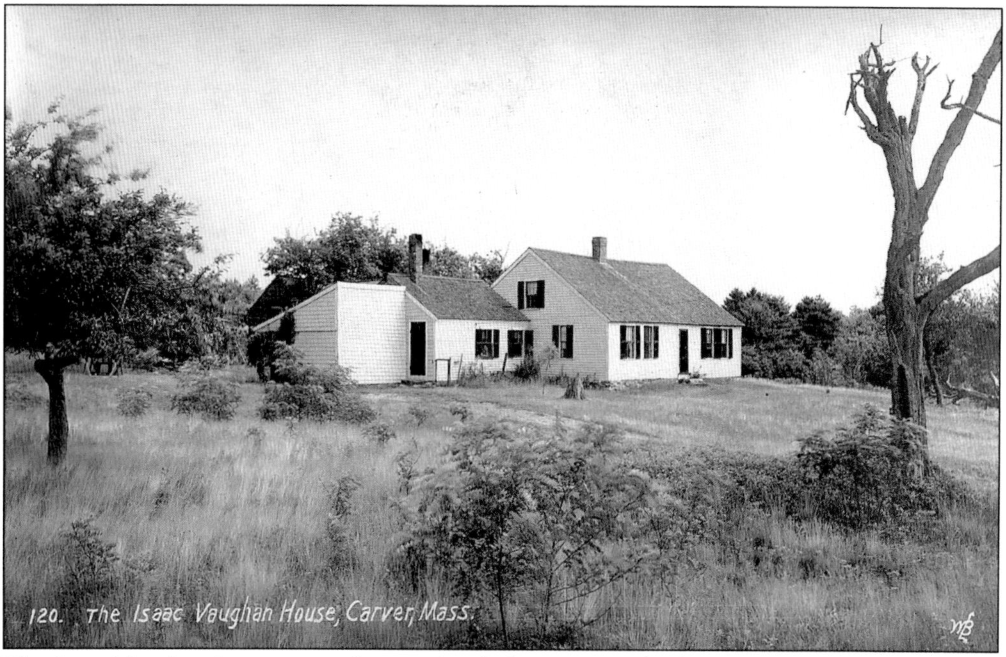

The Isaac Vaughan home, according to family history, was built *c.* 1770. Isaac Vaughan was active in town affairs, holding the positions of town clerk, treasurer, assessor, and member of the school committee.

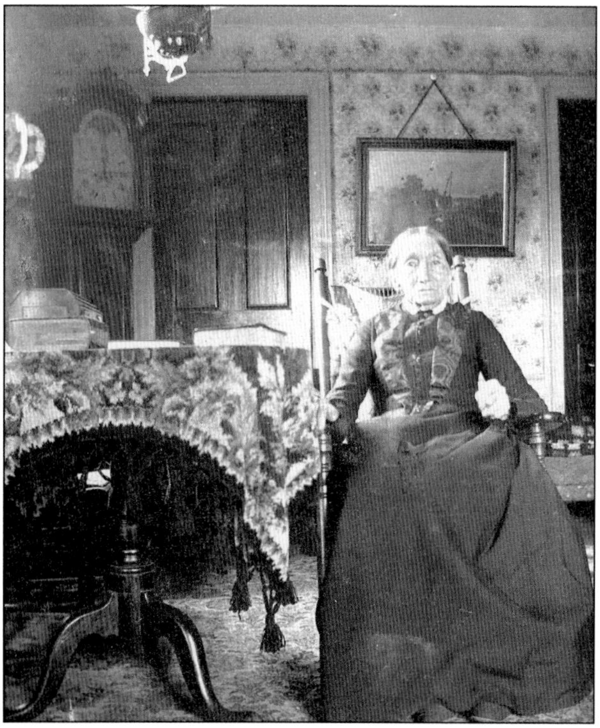

Mercy C. (Sherman) Vaughan was the wife of Thomas Vaughan. They had nine children, but only six of them lived to be adults. Their sons James and Theodore T. became prominent Carver citizens. (Courtesy of Michael Mazalewski.)

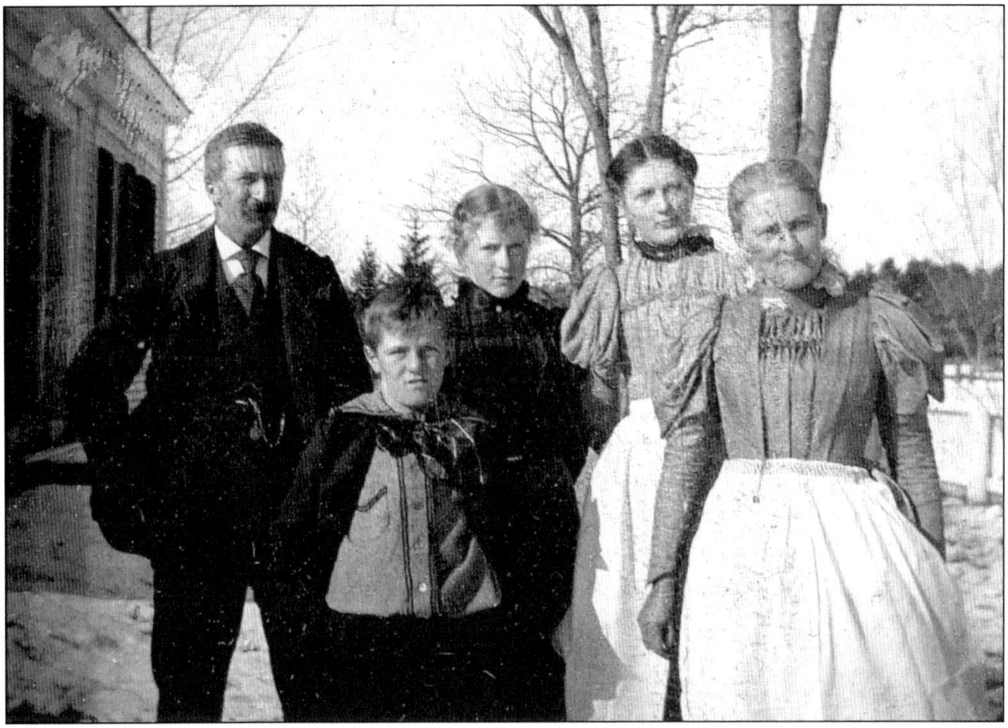

On Thanksgiving Day in 1897, the Theodore T. Vaughan family gathers outside the home on Main Street. Family members are, from left to right, T. T. Vaughan; his son Herbert; his daughters Florence (Vaughan) Weston and Lillian (Vaughan) Atwood; and his wife, Elizabeth (Leach) Vaughan. (Courtesy of Michael Mazalewski.)

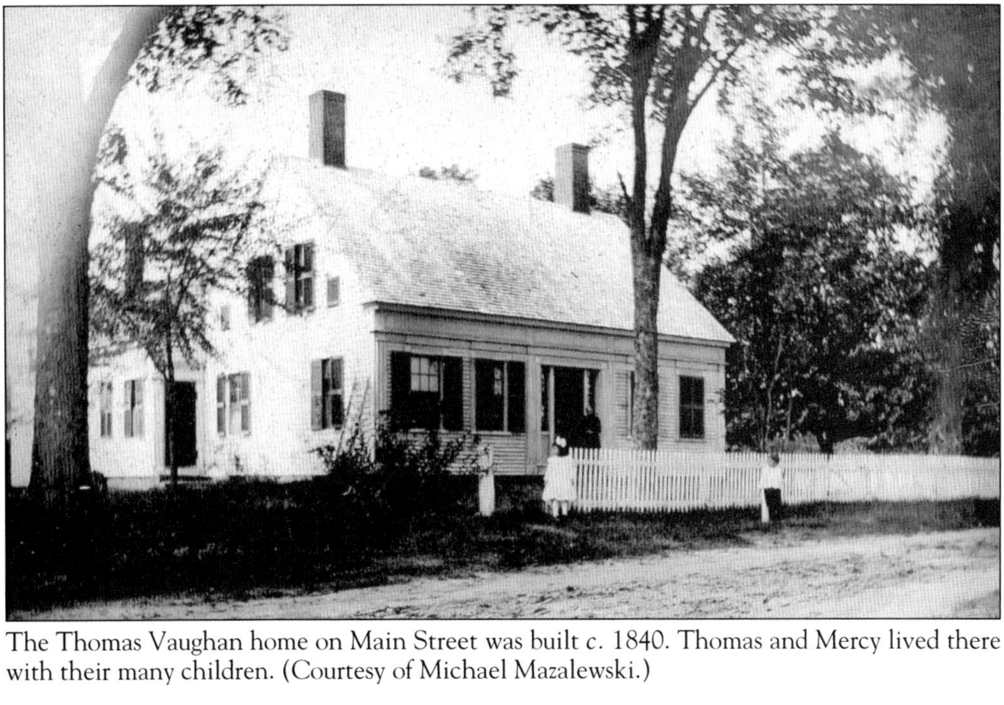

The Thomas Vaughan home on Main Street was built *c.* 1840. Thomas and Mercy lived there with their many children. (Courtesy of Michael Mazalewski.)

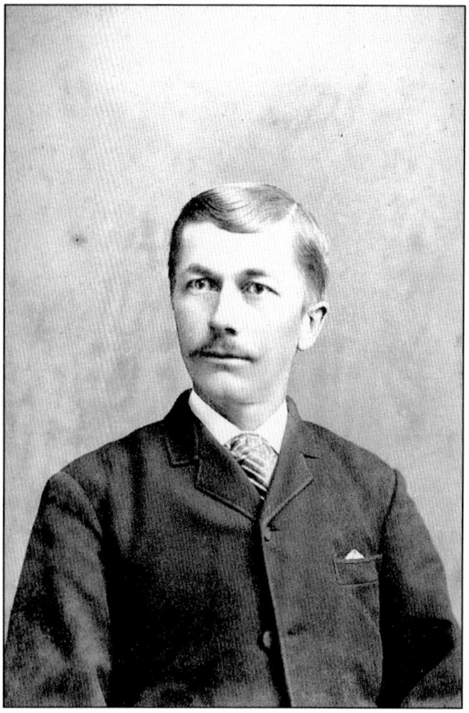

James A. Vaughan (1849–1919) was one of Carver's first postmasters during the first half of the 19th century. He was a local businessman who grew and sold trees, vines, and seeds. (Courtesy of Michael Mazalewski.)

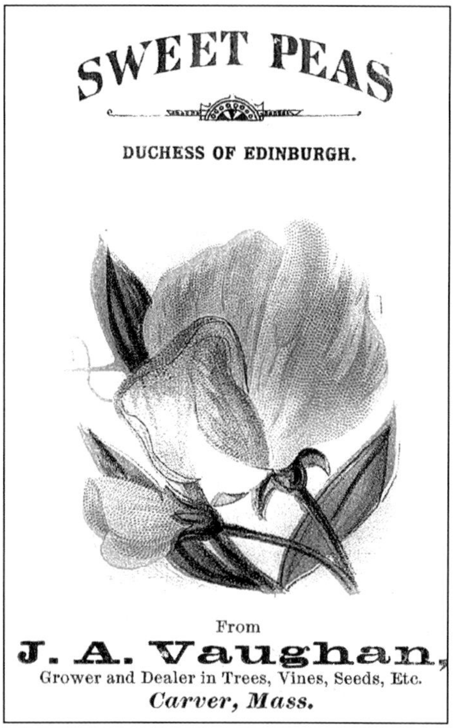

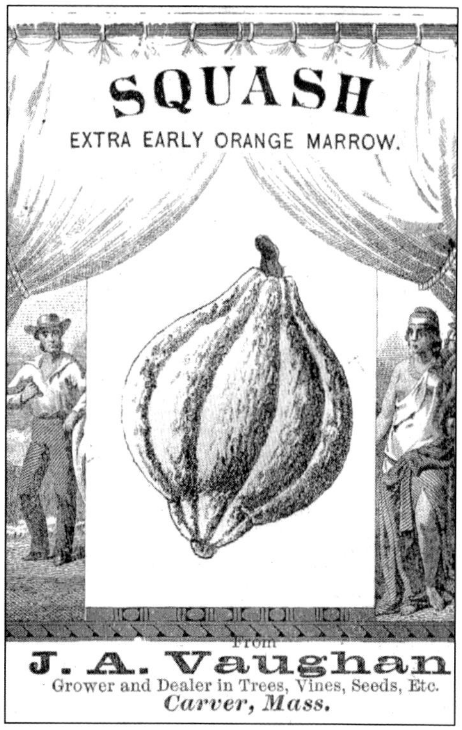

These seed packets represent one part of James A. Vaughan's local nursery business. (Courtesy of Michael Mazalewski.)

Five

Old Home Day

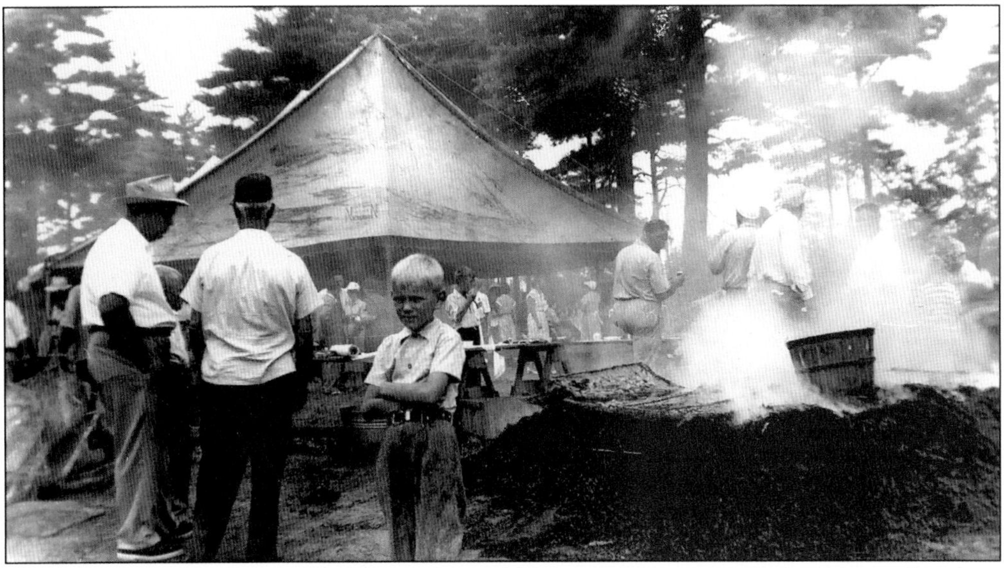

The first Old Home Day was held in 1901 and began with a service in the Baptist church in Center Carver. Afterwards, food was served across the street. The meal included Aunt Jane Barrow's clam chowder, a banana dessert, ice cream, and soda. Old Home Day has become an annual event, a day of festivities, and a day to renew connections with old acquaintances. It is still celebrated on the last Saturday of July in Shurtleff Park.

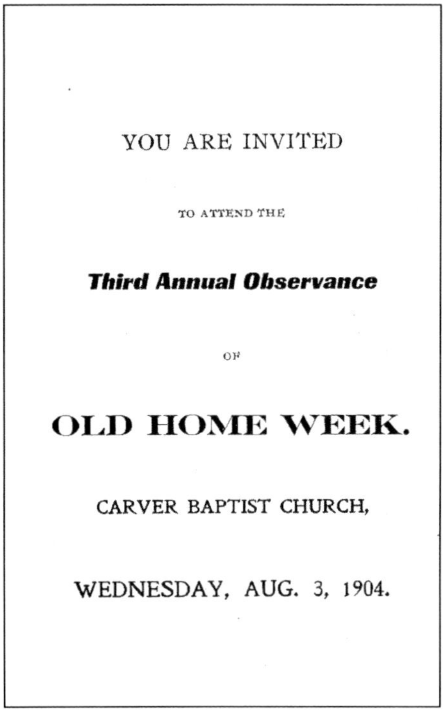

YOU ARE INVITED

TO ATTEND THE

Third Annual Observance

OF

OLD HOME WEEK.

CARVER BAPTIST CHURCH,

WEDNESDAY, AUG. 3, 1904.

This 1904 program invites people to the third Old Home Day celebration, which was held on August 3, 1904. Some of the musicians who entertained the crowd that day were Ira Murdock's Quartette, Bernice Barrows on guitar, and Carl and Justin Southworth, both on coronet.

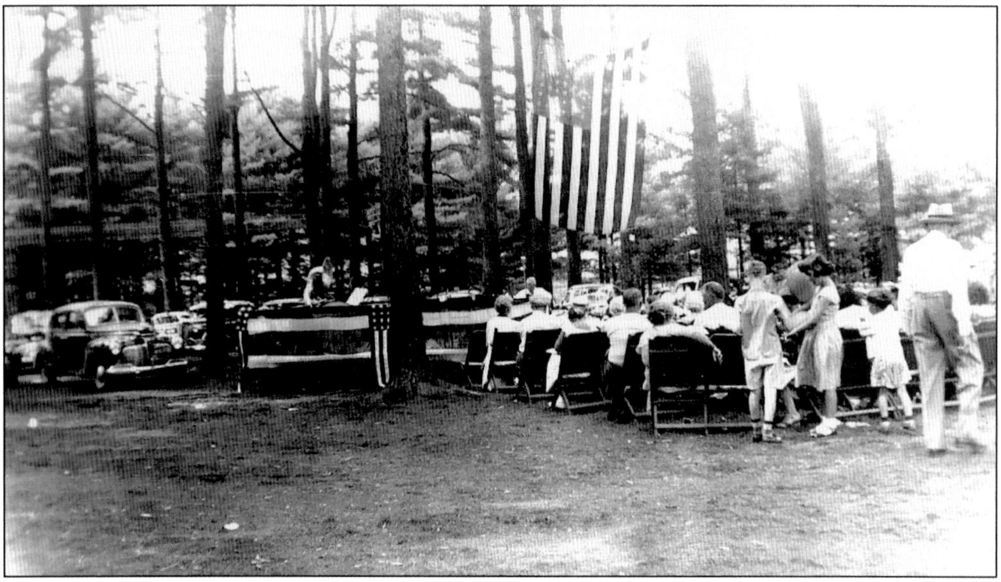

A group of people listens to lively music in front of the bandstand in Shurtleff Park before the clambake is served. Approximately 500 people usually attend the clambake. A more recent tradition at Old Home Day is the five-mile Carver Road Race, which starts the day with a bang.

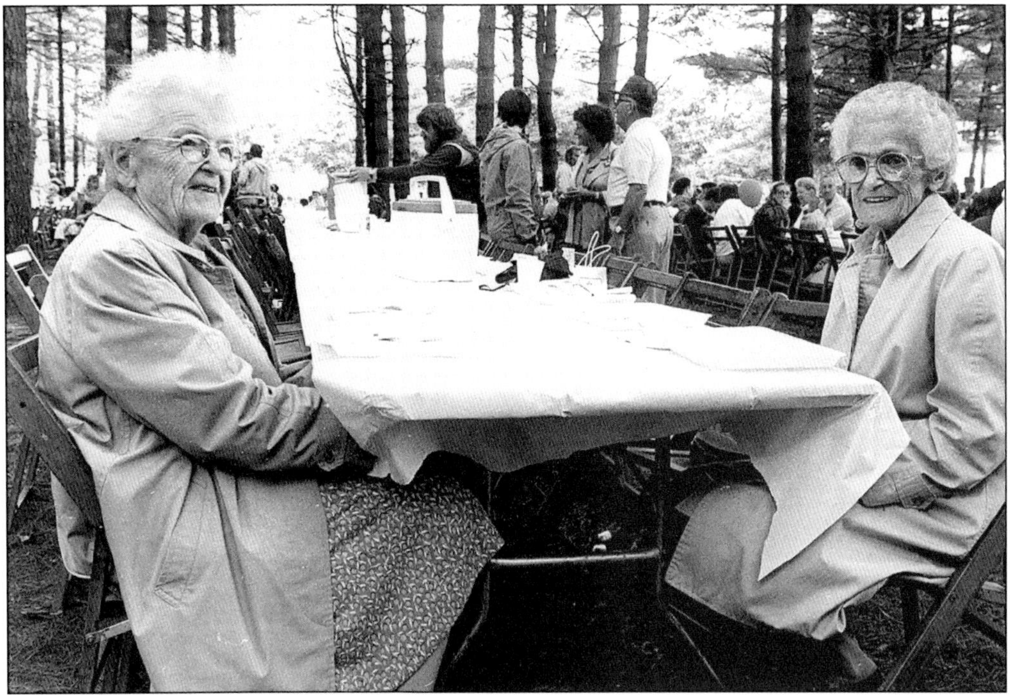

Jennie Bailey Shaw (left) and her sister-in-law, Eunice Atwood Bailey (right), wait to be served at an Old Home Day celebration. (Courtesy of Marjorie Mosher.)

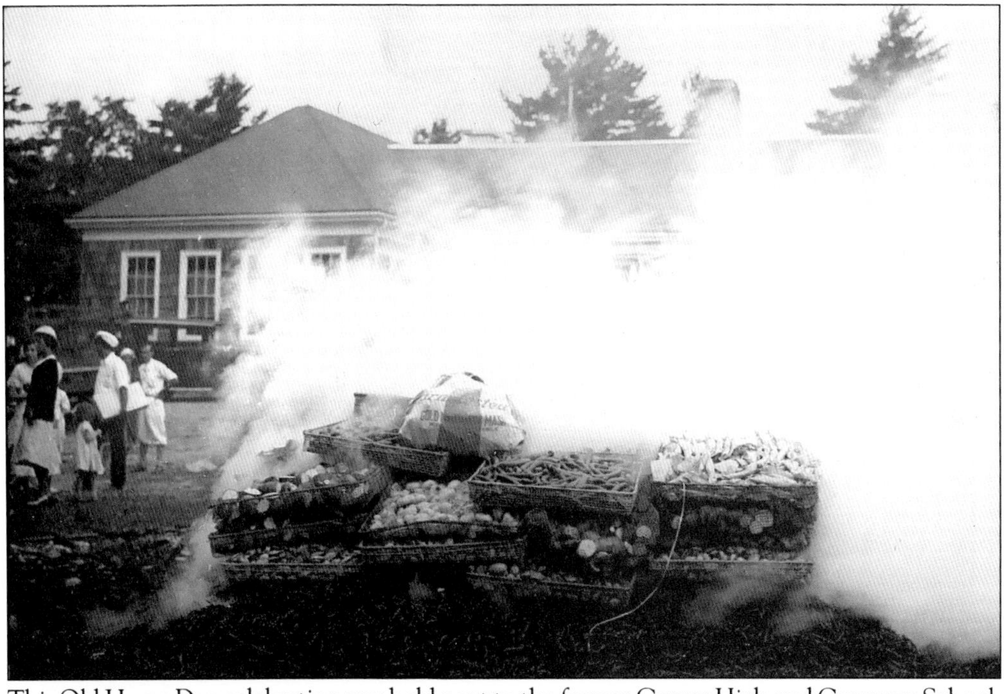

This Old Home Day celebration was held next to the former Carver High and Grammar School. The canvas has just been removed from the bake, exposing the racks of food on top of seaweed ready to be served.

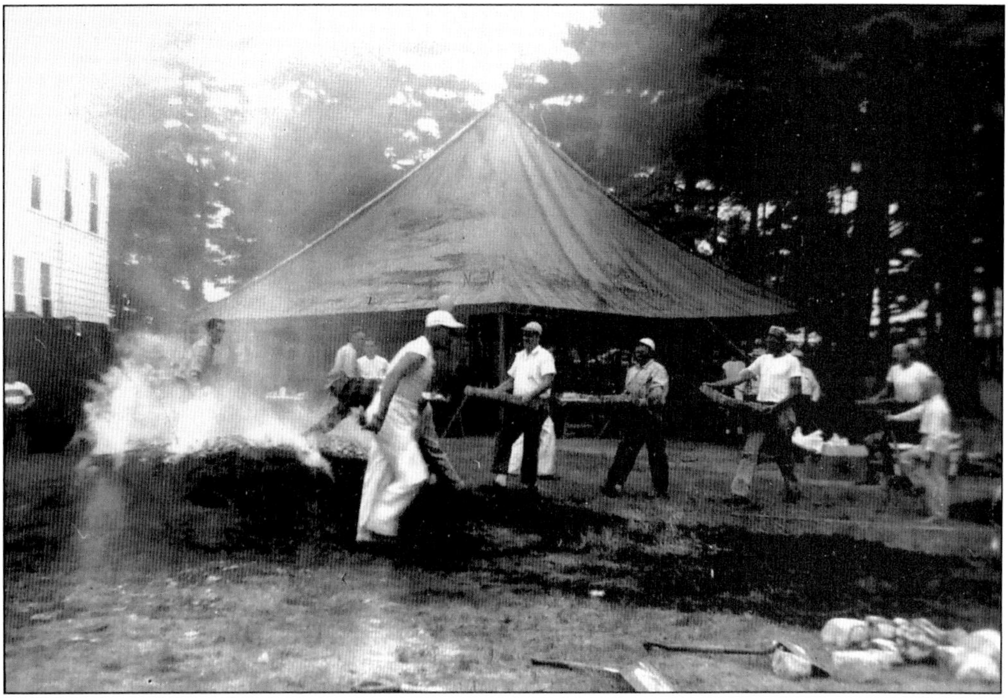

Old Home Day workers carry racks of food that will soon lie sandwiched between layers of seaweed. (Courtesy of William Holmes.)

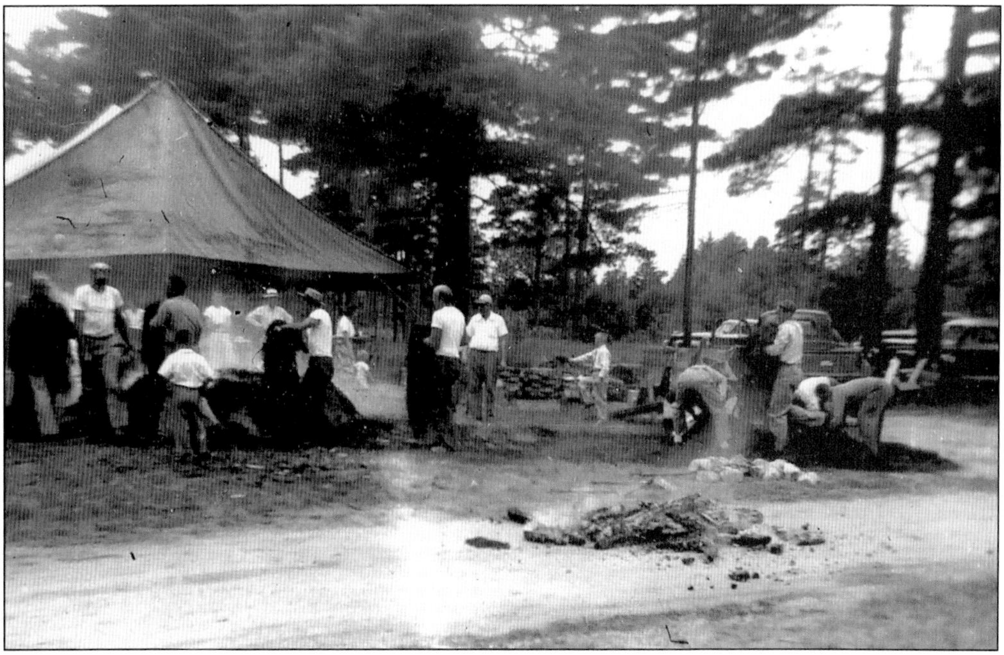

Due to rain, this was one of the few Old Home Day celebrations that was located behind town hall and protected by a tent. Although the rain was an inconvenience, it was also a blessing because a devastating forest fire had started the previous day in Wareham and South Carver. (Courtesy of William Holmes.)

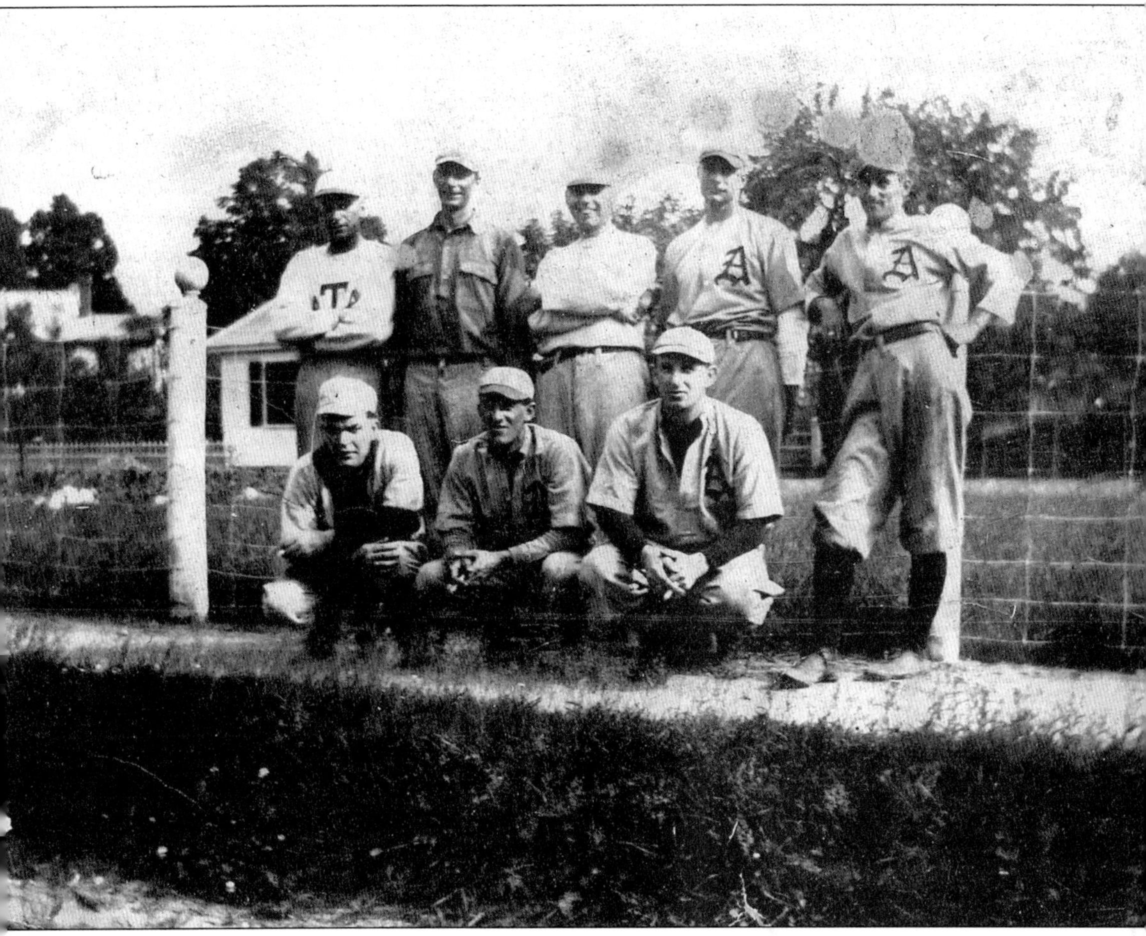

Members of the Carver Athletics baseball team pose at Johnson's Field across from the South Carver Grange Hall on the day of the grange clambake. From left to right are the following: (first row) Donald "Jack" Bailey, Arleigh Pink, and Henry Pink; (second row) Duffy Lewis, Gene Wright, Birt Perkins, Ken Shaw, and Frank "Bugs" Shaw. (Courtesy of Dana Ward.)

The Carver Old Home Week Association

Announce

That Wednesday, July Twenty-Ninth, Nineteen Hundred and Three, will be celebrated as

Old Home Day.

BAPTIST CHURCH, CARVER, MASSACHUSETTS.

Morning Session, 10. Afternoon Session, 2.

Invitation.

That this meeting may be a success and that all may have a royal good time,

Come ye sons and daughters of Carver.
Come ye whose old home is here.
Come ye every one.
Come ye all.

OSCAR FRANK STETSON, Secretary,
NORTH CARVER, MASS.

Notices.

Train leaves Middleboro for North Carver at 8.09 a. m. Returning leave North Carver at 5.35 p. m.

Leaves Plymouth for North Carver at 7.20 and 11.20 a. m. Returning leaves North Carver at 2.26 and 6.26 p. m.

Carriages will connect with trains to convey passengers from North Carver Station.

Dinner will be furnished at a reasonable price.

The 1903 Old Home Day program includes the train schedule for the North Carver Train Station to assist people coming to Carver for the day from Middleborough and Plymouth.

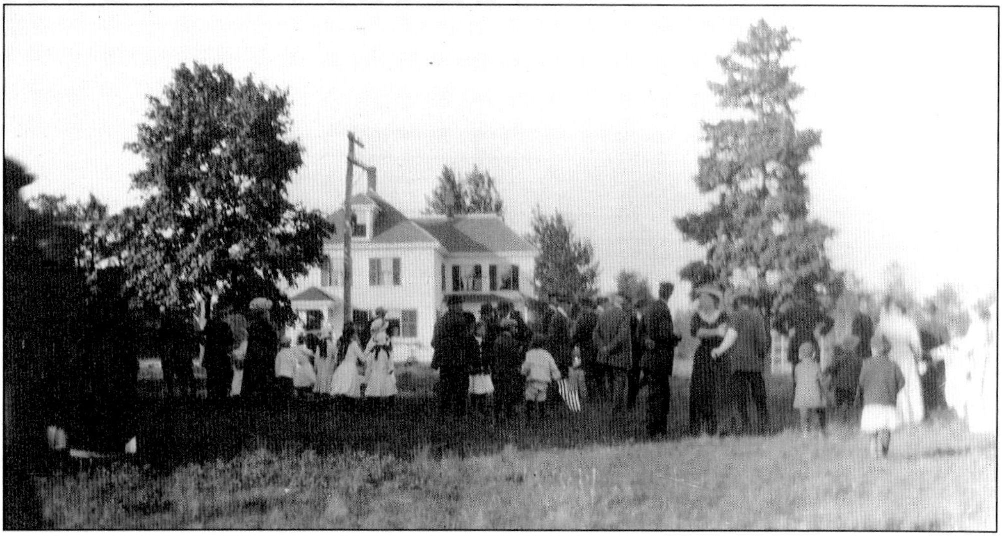

The crowd in this photograph, from the 1912 Old Home Day, is gathered by the Baptist church, and the parsonage is visible behind the crowd. The land in the center of town was donated by Dr. Benjamin Shurtleff from his estate in 1908 and became known as Shurtleff Park.

Six

South Carver

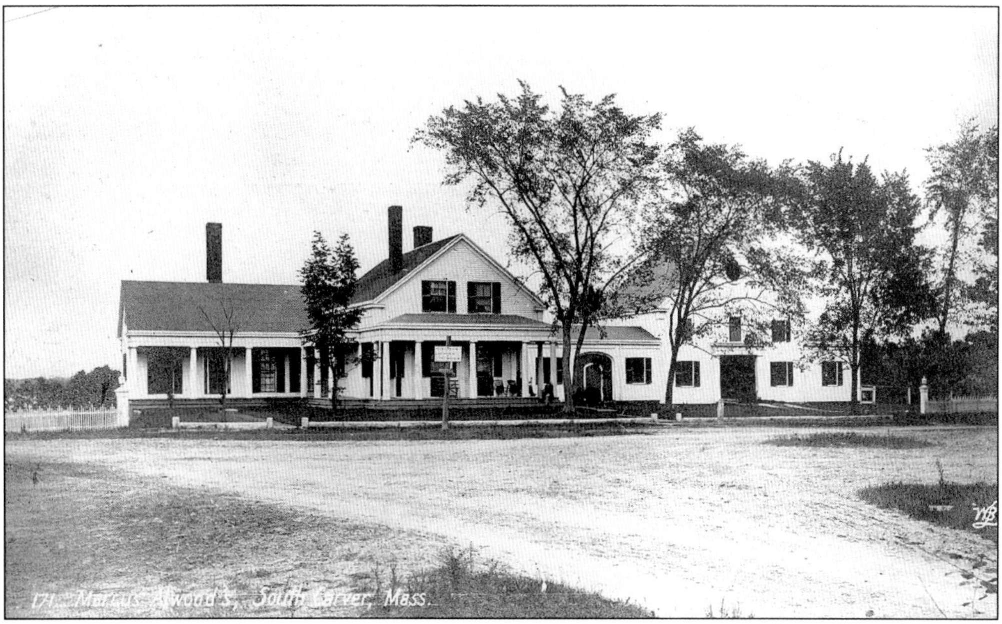

Jesse Murdock lived in this home on Tremont Street in South Carver. The house was built in 1845, and Jesse and his sister Susanna lived there until Susanna died in 1902. She left the property to Marcus Atwood, who had been a dedicated caretaker for many years. Ellis D. Atwood acquired the home from his uncle, and his widow, Elthea, made it possible for the town to acquire the home. It is now used by the Council on Aging.

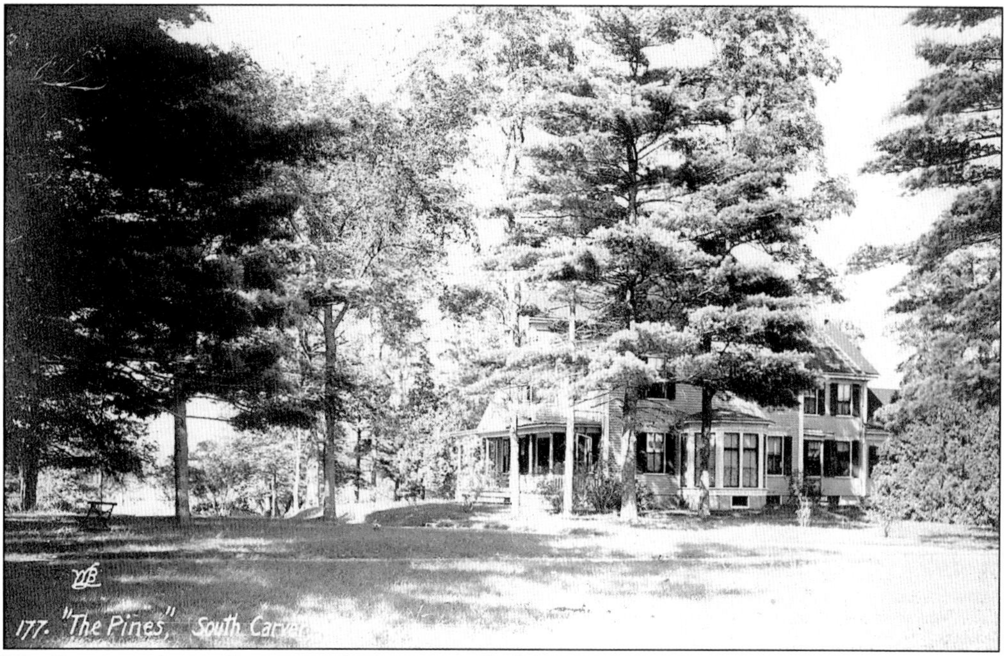

The Pines was located opposite the Jesse Murdock home on Tremont Street. The distinguished structure was built by Peleg McFarlin in 1887 and then sold in the 1920s to a couple who took in summer boarders. The last owner was the Ruel Gibbs family, who owned it until it burned in the early 1930s. Benjamin Ellis built his grand home on the same site in the early 1800s, but the house was later destroyed.

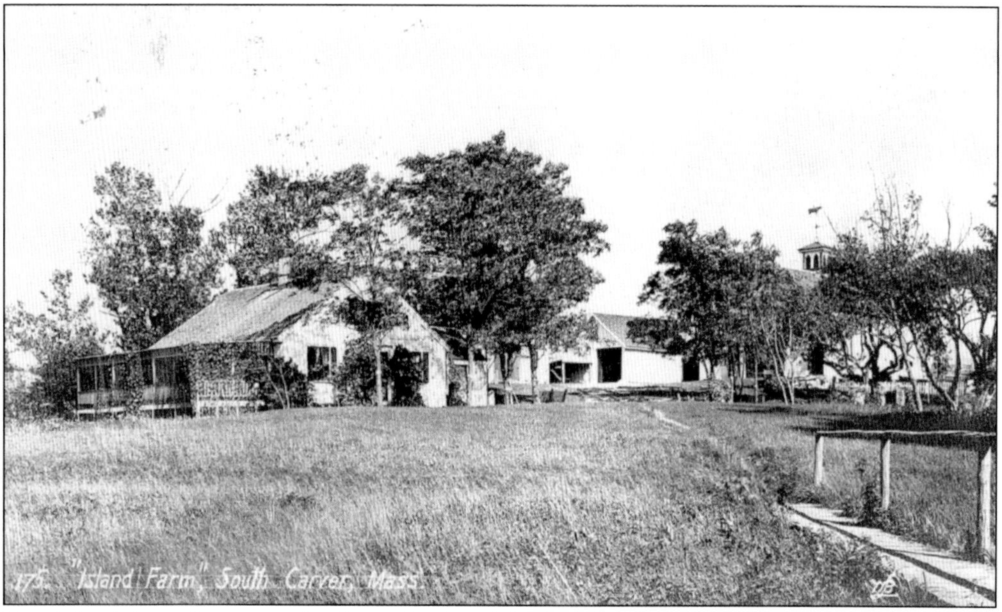

The Island Farm house was built by Bartlett Murdock in the 1760s. He was the founder of the Charlotte Furnace, which later became the Ellis Foundry. Now hidden by trees, the house remains a residence on the original site, across from the remaining Ellis Foundry building on Foundry Pond.

Frank and Elizabeth (Atwood) Costello are shown in front of their home at the Island Farm estate on their wedding day. Frank became the owner of the Cranebrook Cranberry Company after the previous owner, his uncle Andrew O'Brien, died. (Courtesy of Michael Mazalewski.)

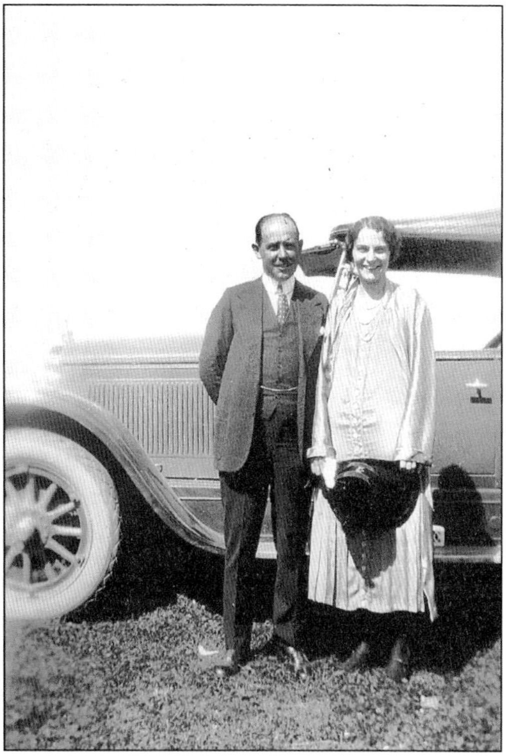

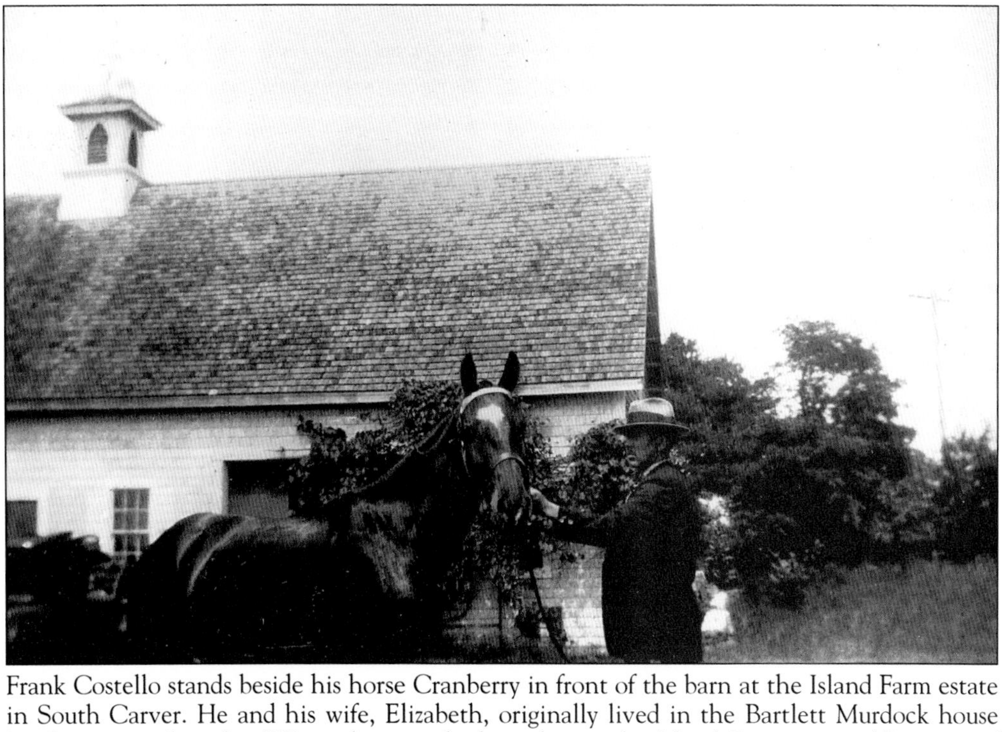

Frank Costello stands beside his horse Cranberry in front of the barn at the Island Farm estate in South Carver. He and his wife, Elizabeth, originally lived in the Bartlett Murdock house but later moved to the O'Brien house, which is also on the Island Farm estate. (Courtesy of Michael Mazalewski.)

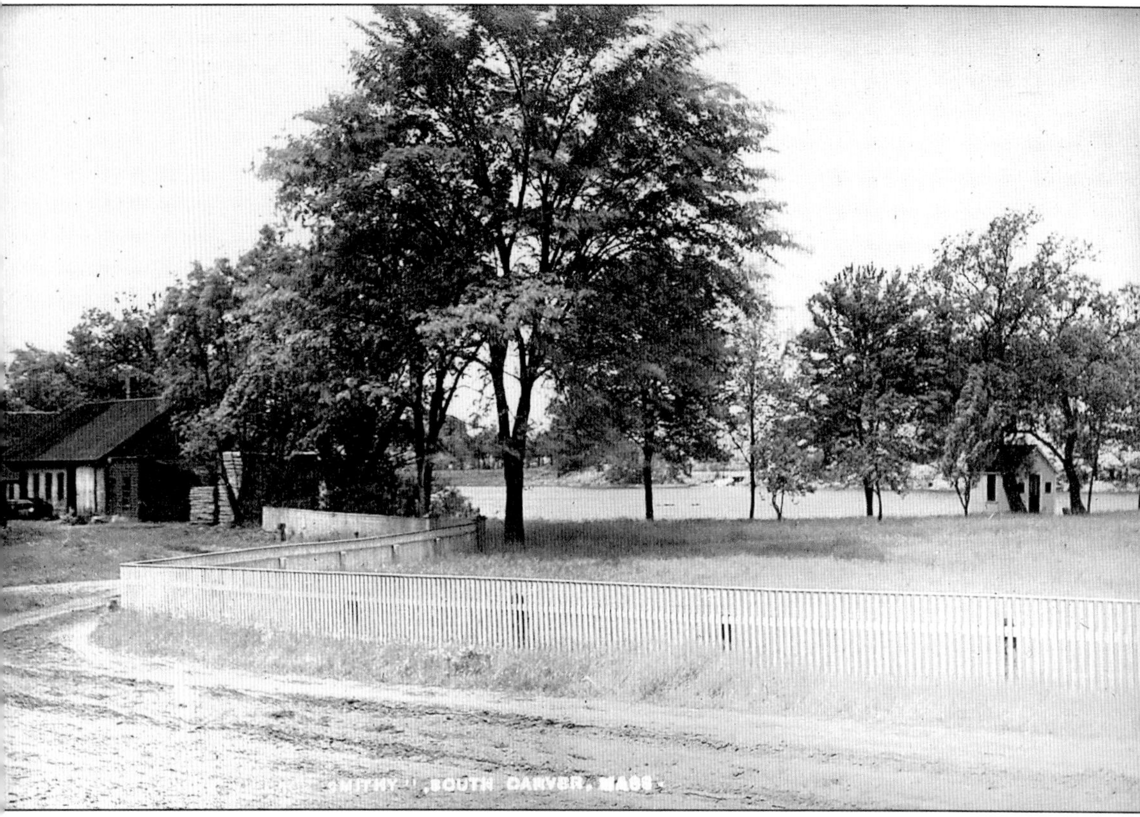

In this photograph, H. R. Bailey's Blacksmith Shop can be seen to the left; Foundry Pond and Sampson's Pond are in the background.

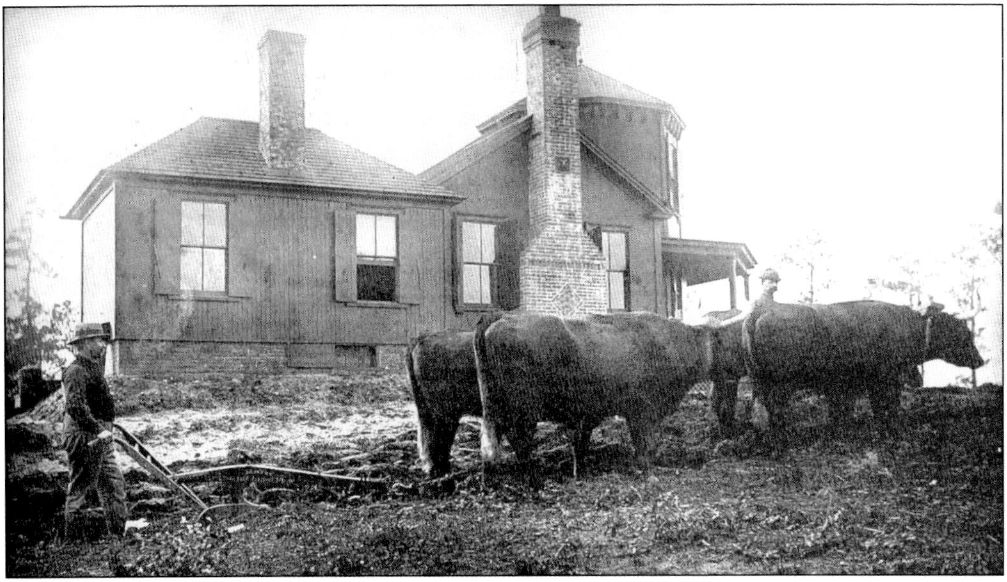

The Job A. Turner Farm was located in the vicinity of the present-day Myles Standish State Forest headquarters. The house on the hill, originally a summer home for Turner, eventually became the residence of the forest supervisor. (Courtesy of William Holmes.)

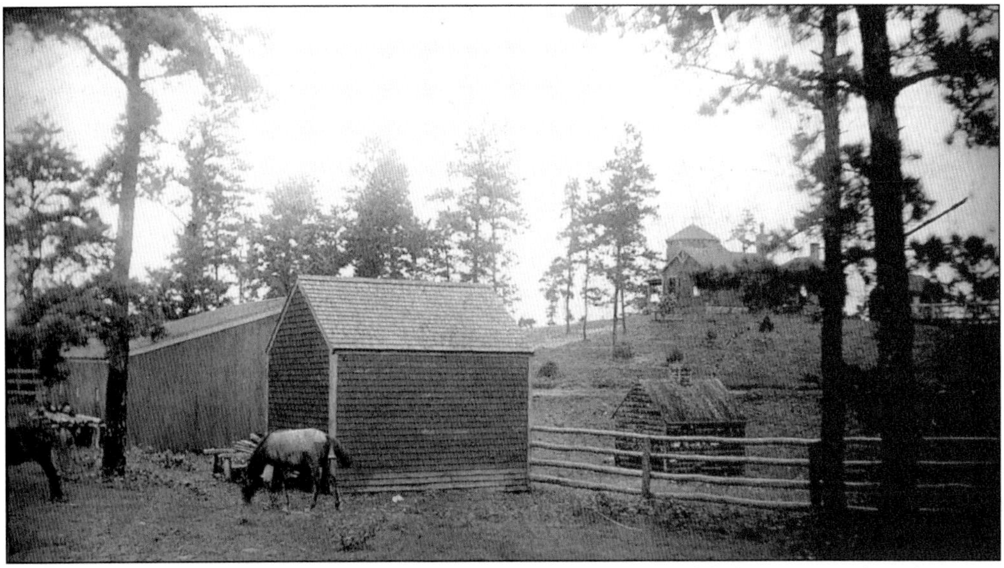

Prior to becoming a state forest, the Turner Farm property was a wildlife sanctuary for a few years c. 1911. Barrett's Pond is behind the house in this picture. (Courtesy of William Holmes.)

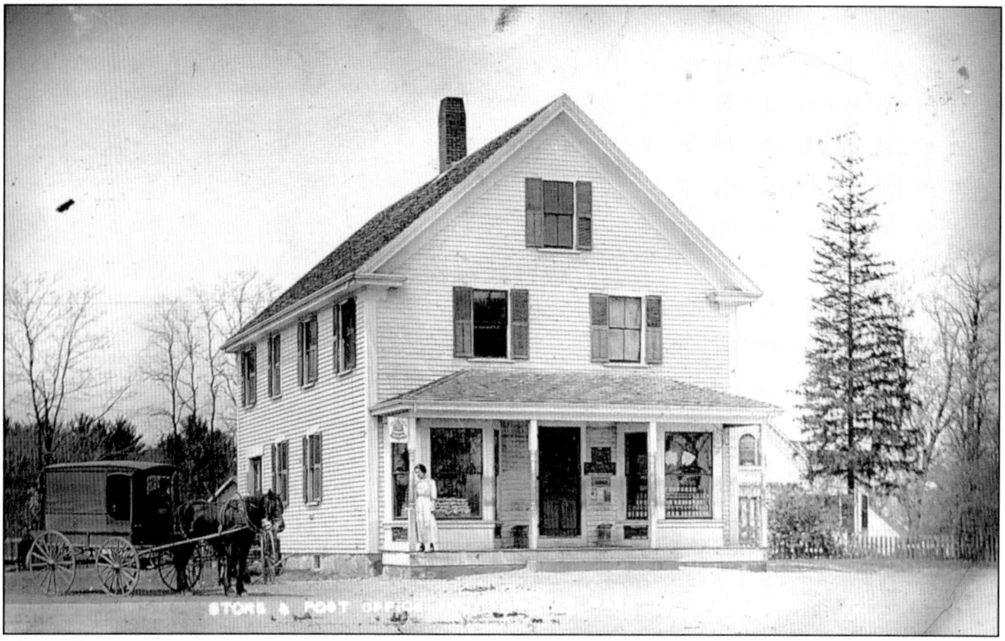

The Ellis Foundry Company Store was built in 1852 on the corner of Tremont and Lakeview Streets. The original foundry store was located near Furnace Pond, and supplies were provided using credit and the barter system. The store also served as a bank, a bar, and starting in 1850, a post office. The post office and store moved up the hill in 1852.

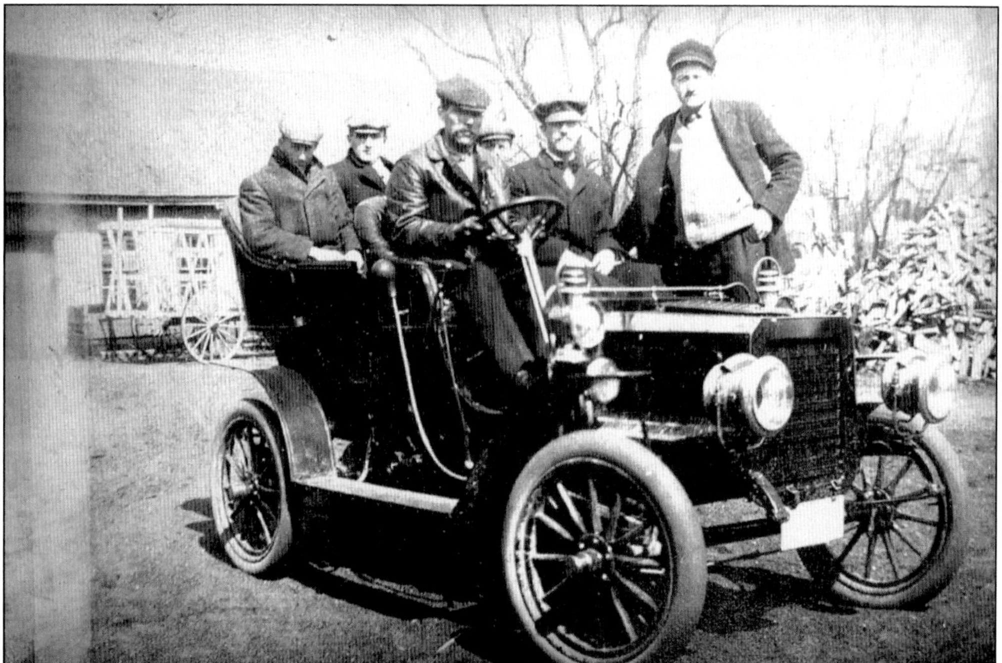

H. R. Bailey sits behind the wheel of his car in the company of the following friends, from left to right: (first row) H. R. Bailey, Arthur Nickerson, and Donald McFarlin; (second row) Bill Westgate, Joshua Southworth, and Bernard Shaw.

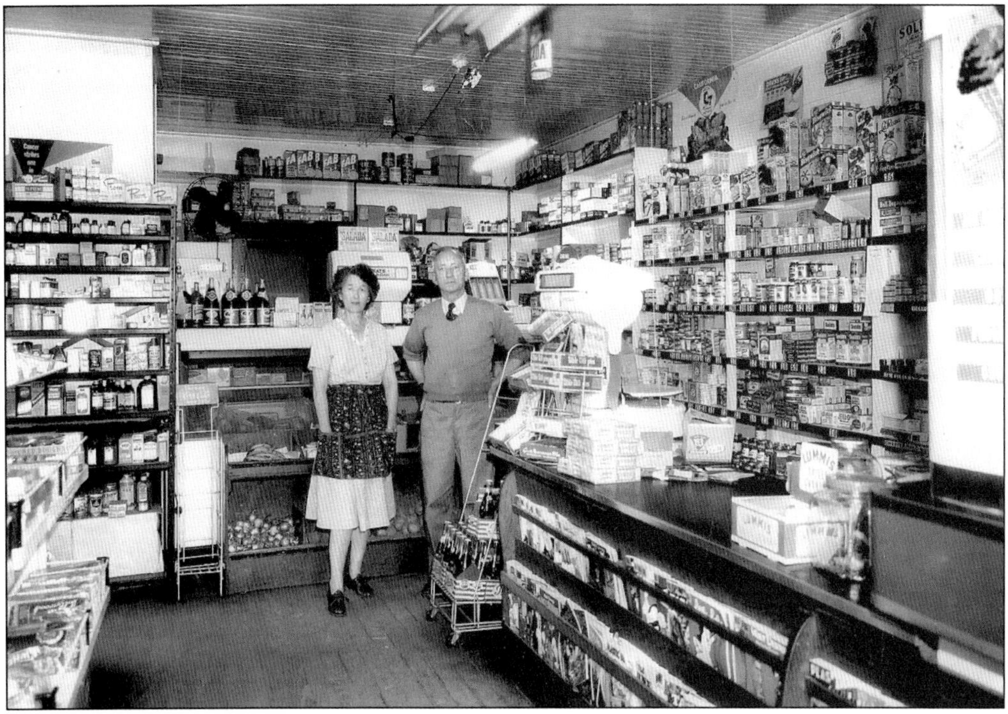

Postmaster Lewis W. Jenney and his wife, Dorothy (Perkins) Jenney, appear in their South Carver store. Lewis was the fifth owner of the property after the original building was destroyed by fire *c.* 1904. The building housed the post office, a general store, and the family's living quarters. The Jenneys sold the store in 1957 after serving the community for 20 years. (Courtesy of Constance Jenney Shaw.)

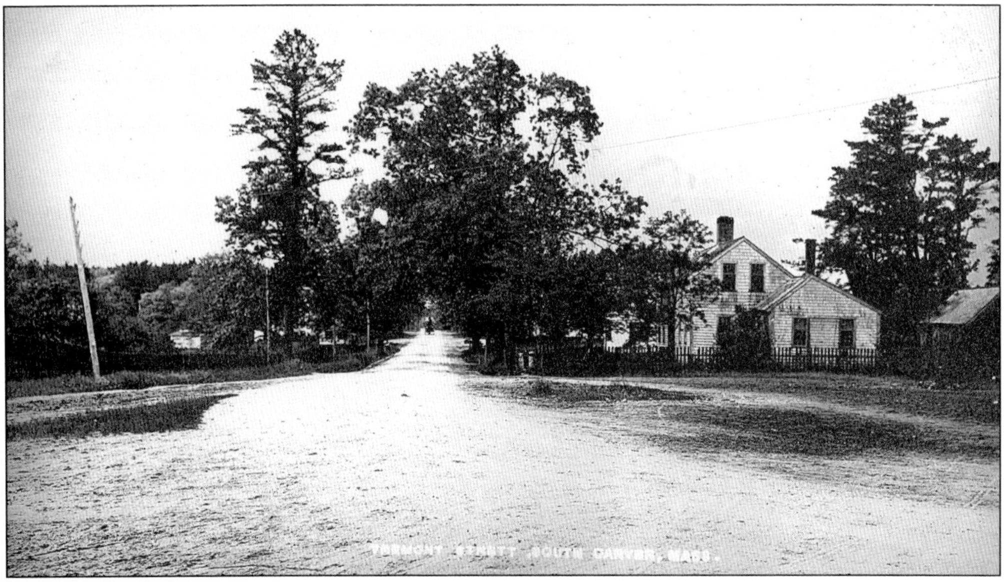

This view looks south down Tremont Street from the corner of Tremont and Lakeview Streets in South Carver. The village of South Carver was originally known as Furnace Village, or Ellis Furnace Village, until after the Civil War. (Courtesy of Christine Demers.)

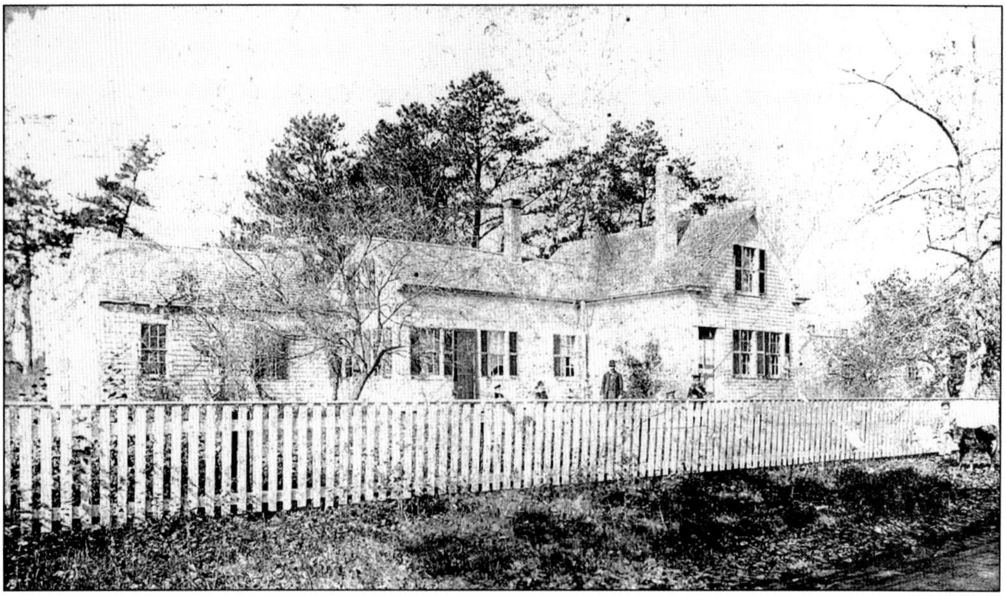

This house originally belonged to Ira Bent, a foundry molder. It is believed that the ell on the house was brought from the Federal Furnace. The residence became a two-family home in the 1900s.

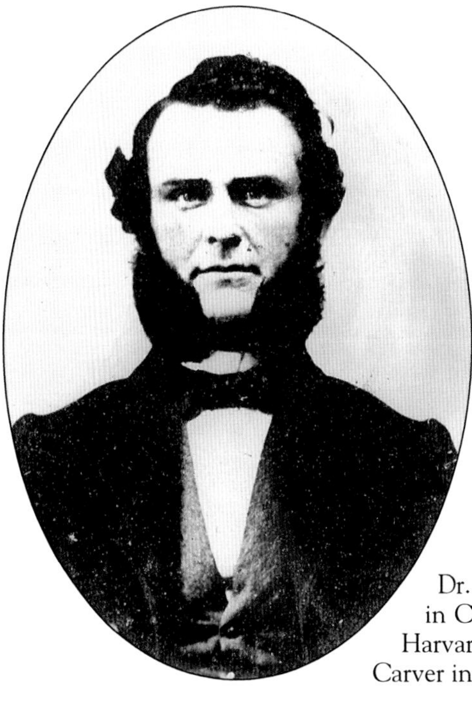

Dr. Ellis Holmes Cornish was a well-loved physician in Carver for more than 40 years. He graduated from Harvard Medical School and opened his practice in Carver in 1868.

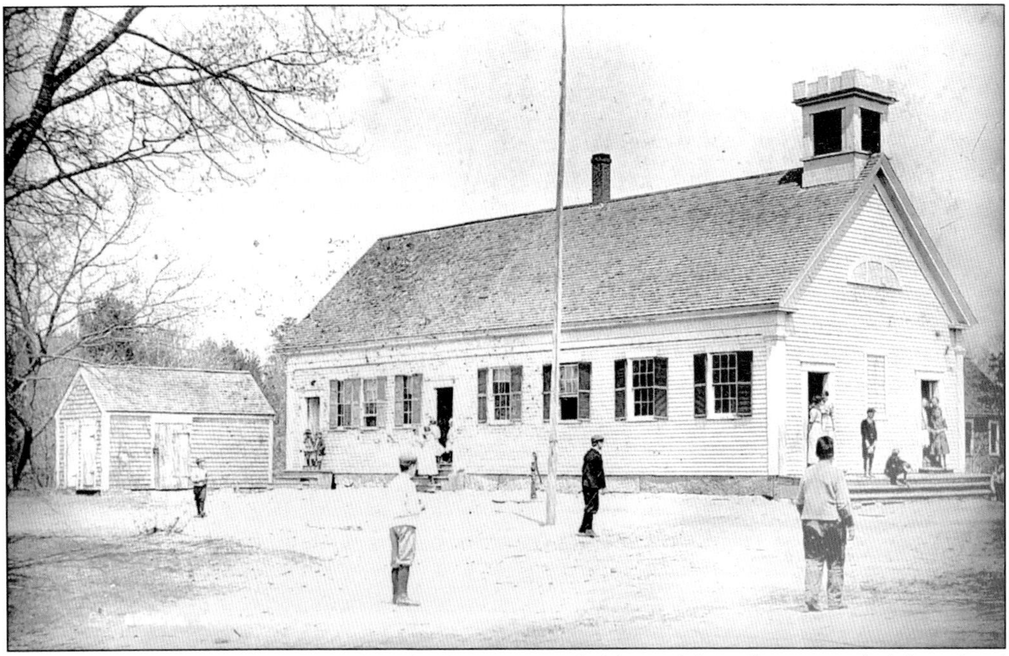

The South Carver Primary School was built in 1852. Children of the village attended the school until 1932, when the present Benjamin Ellis School was constructed. William Savery provided a large bell for the school.

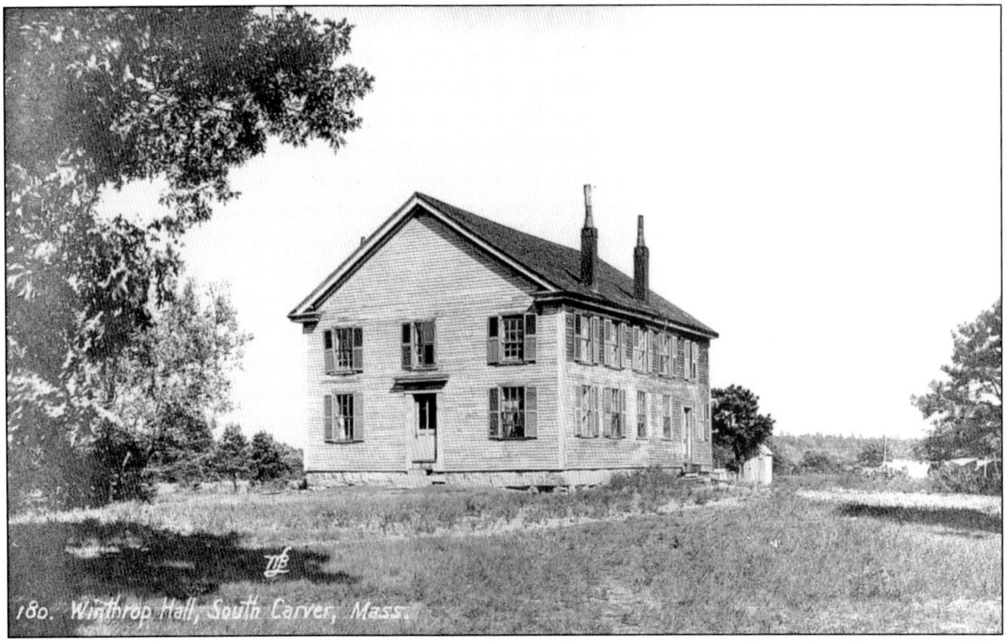

Winthrop Hall, located on Tremont Street in South Carver across from the Benjamin Ellis School, was built in 1879 for use as a community hall. The building was used for church services, Sunday school classes, performances, dances, debates, and a library. In later years, Finnish families who had just moved to Carver lived in the hall until they found permanent homes. The building was razed during the 1930s.

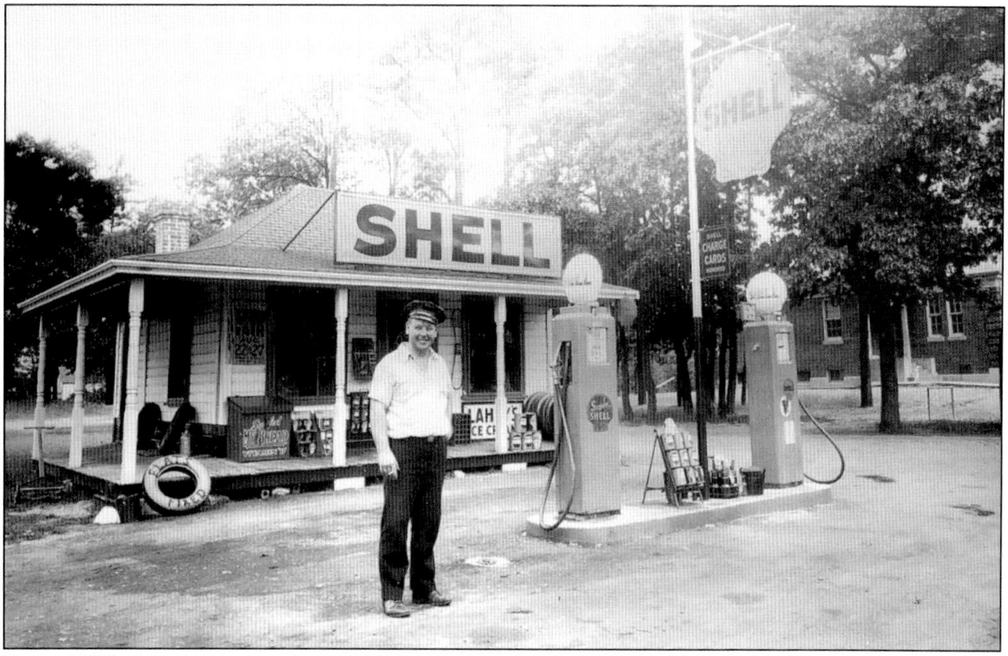

Roger Williams appears in front of his gas station known as "the Stand" in 1938. He leased it from Charles Carlson, who owned the property and lived in the house to the left of the station. Roger and his wife, Eunice, also drove school buses for the town for many years. The house was torn down, but the station is still in business after changing owners numerous times. (Courtesy of Henry S. Williams.)

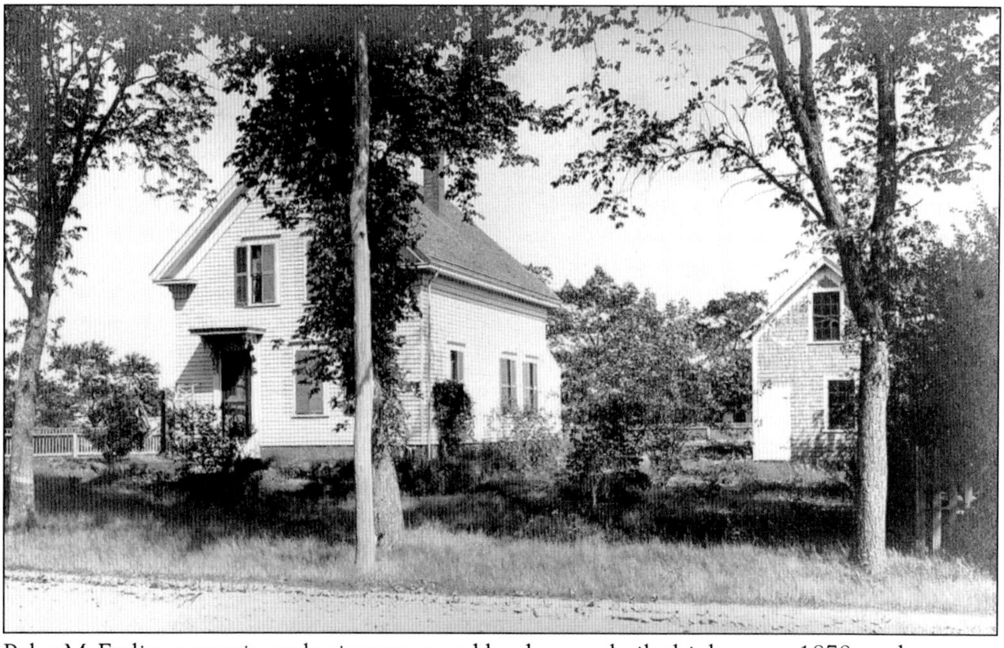

Peleg McFarlin, a prominent businessman and landowner, built this house *c.* 1878 on the corner of Wareham and Tremont Streets. He was one of the owners of the Ellis Foundry. He was also a writer of political and economic essays under the pen names Ruralis and Logan.

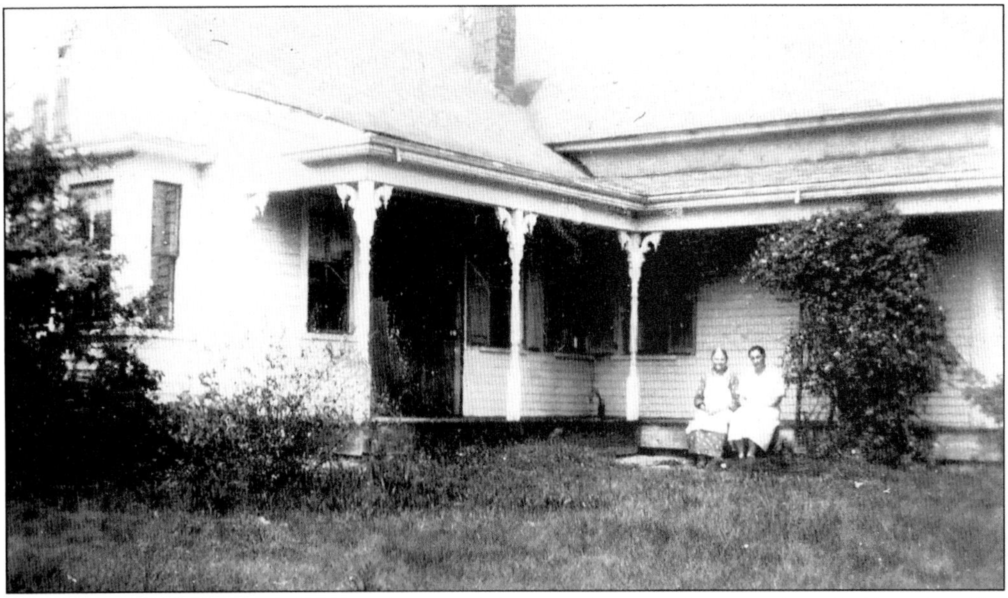

Anna Salmi sits on the porch of her home on Tremont Street with an unidentified boarder. She and her husband, Otto, came from Finland in the early 1900s, as did many others at that time, to work in the cranberry industry. In 1926, they purchased this home where their three daughters were born. (Courtesy of Mary Korpinen.)

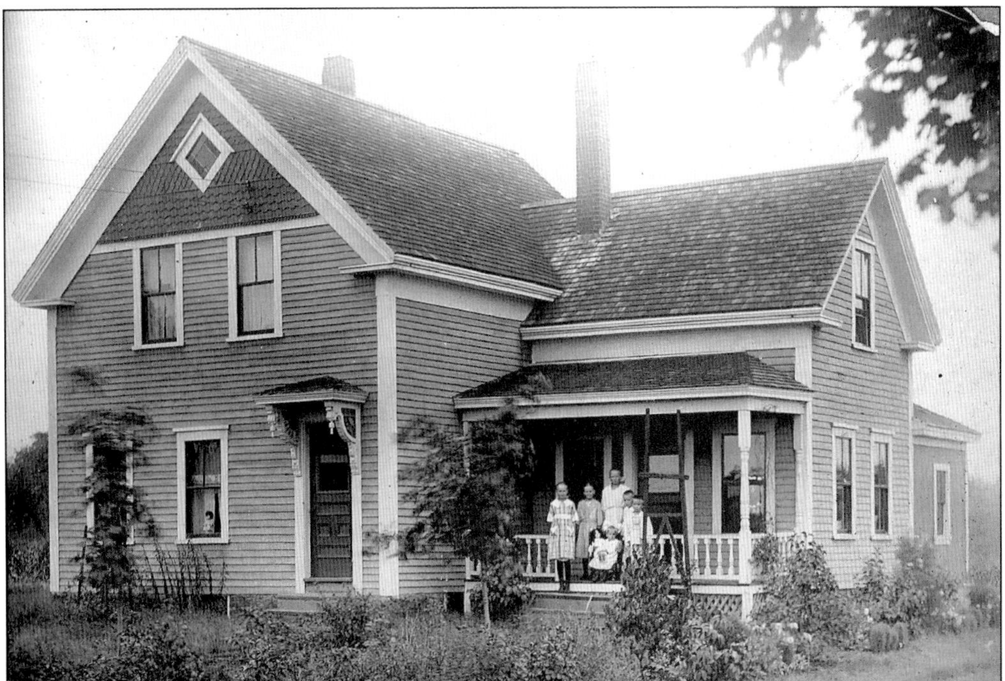

This was the home of Alex Johnson on Tremont Street in South Carver. Both Alex and his wife, Hulda, came from Finland. They first settled in Maine but then moved to Carver in 1896. Alex worked for other cranberry growers and eventually became the owner of a number of bogs. His five children married and settled in South Carver. (Courtesy of Henry S. Williams.)

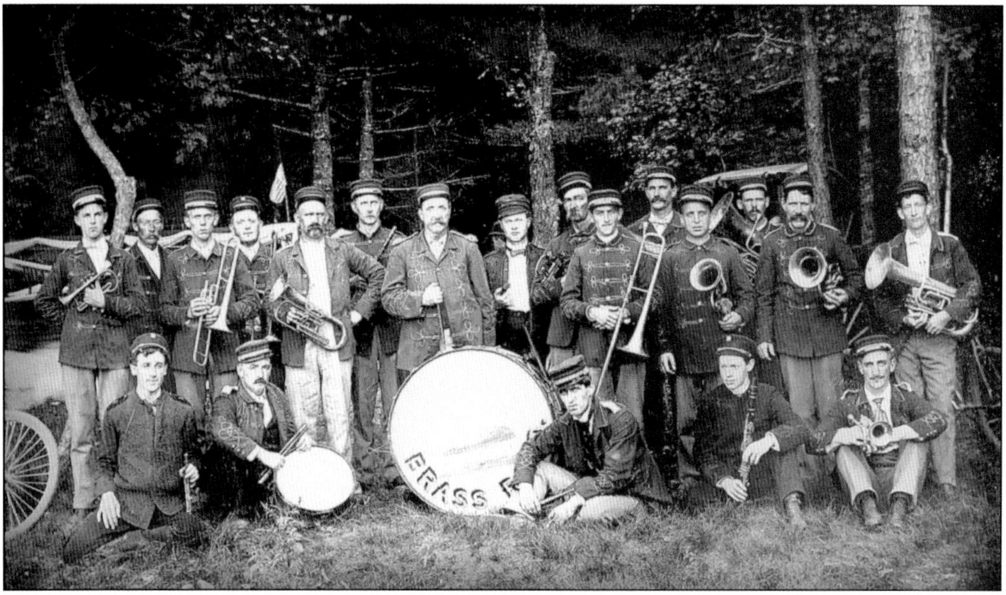

The Thomas Southworth Brass Band was active in the late 1870s and 1880s. Southworth was a foundry worker and a musician from South Carver. Posing for the photograph, from left to right, are the following: (first row) unidentified, Arthur Burbank, Harvey Swift, unidentified, and Carl Southworth; (second row) Arthur Nickerson, Harvey Raymond, unidentified, Walter Shurtleff, L. Hayden, unidentified, Mozart Southworth, Chester Poole, Ira Ward, Don McFarlin, Everett Tillson, Jimmy Lee, Skip Griffith, Chet Tillson, and Frank Raymond.

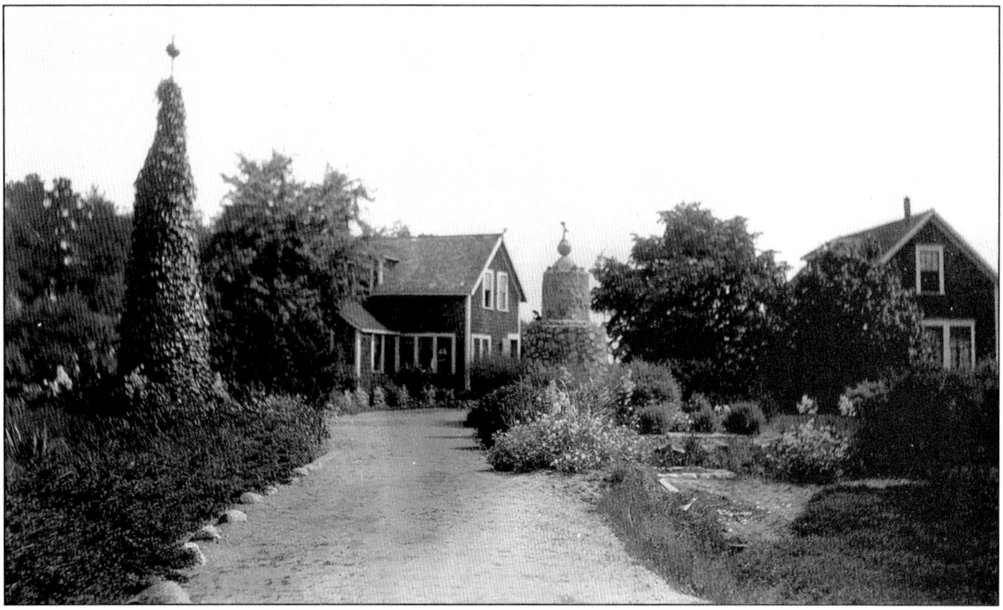

Frederick Anderson, a Swedish immigrant and ironworker, built a monument in his elaborate gardens on Wareham Street in South Carver. The monument was dedicated as the Liberty Column at a special ceremony after World War I and represented Anderson's hope for peace and freedom for all.

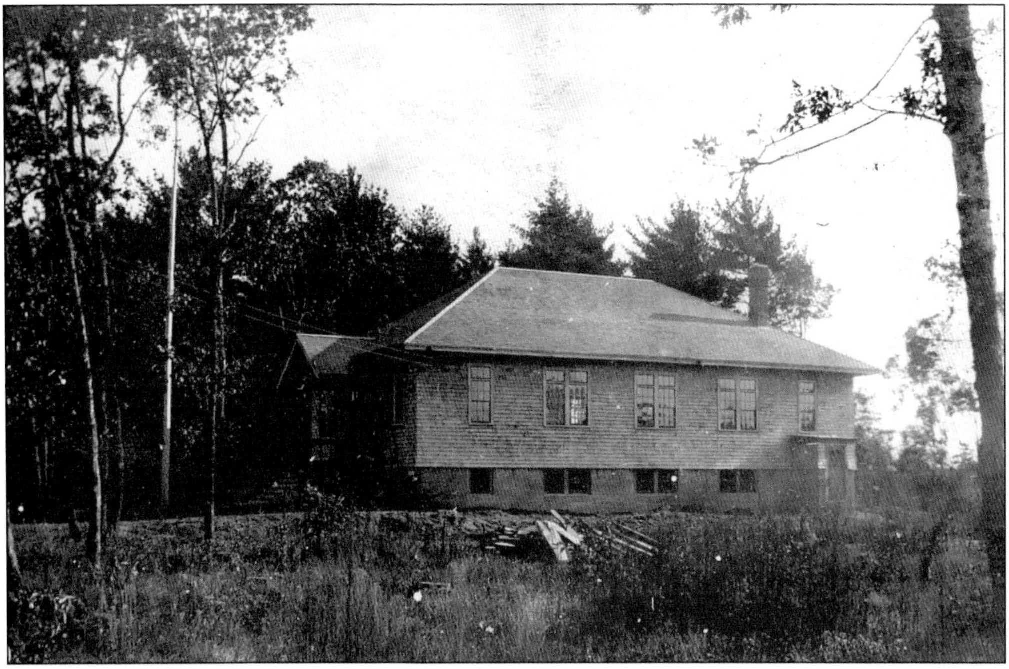

The grange hall was built in 1915 on Wareham Street in South Carver. A stone plaque was placed in the grove next to the building to commemorate Julian Southworth, a South Carver man who was killed in World War I. The pine grove was the site of clam bakes held by the Ladies' Aid Society and the grange until the hurricane of 1938 destroyed the grove.

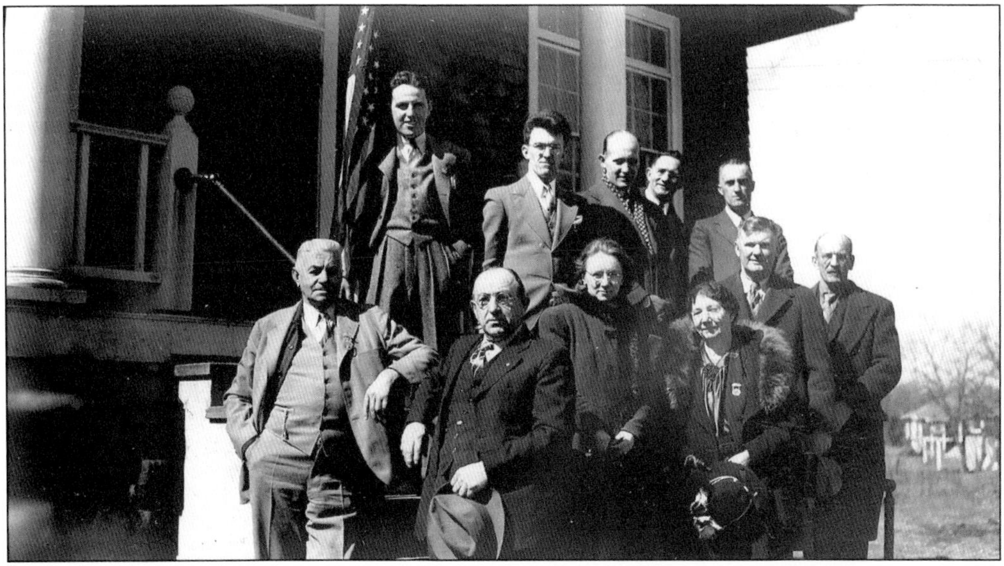

Members of the South Carver Grange pose in front of their building on Wareham Street. From left to right are the following: (first row) Frank Barrows, William E. Holmes, Hattie Griffith, and Florence Washburn; (second row) David Barry, Edward Adams, Norman Holmes, Rodney Griffith, Ralph Washburn, Andrew Griffith, and Ellis Bumpus. (Courtesy of William Holmes.)

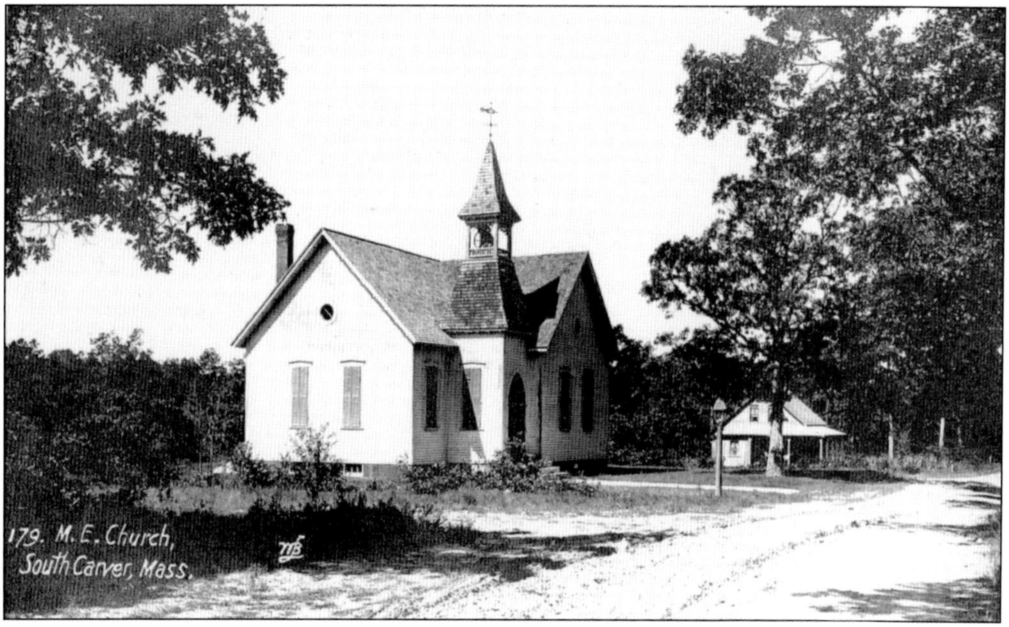

The Methodist church in South Carver was built in 1896, when attendance at the Methodist Episcopal church at Huckleberry Corner had fallen due to the increase of other churches in that area.

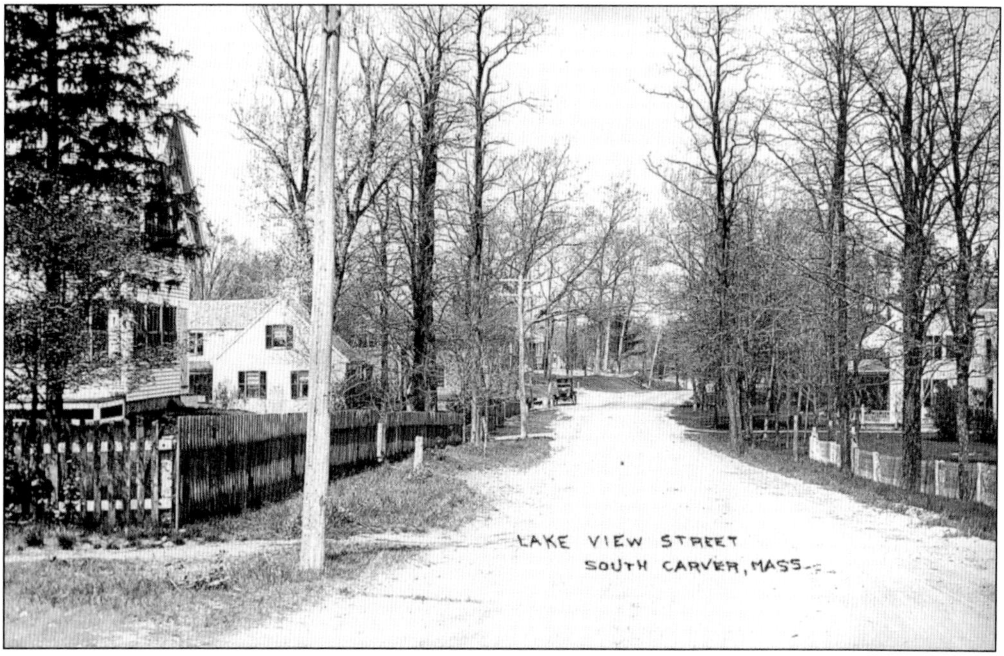

This westerly view shows Lakeview Street from the front of the Ellis Foundry Company Store. Sampson's Pond is to the right, and the first house on the left was the home of H. R. Bailey, local cranberry grower and inventor of cranberry-growing equipment.

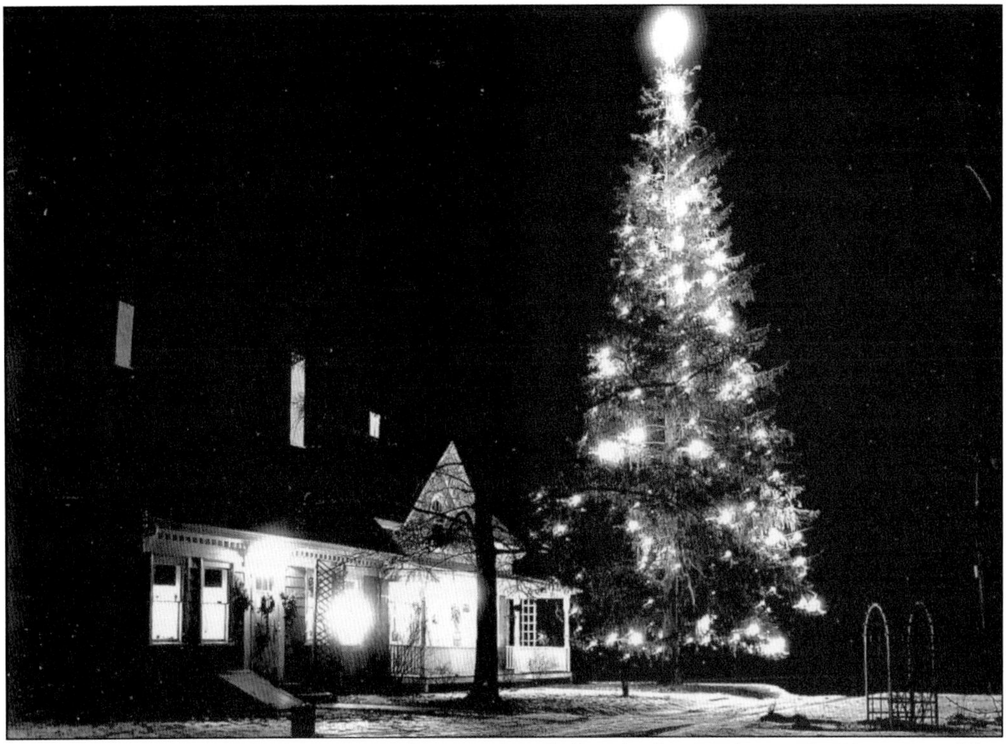

H. R. Bailey's 79-foot-high tree was decorated with hundreds of lights each Christmas. This custom began a couple of years after Ellis Atwood drew hundreds to his Christmas displays at his residence on Lakeview Street, just down the road. Each year, local carolers gathered at H. R. Bailey's home to sing and were served hot chocolate by his wife, Ina Bailey.

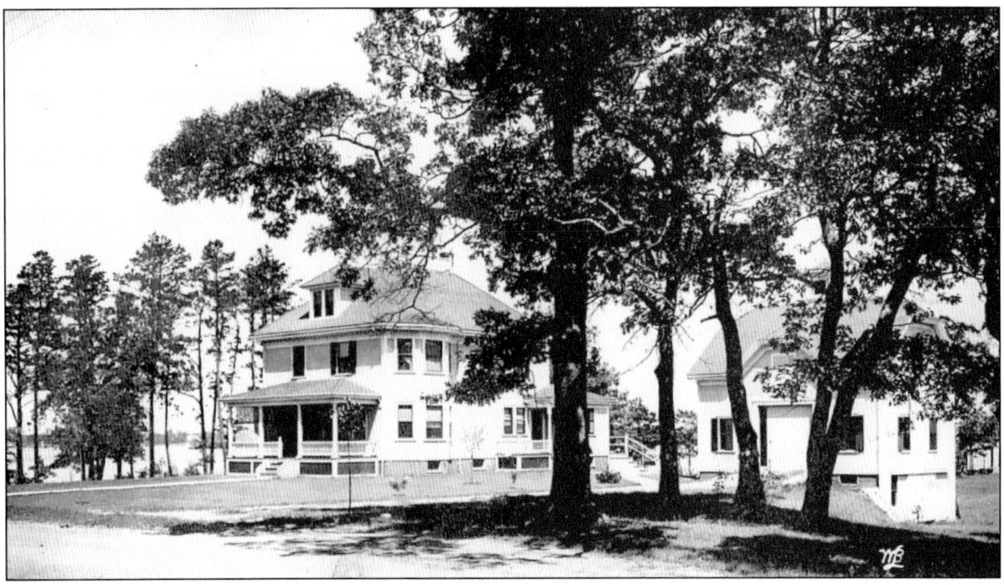

Stephen Dexter Atwood, a local cranberry grower, built this home *c.* 1915. Upon his death, his son Ellis lived here. Ellis D. Atwood founded the Edaville Railroad and oversaw the largest privately owned cranberry business in the Commonwealth during the 1930s and 1940s.

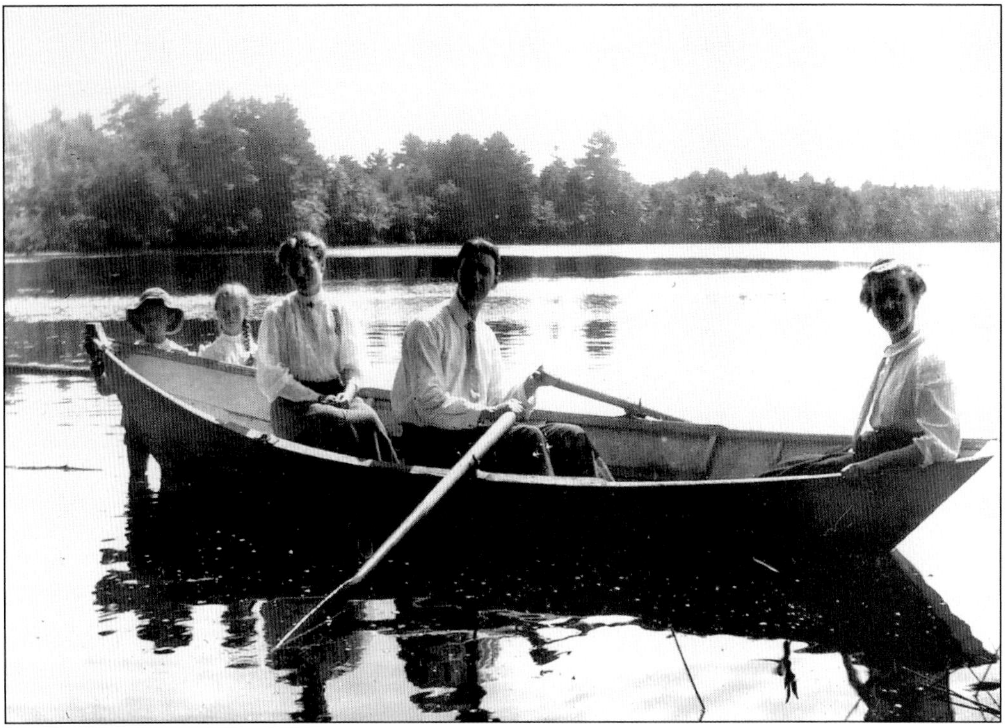

Local townspeople enjoy an outing on Sampson's Pond. (Courtesy of Charles Bezanson.)

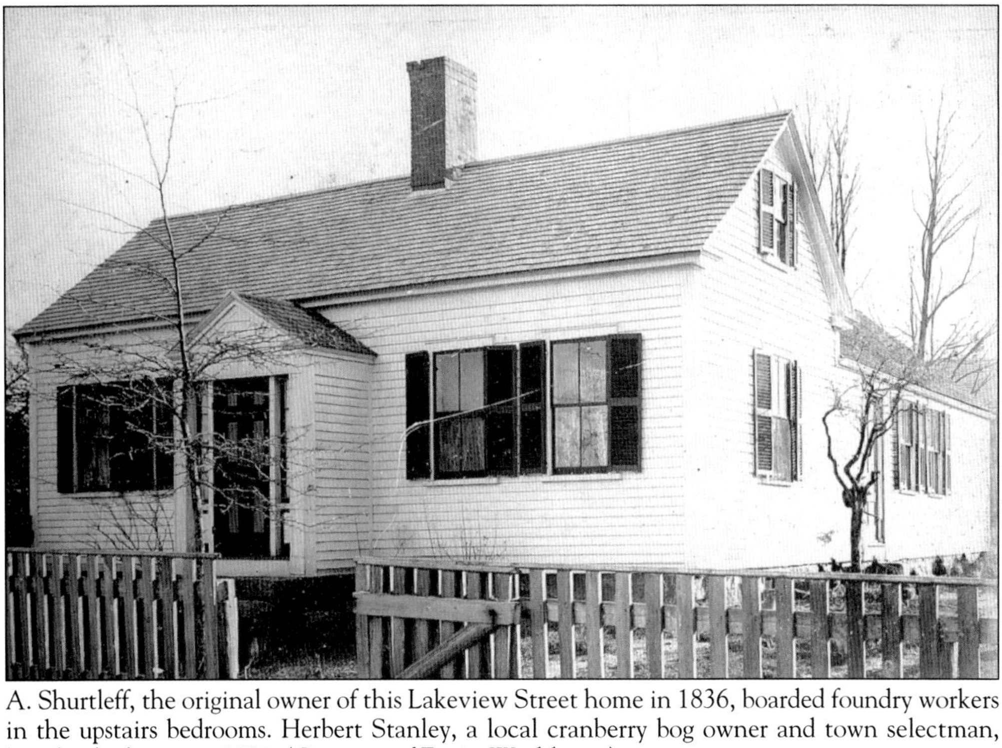

A. Shurtleff, the original owner of this Lakeview Street home in 1836, boarded foundry workers in the upstairs bedrooms. Herbert Stanley, a local cranberry bog owner and town selectman, bought the house in 1894. (Courtesy of Erwin Washburn.)

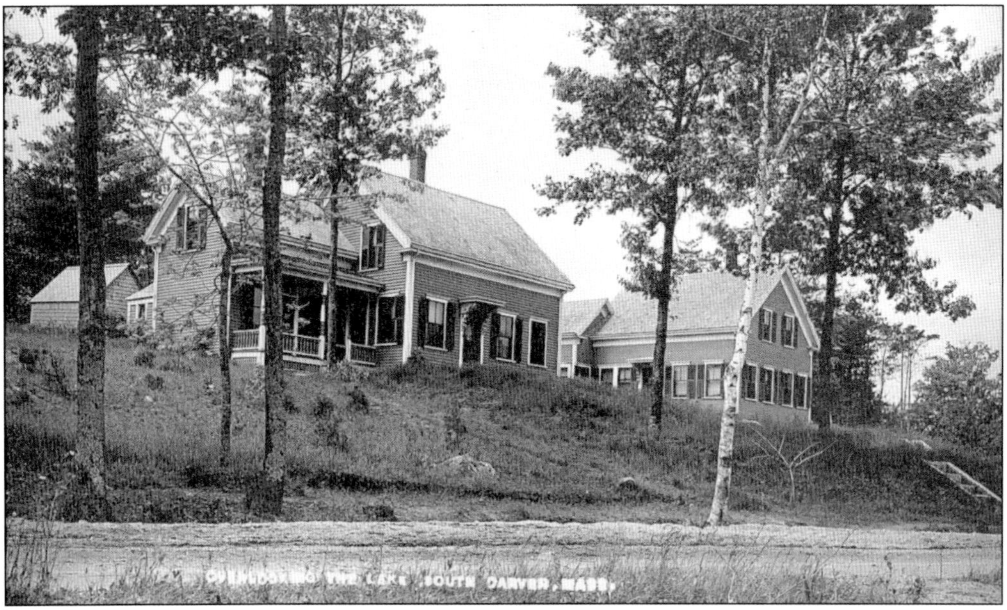

These two homes on the hill facing Sampson's Pond on Lakeview Street were built *c.* 1899 by Henry Griffith, author of *History of the Town of Carver, Massachusetts,* and town clerk. The home on the left was built for his mother, Martha. Griffith's home on the right had a small building in the rear that served as his office.

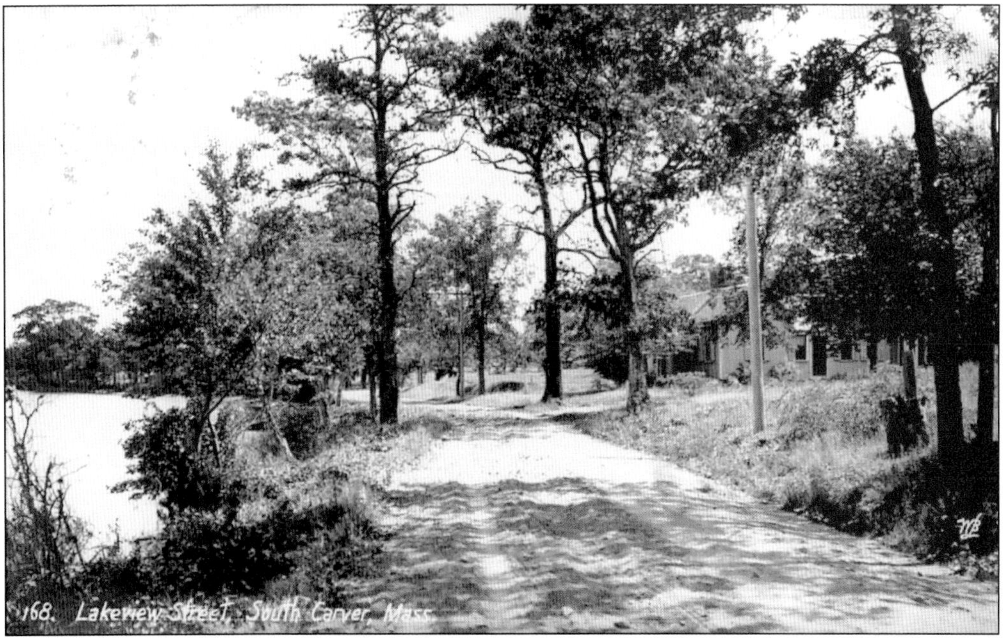

Sampson's Pond appears on the left in this photograph as Lakeview Street heads east. In early records, this part of the territory was called Samsons Country. The name Samsons is believed to be associated with an American Indian name, but the land was called Samsons Country prior to the granting of 200 acres of land to an American Indian named Samuel Sonett on the south side of the pond.

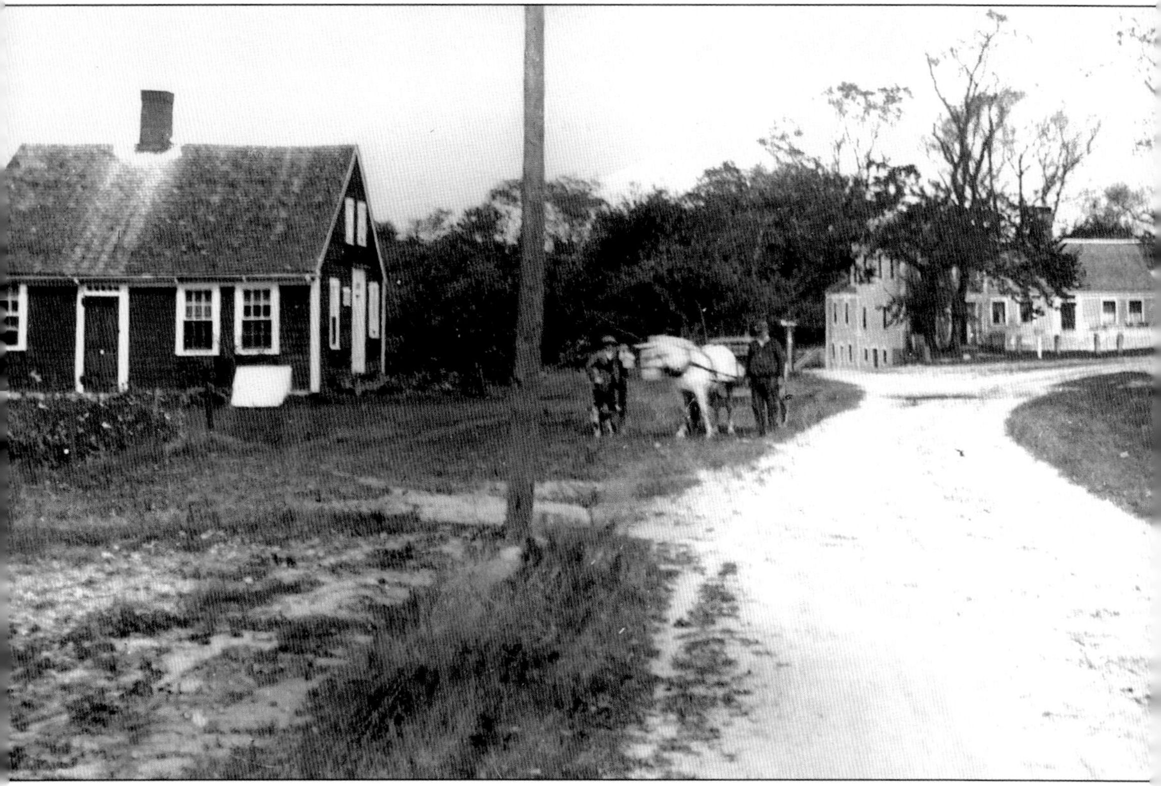

John Maxim Jr. was born in this house at Huckleberry Corner in 1795. He was a molder at a local foundry, a musician, and a writer for local newspapers using the pseudonym Bemis. He wrote witty songs during political campaigns and became famous for the slogan "Tippicanoe and Tyler Too" for William Henry Harrison's 1840 presidential campaign. Ryder's Store can be seen up the road on the right. The store operated in the 1850s. The building was later owned by Clayton McFarlin and his sister, who used the building as a millinery shop and a screen house. (Courtesy of Mary Asiaf.)

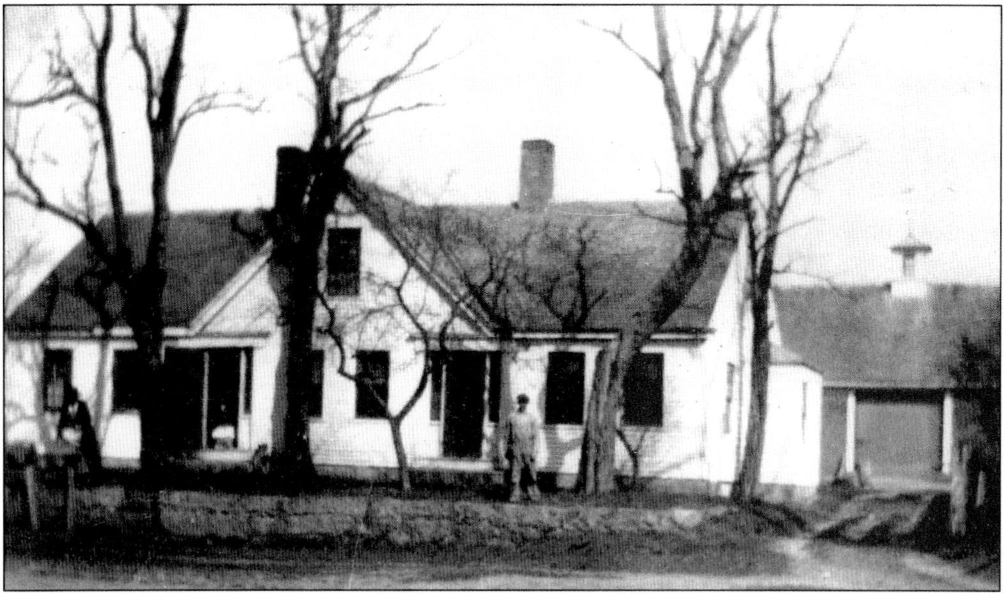

The Gustavus Atwood House on Rochester Road, built *c.* 1812, was passed from father to son until it was sold out of the family in 1963. The property served as a farm and lumber business for many years, and the house has seen many additions. Gustavus Atwood was a committed town resident who was very active in local government.

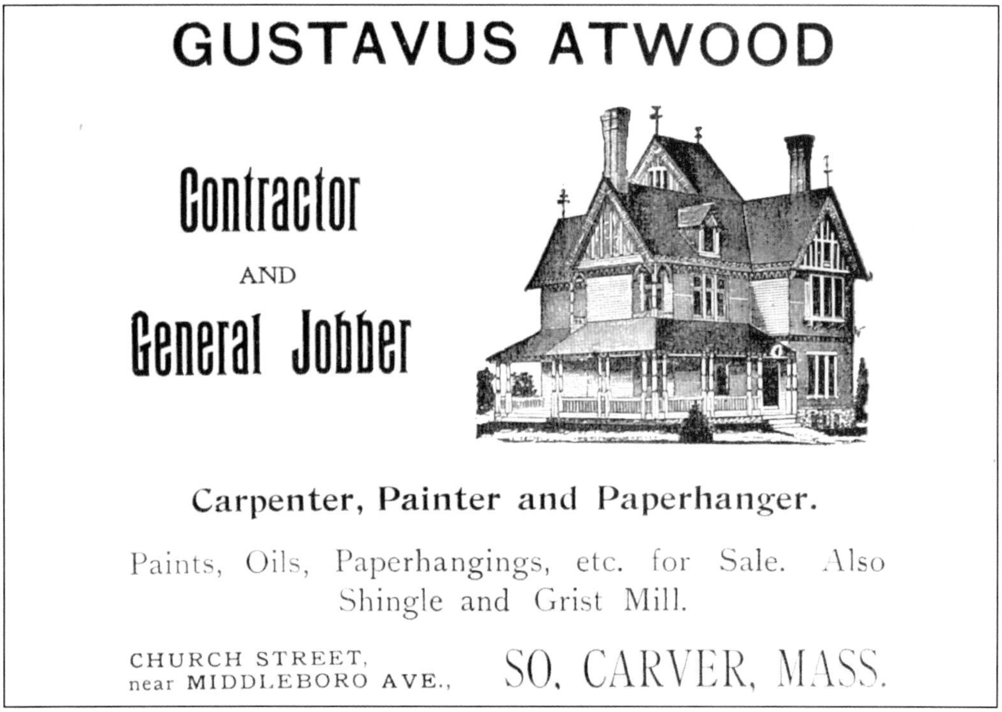

An advertisement for Gustavus Atwood's business appears in *The 1902–1903 Resident and Business Directory of Carver, Halifax, Hanson, and Plympton*. Middleboro Avenue was the main road between South Carver and Middleborough. Middleboro Avenue and Church Street merged at Huckleberry Corner.

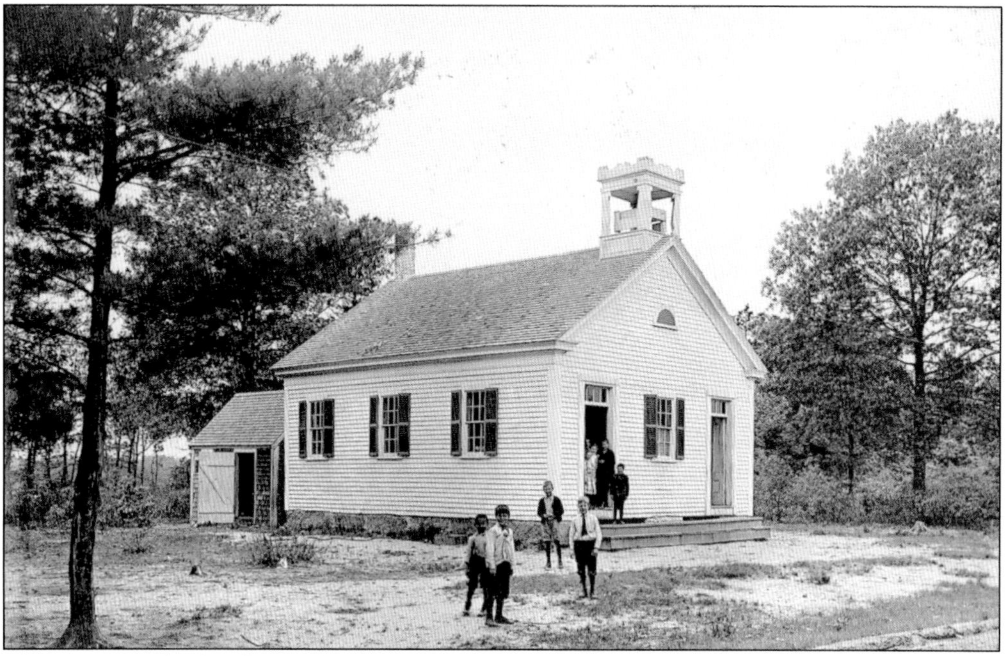

The Bates Pond Schoolhouse, built in 1852, was located on Rochester Road and served District 8 in the town school system. The building was moved near Bates Pond on Rochester Road in 1900. In 1975, it was moved again to its present site on Indian Street near the Rochester Road intersection, where it has been converted to a private residence.

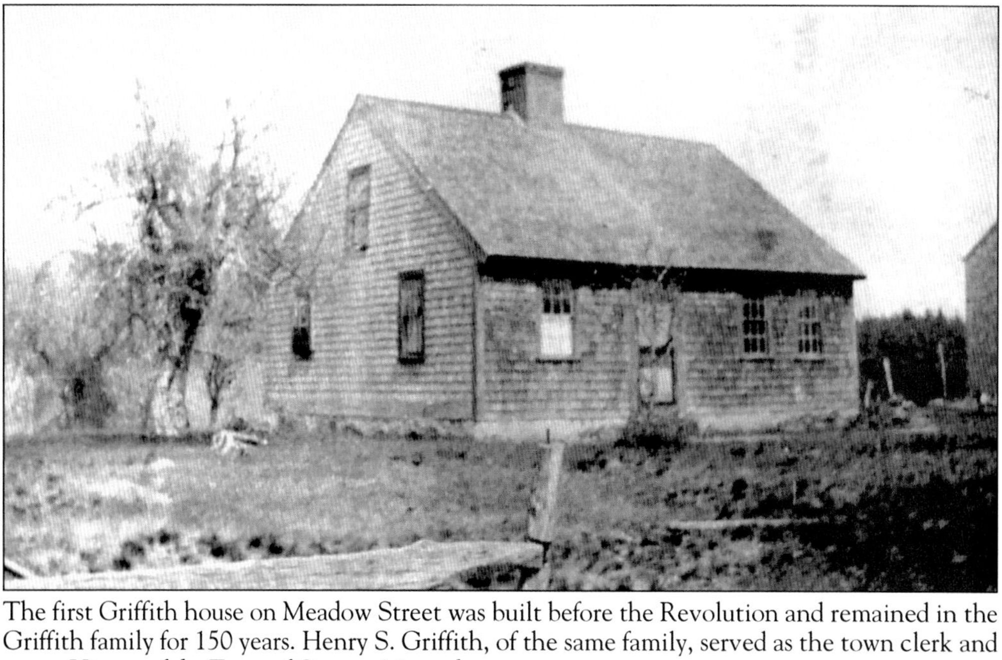

The first Griffith house on Meadow Street was built before the Revolution and remained in the Griffith family for 150 years. Henry S. Griffith, of the same family, served as the town clerk and wrote *History of the Town of Carver, Massachusetts*.

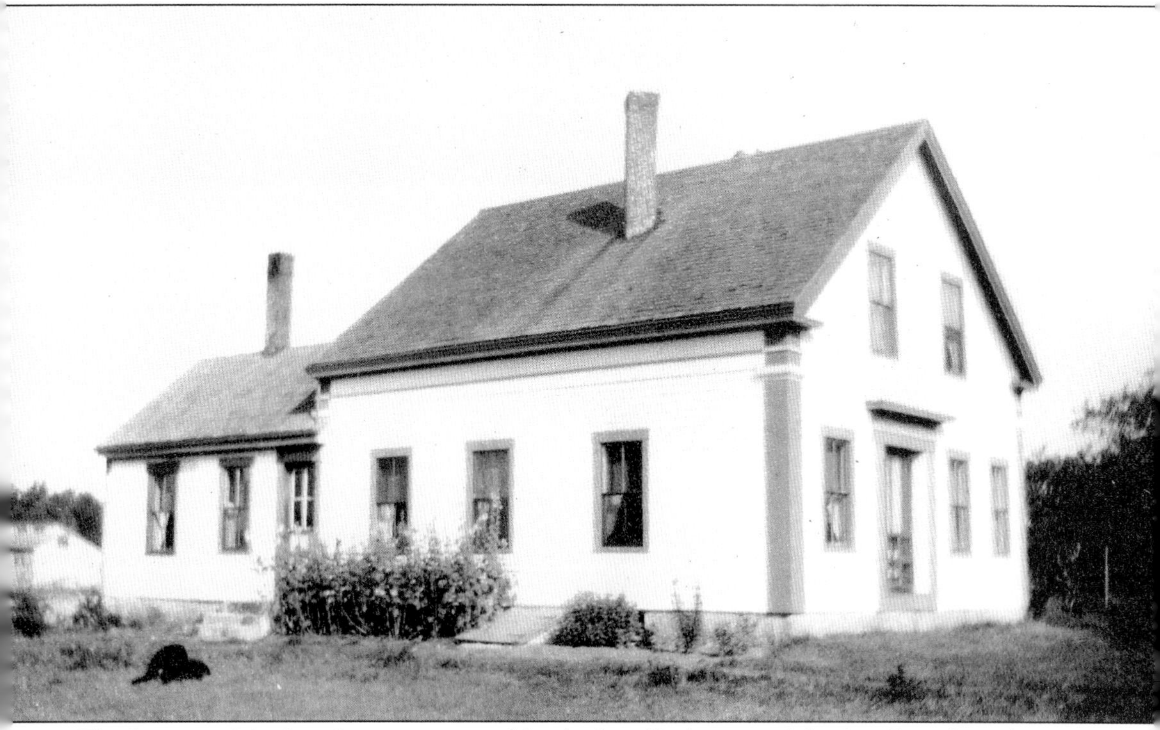

This home on Meadow Street was owned by Andrew Kaski, one of the first Finnish settlers in Carver. He and his wife helped other Finnish immigrants get settled, as was the custom of Finnish families. One goal of these families was to earn enough money to buy a home and build a sauna, for the sauna allowed them to continue an important Finnish custom. Finnish immigrants farmed the land, and many became cranberry bog owners. (Courtesy of Sally Merritt.)

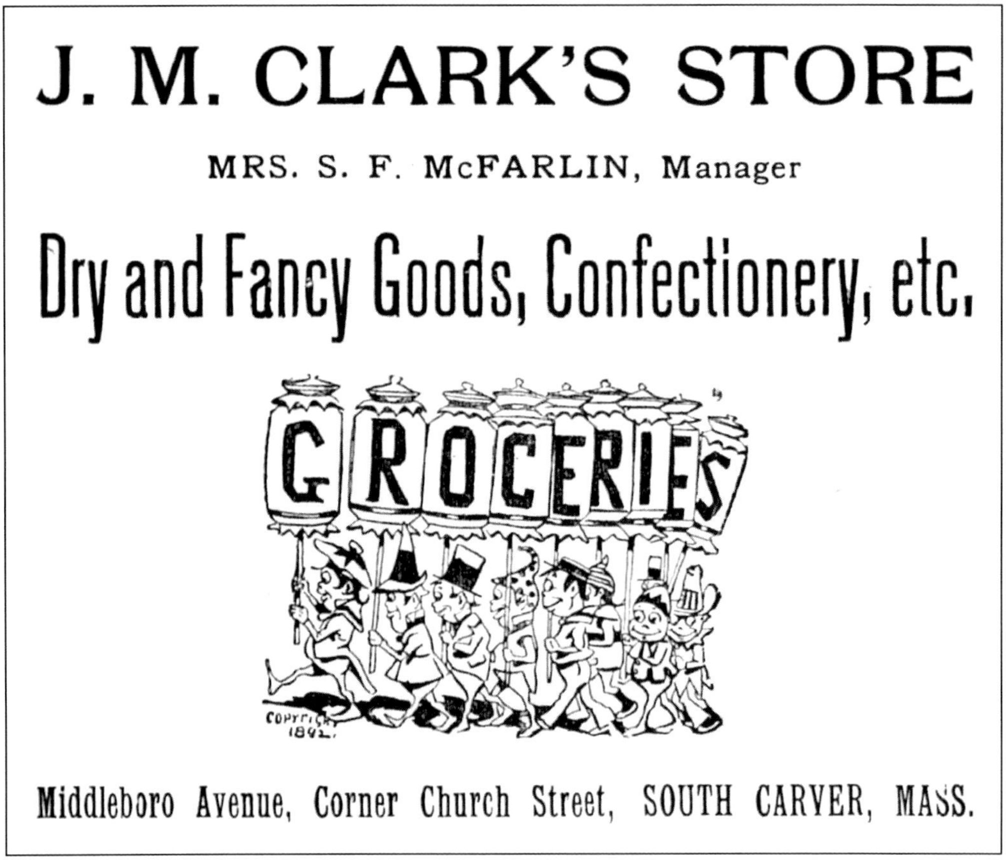

An advertisement for Clark's Store appears in *The 1902–1903 Resident and Business Directory of Carver, Halifax, Hanson, and Plympton*.

Seven

Cranberries

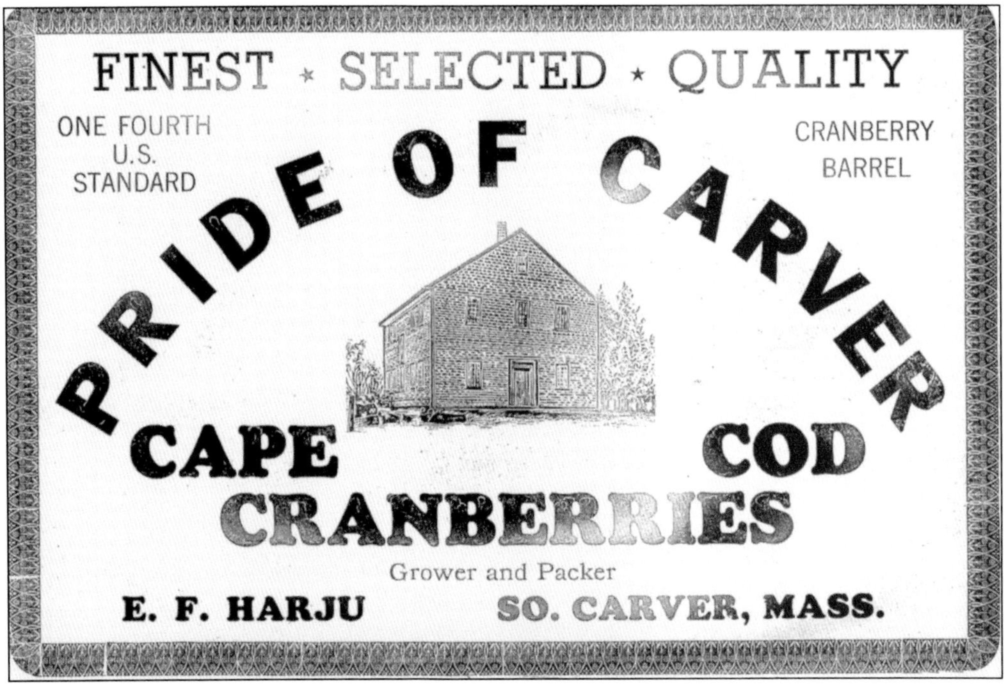

The Pride of Carver cranberry label belonged to Eino F. Harju, who was a member of the Cape Cod Cranberry Growers Association. (Courtesy of Larry Cole.)

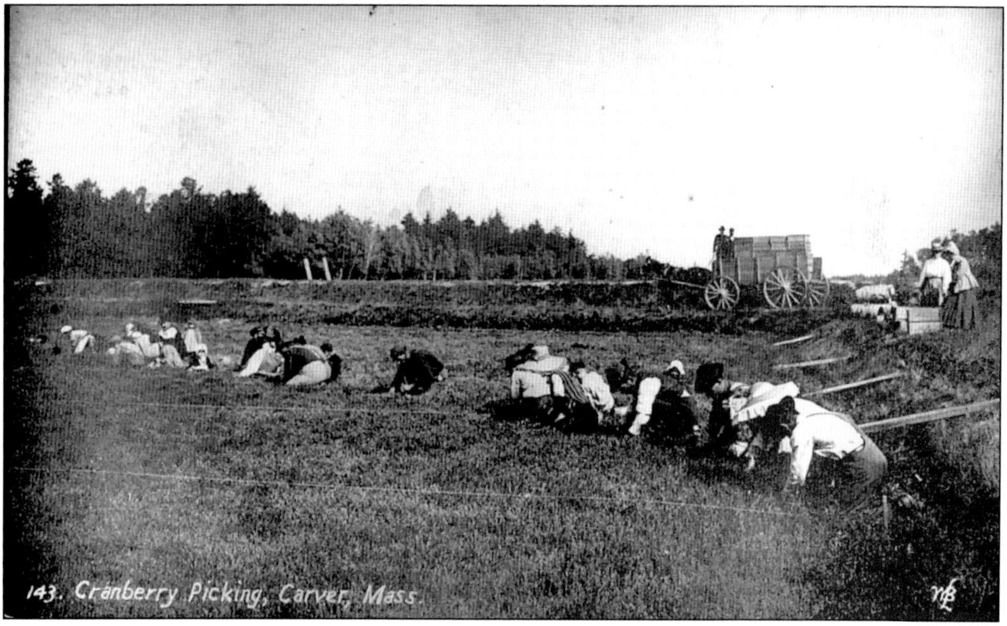

The many cranberry bogs in Carver drew people to town for the annual harvest of the berries. The cranberries were individually hand-picked, and lines of string marked off a picker's designated area. (Courtesy of Christine Demers.)

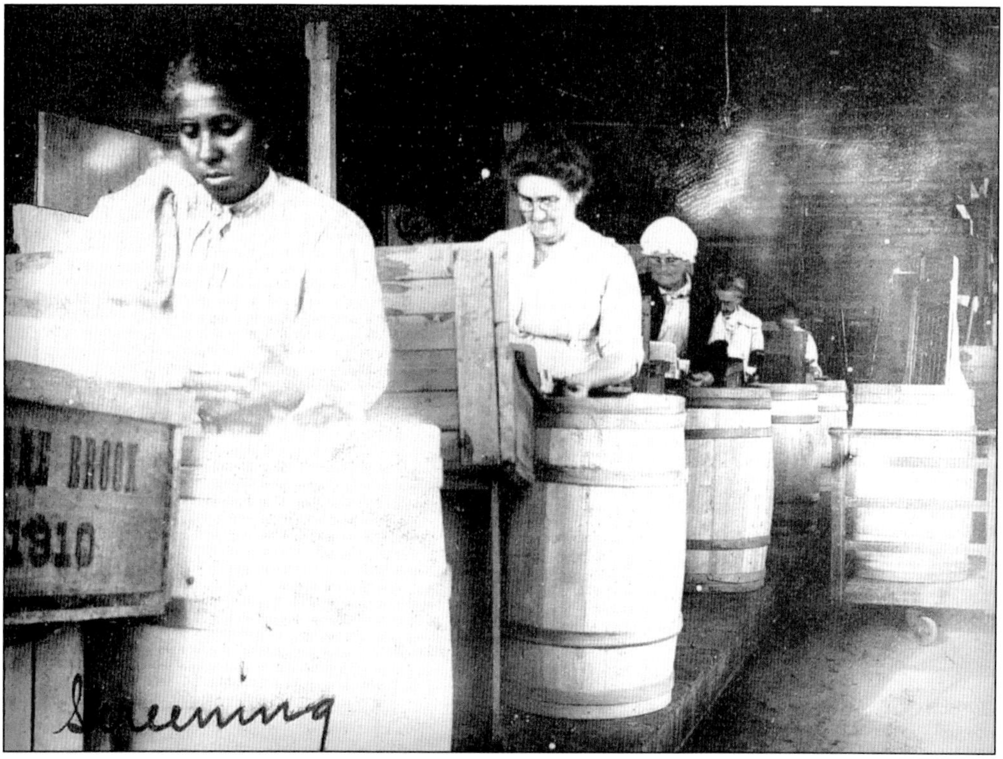

Local women, including those related to the growers, had the long, tedious task of screening cranberries and filling barrels without the aid of machinery.

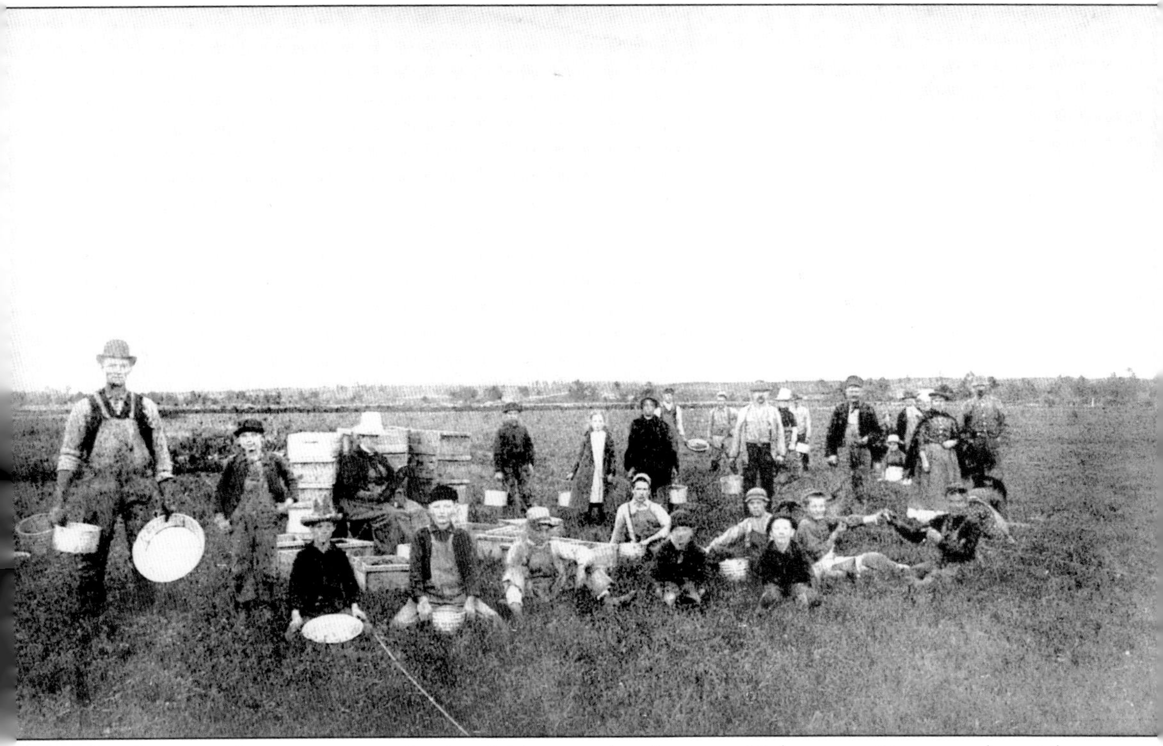

Cranberry workers prepare to begin picking cranberries on a Makepeace Company bog. The cranberry industry drew immigrants in great numbers from Finland. Many Finns arrived toward the end of the 1800s, and by the early to mid-1800s, Carver had the largest number of Finnish residents among the surrounding towns. (Courtesy of William Holmes.)

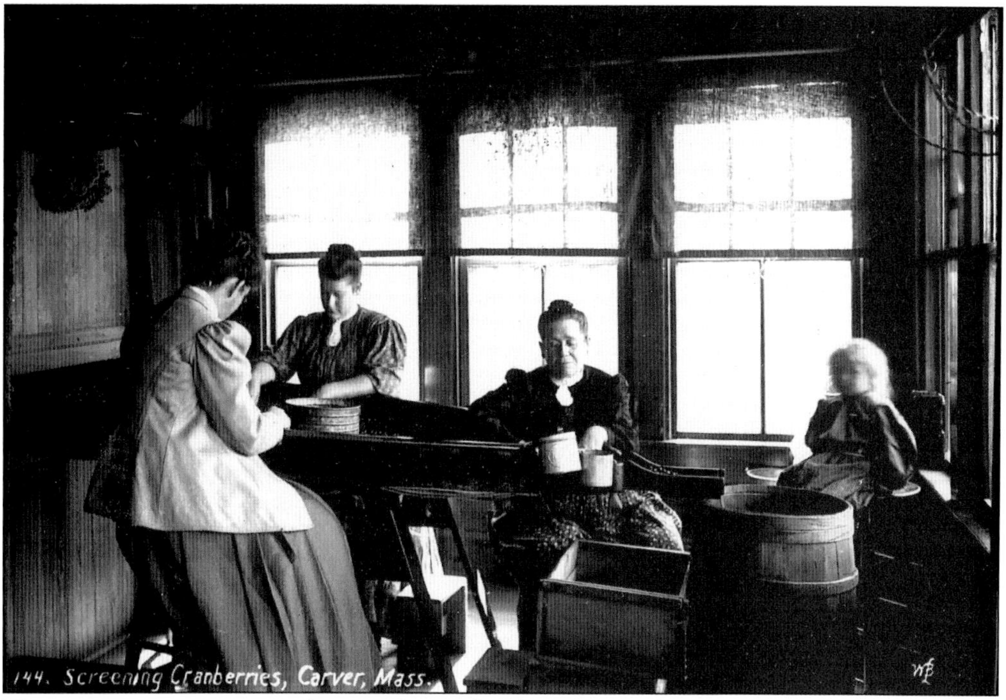

These women screen cranberries for a local grower. The good berries go into the shipping barrels.

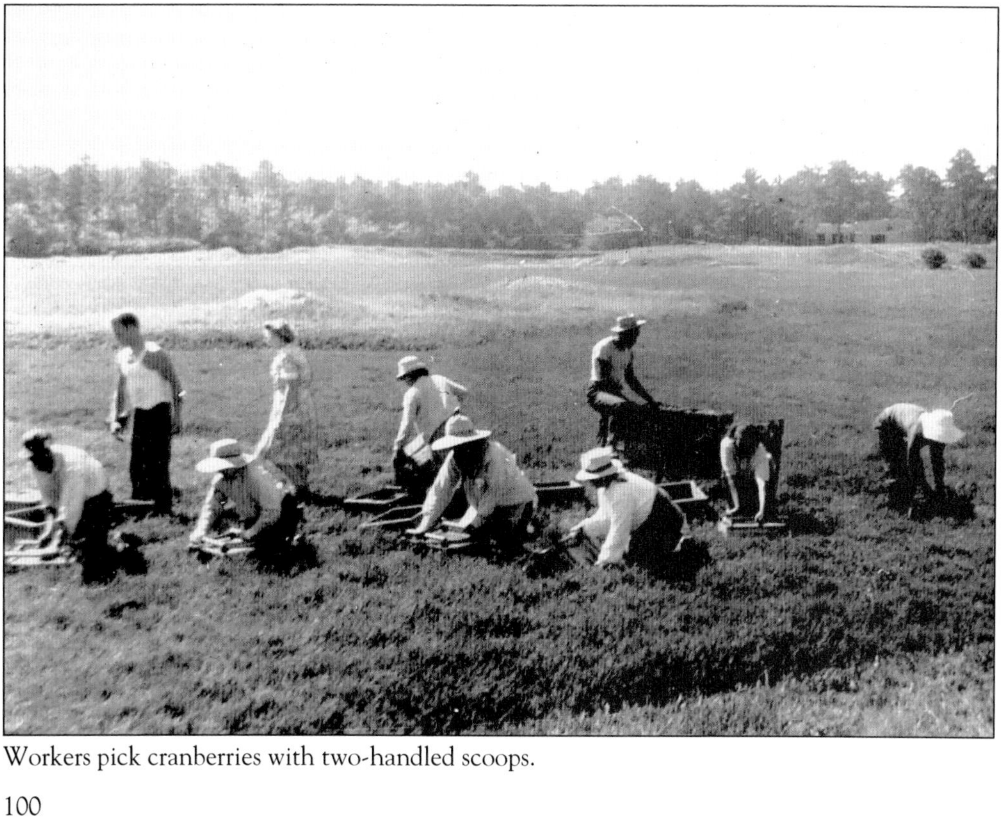
Workers pick cranberries with two-handled scoops.

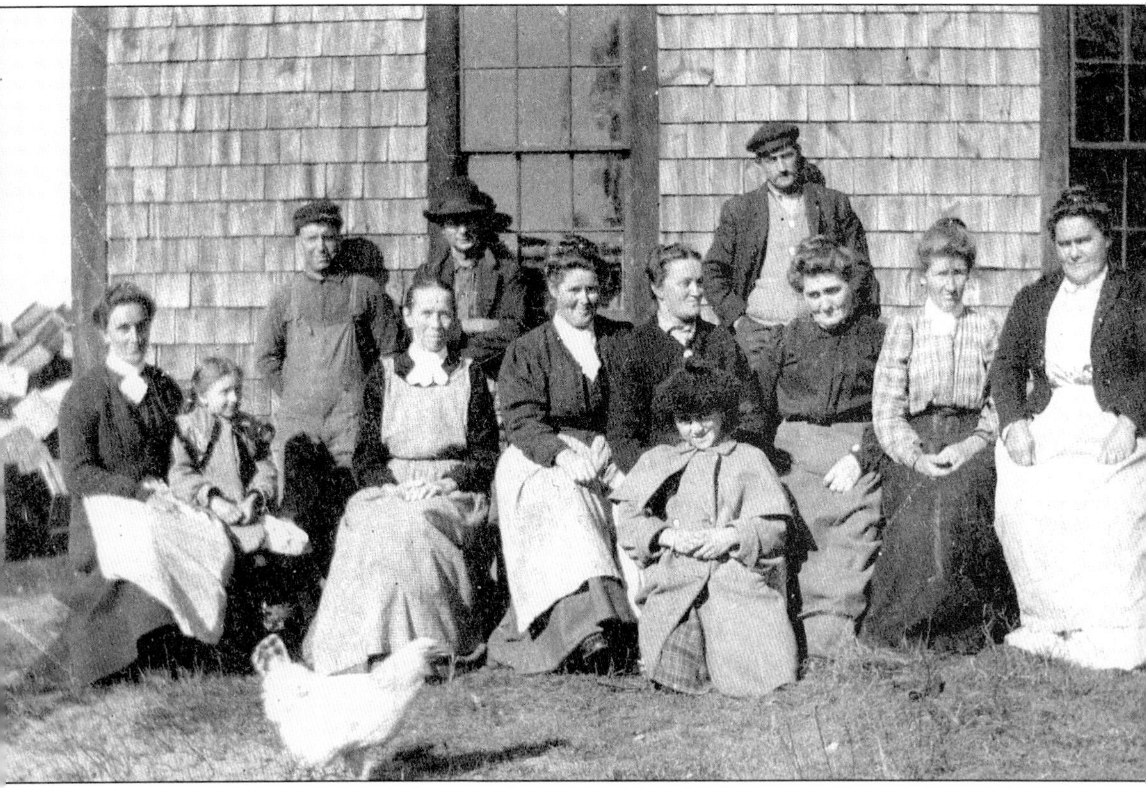

Cranberry workers pose for a photograph at Donald McFarlin's bogs. From left to right are Mrs. James Lus, her daughter Alice, James Lus, Mrs. Isadore Howland, Orville Griffith, Hilma Williams, Rose Morris, her daughter Lidia, Don McFarlin, Lucy Southworth, Carrie Jefferson Kelly, and Mrs. Henry Griffith.

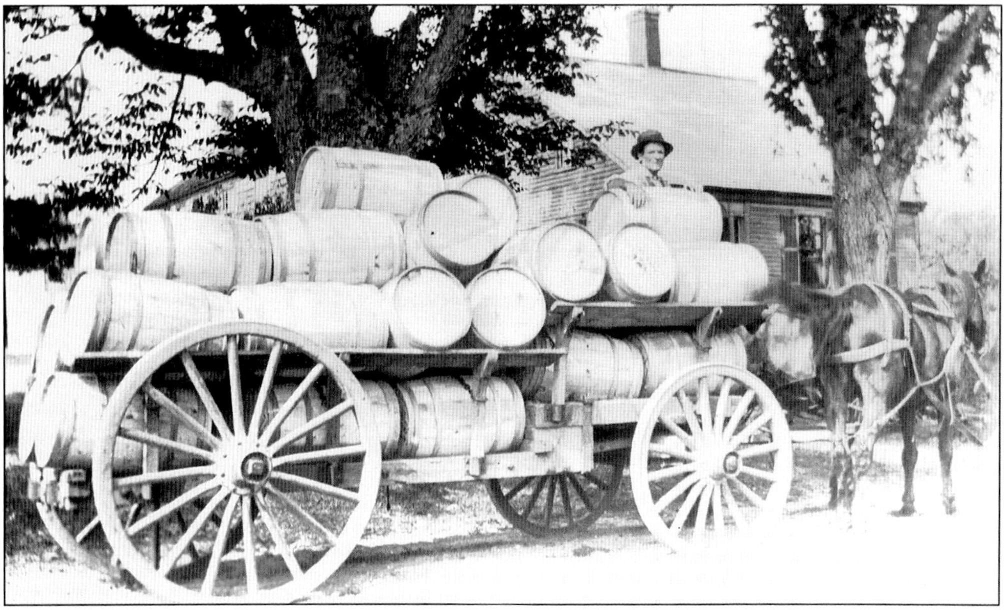

Alton Chandler is in front of his home with a wagonload of barrels filled with cranberries. (Courtesy of Larry Cole.)

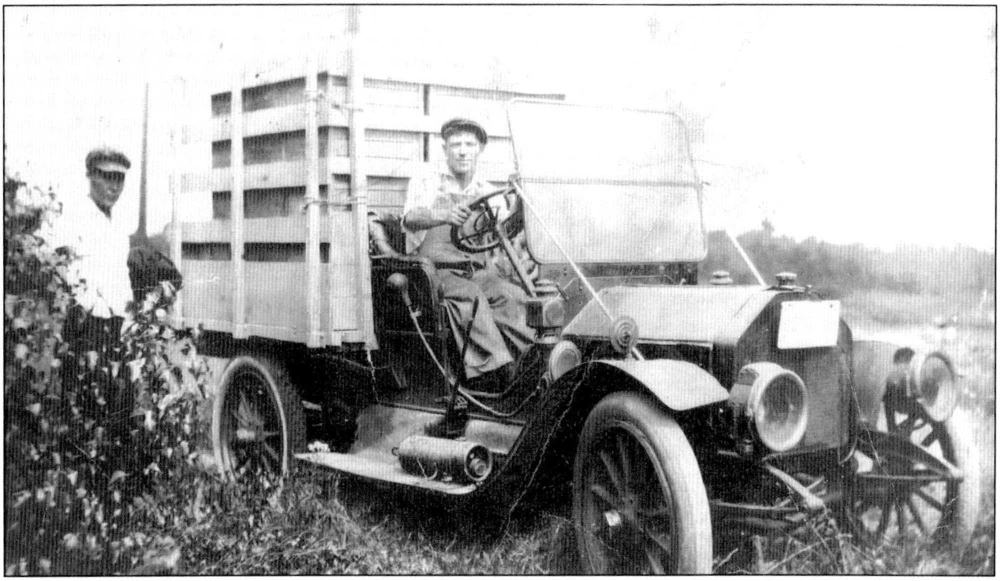

John Hill (formerly Gummerus), a foreman at Federal Bogs, drives a truckload of cranberry boxes to a bog. His parents, Robert and Ida Gummerus, were early Finnish settlers. (Courtesy of Wilho Harju.)

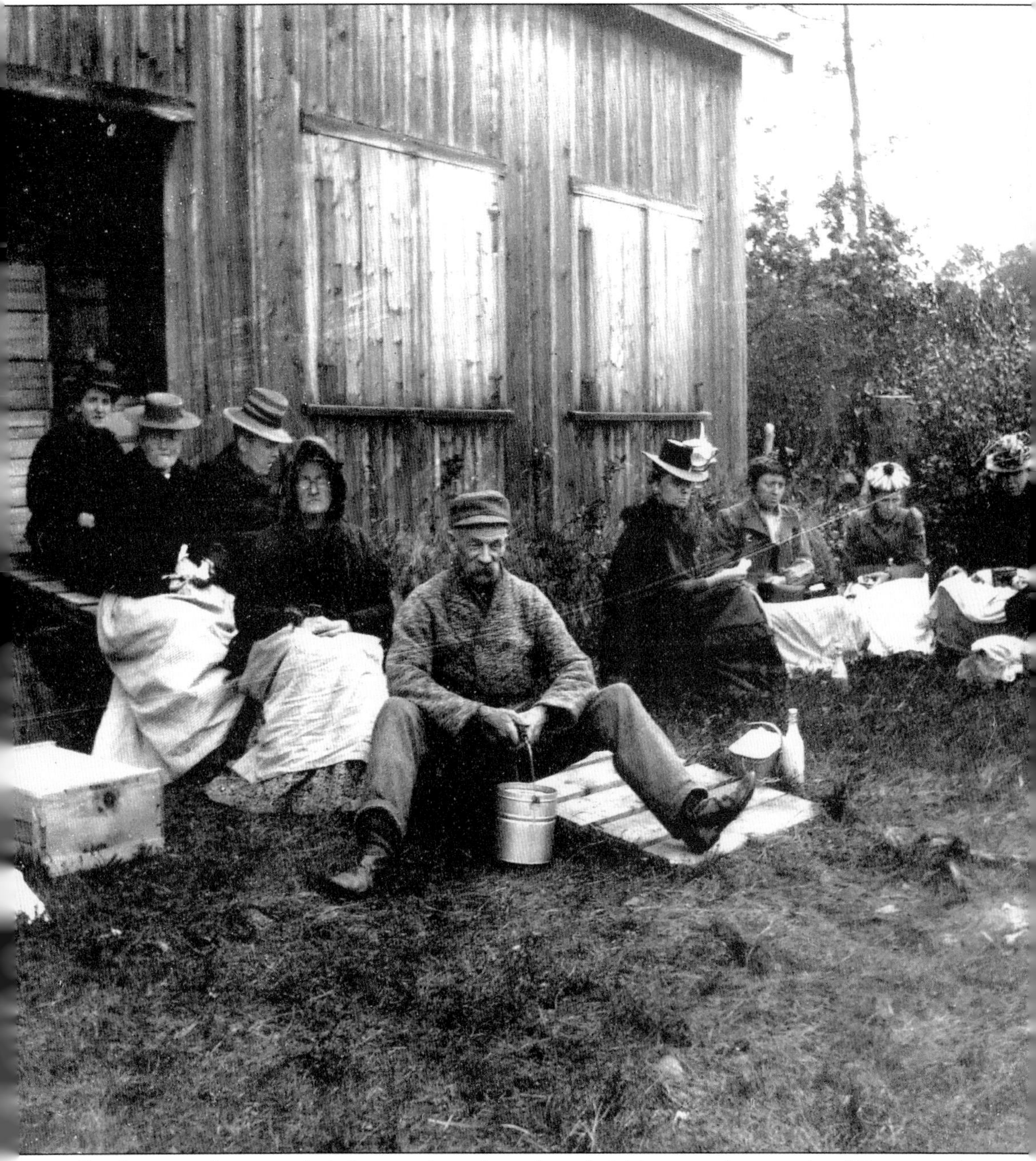

Cranberry workers rest their knees after a long day of picking on a bog nearby. (Courtesy of Charles Bezanson.)

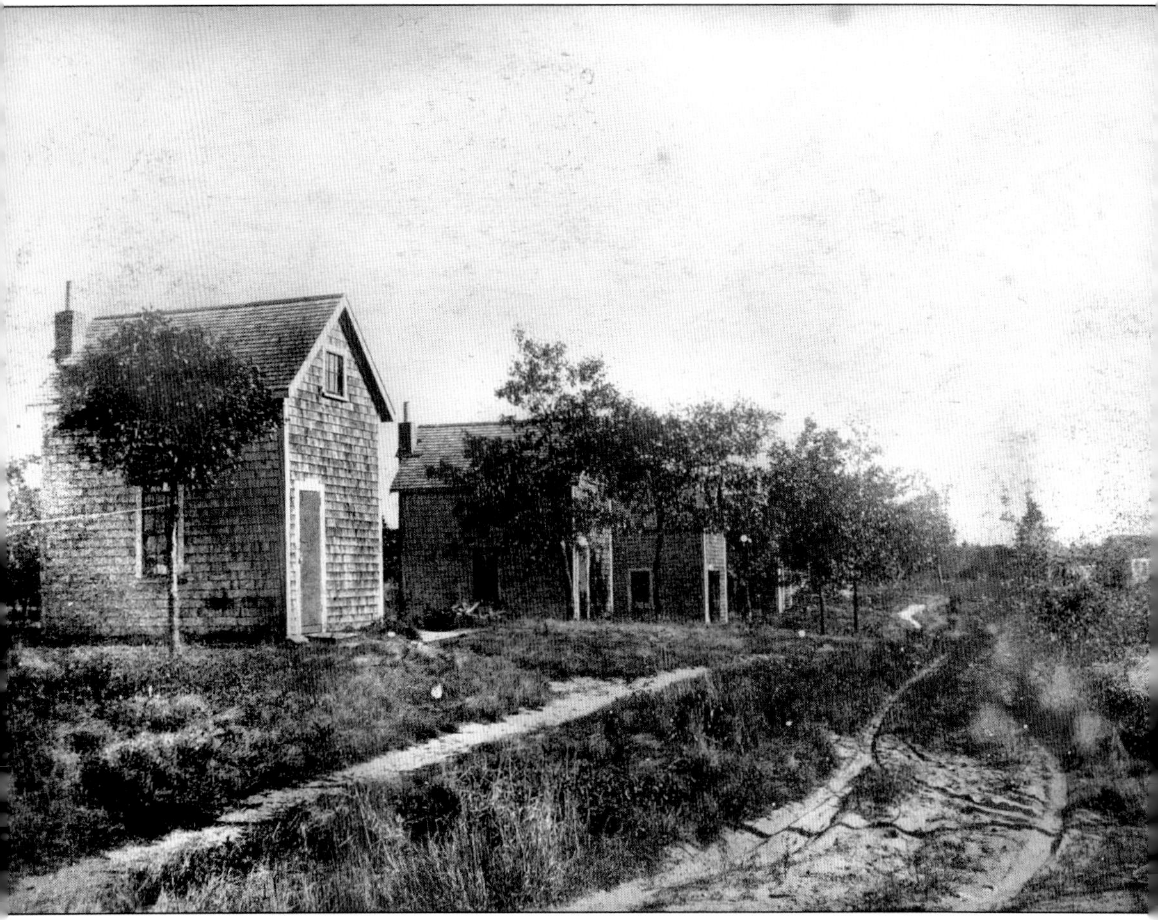

These buildings at the Crane Brook Cranberry Company are typical of the housing provided for bog workers. Although not all cranberry bog owners provided housing for their workers, the larger growers usually did, and bog camps were scattered around Carver. Many of the camps have now been converted into homes. (Courtesy of Maggie Mills.)

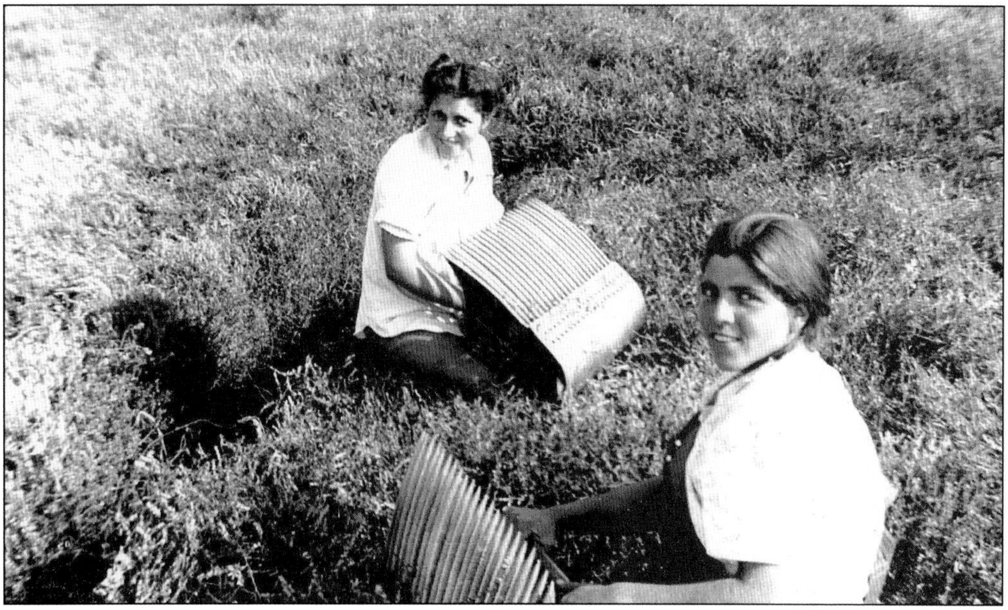

Two women pick cranberries. Toward the end of the 1800s, snap machines came into use and literally "snapped" the berries off the vine. The cranberry scoop replaced the snap machine *c.* 1900. The first scoops used held two quarts, making the scoop fairly heavy but collecting a lot of berries. Pickers emptied their scoops into bushel boxes placed around the bog.

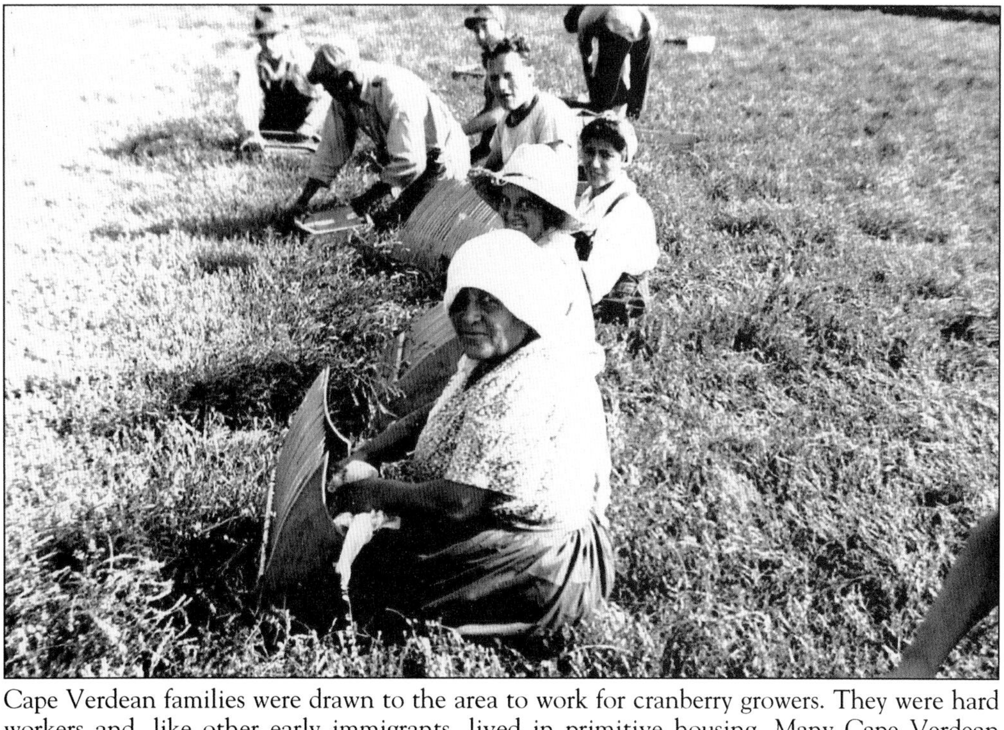

Cape Verdean families were drawn to the area to work for cranberry growers. They were hard workers and, like other early immigrants, lived in primitive housing. Many Cape Verdean families remained in Carver and became productive and respected members of the community.

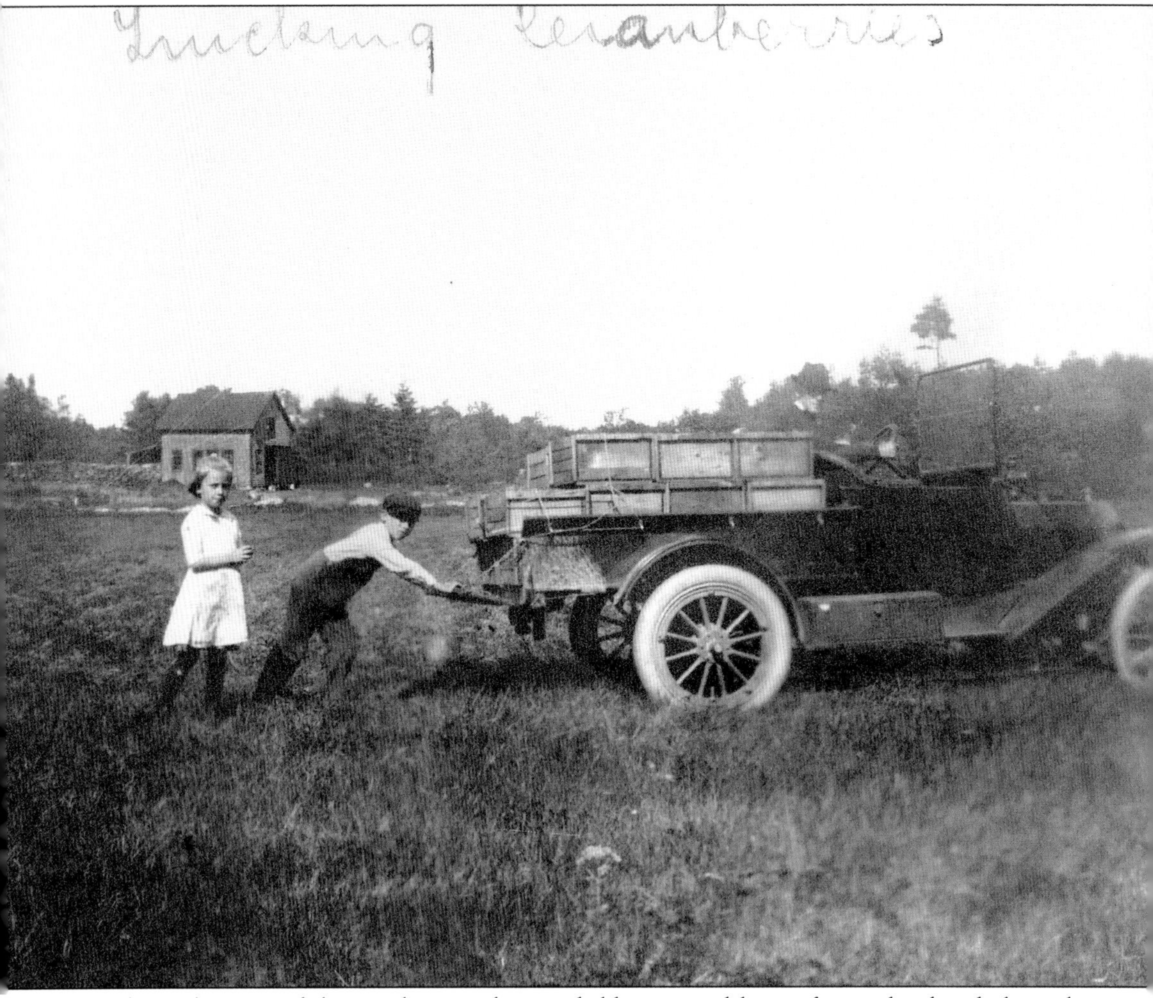

In the early years of the cranberry industry, children stayed home from school to help with the harvest. These children help load a bog buggy, which will take the berries off the bog to be processed.

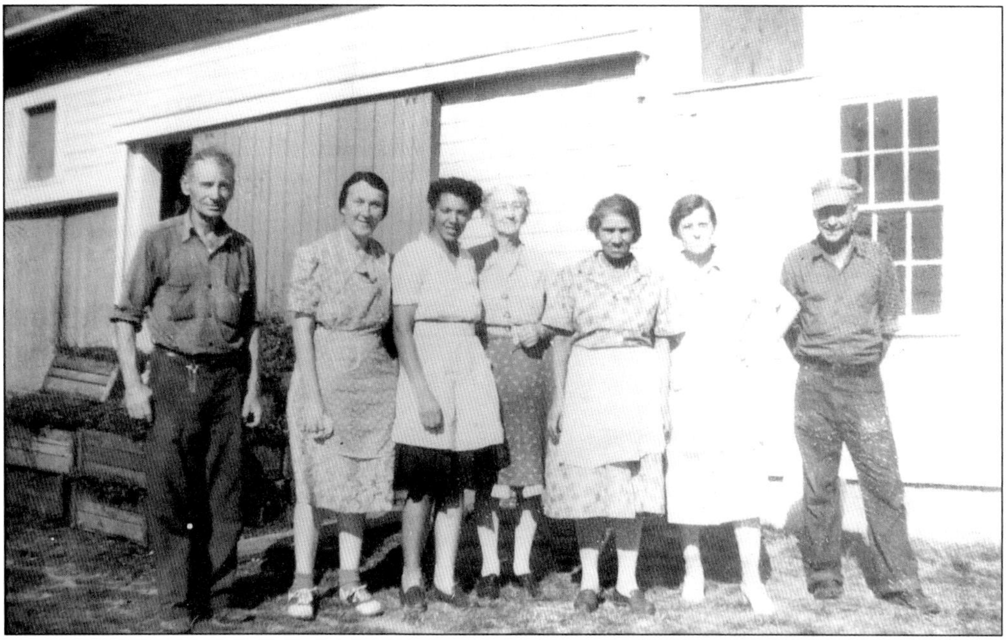

Clayton McFarlin's cranberry screeners stand in front of his screen house at Huckleberry Corner in the 1940s. From left to right are Les Thomas, Amelia Wrightington, Jeanette Barboza, Charlotte "Lottie" Atwood, Celia Fernandes, Lydia Bumpus, and Aaron Arponen. (Courtesy of Enid E. Wainco Harju.)

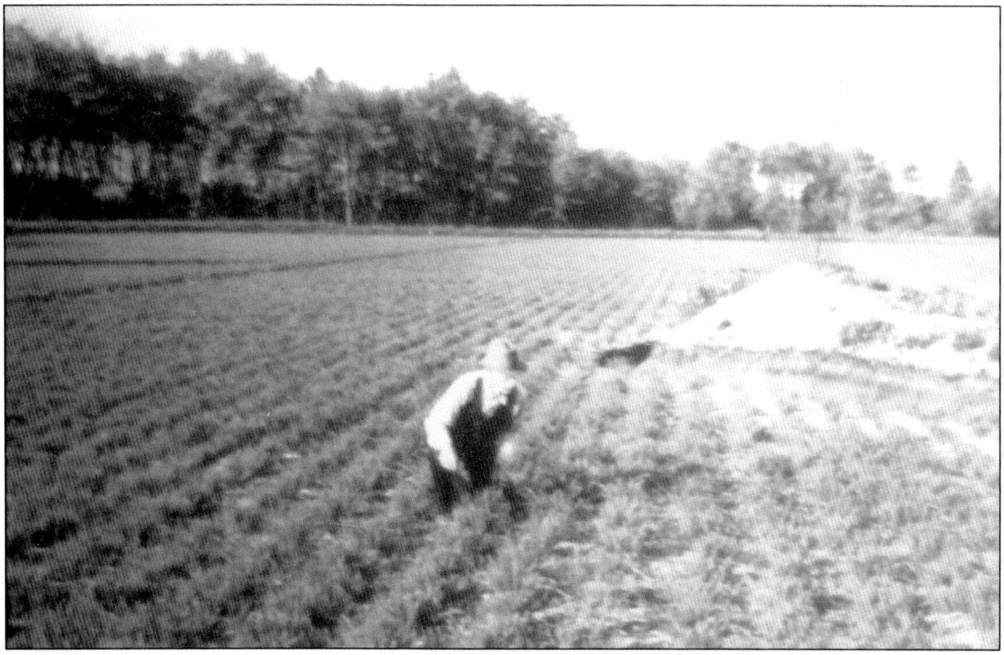

Clayton McFarlin works on one of his bogs. He often pruned and weeded his 30 acres alone. At one time, McFarlin grew more berries of superior quality per acre than any other grower in the industry. He was also a surveyor for 60 years and a Carver assessor from 1916 to 1930.

L. A. HAYDEN,

MANUFACTURER OF

Separators and Cranberry Implements

OF ALL KINDS TO ORDER.

GENERAL REPAIRER of Carriages, Sleighs, Guns, Cranberry Implements, Etc.

MIDDLEBORO AVENUE, NEAR MIDDLEBORO LINE,

An advertisement for L. A. Hayden, manufacturer of separators and cranberry implements, appeared in *The 1902–1903 Resident and Business Directory of Carver, Halifax, Hanson, and Plympton*. The Hayden Separator was first patented in 1912 by L. A. Hayden.

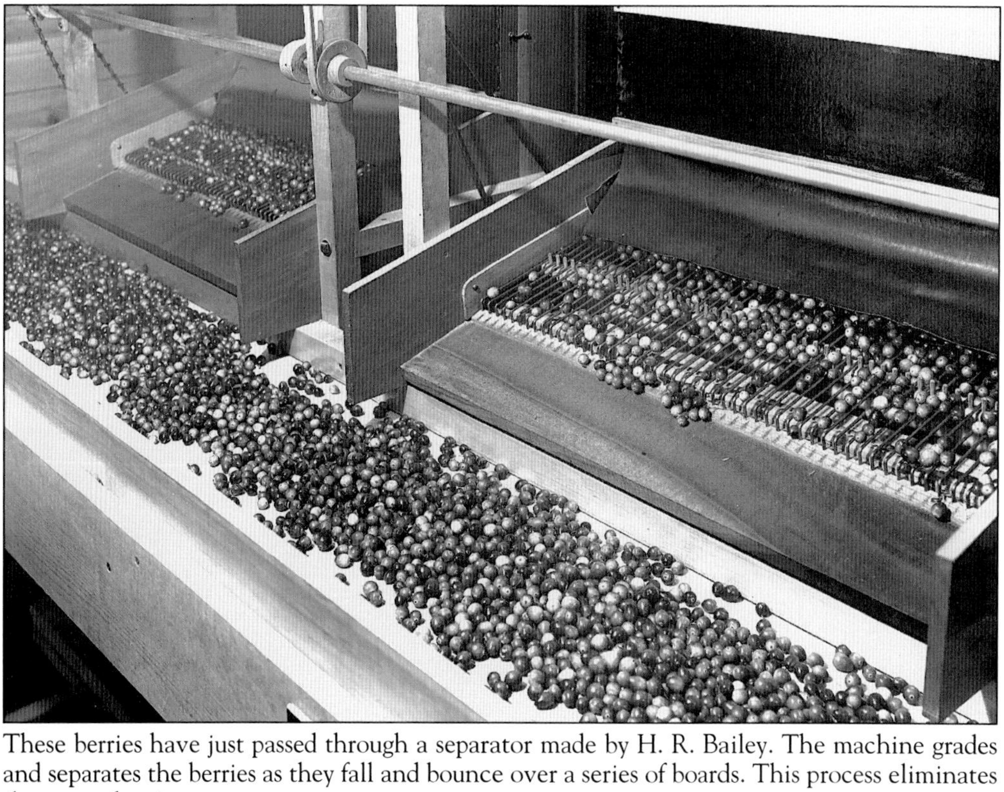

These berries have just passed through a separator made by H. R. Bailey. The machine grades and separates the berries as they fall and bounce over a series of boards. This process eliminates the rotten berries.

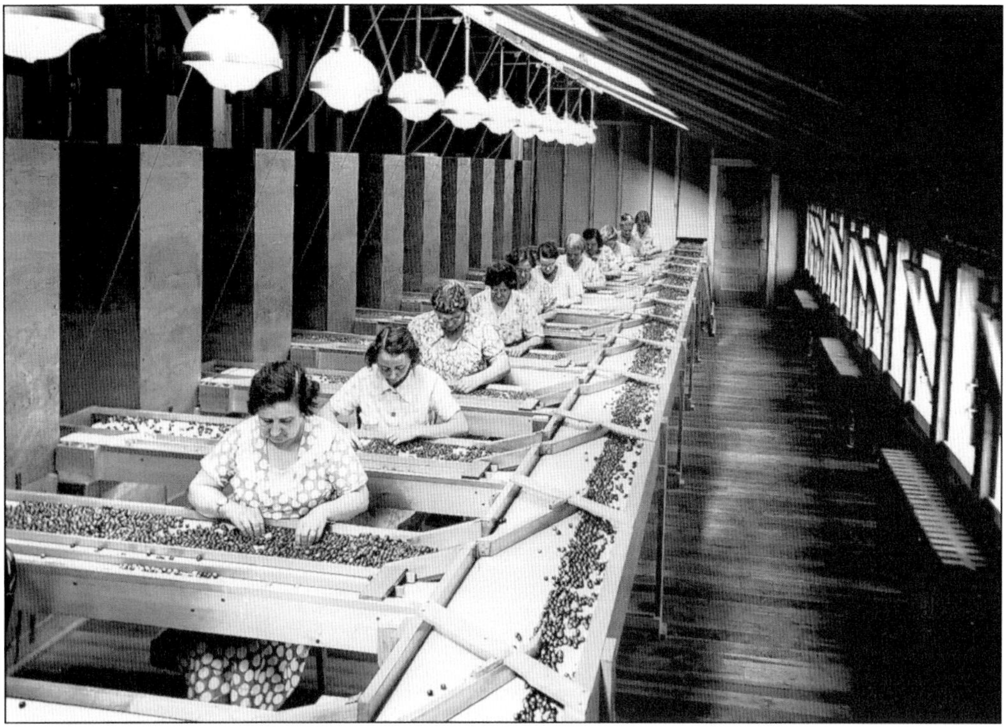

Workers hand screen the cranberries, discarding green and imperfect berries.

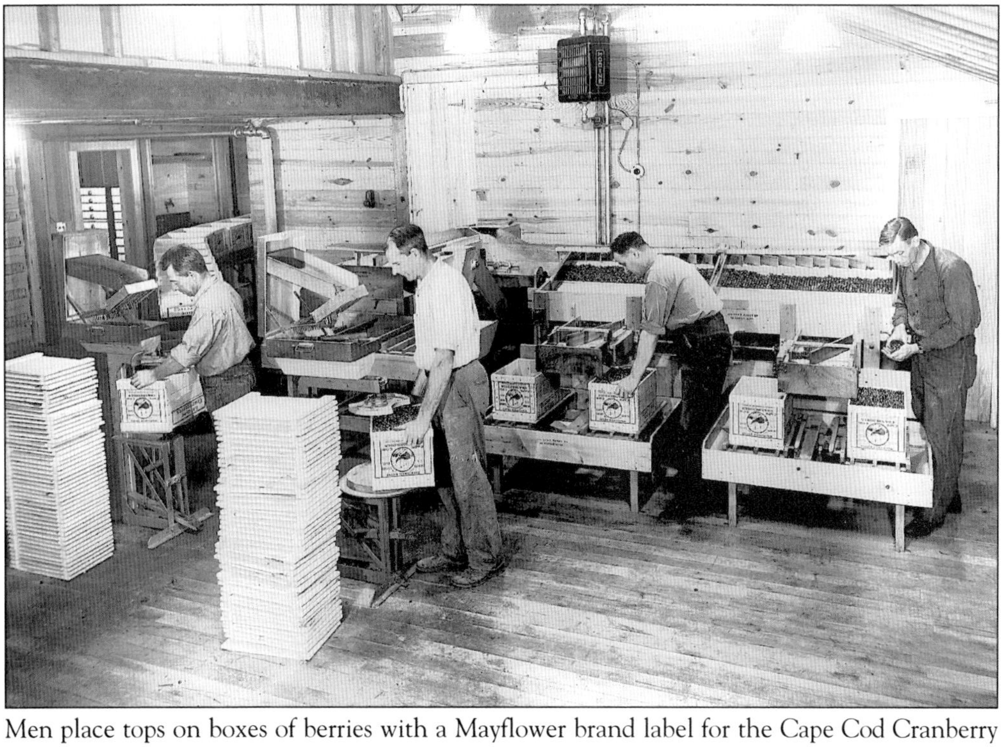

Men place tops on boxes of berries with a Mayflower brand label for the Cape Cod Cranberry Growers Association.

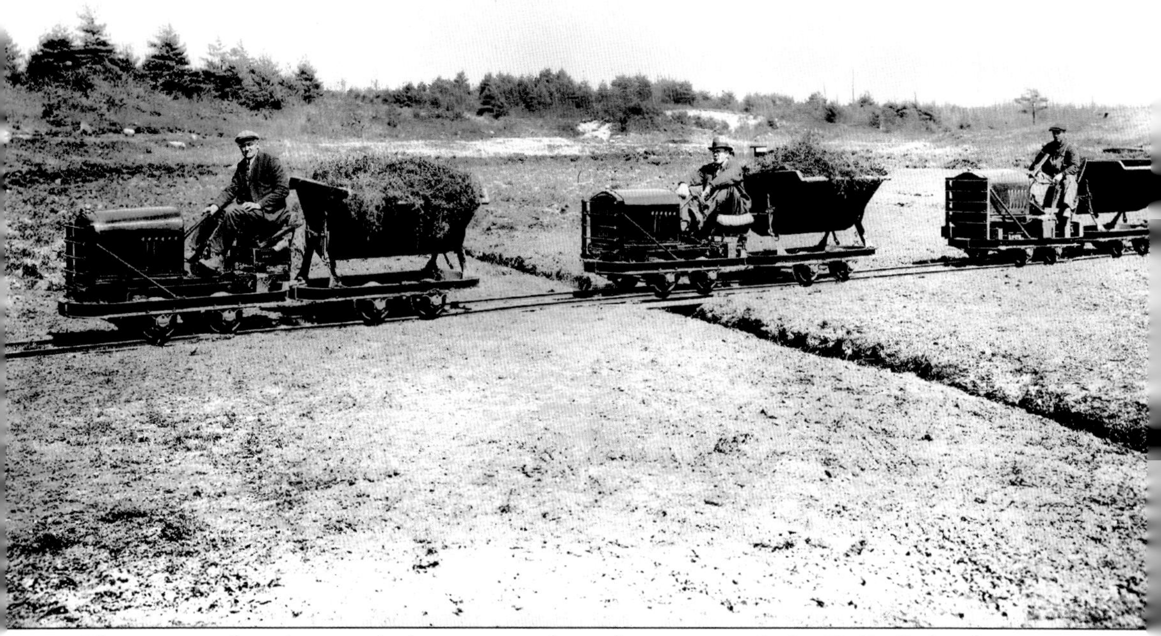

The men in this photograph demonstrate the rail engines made by H. R. Bailey for use on cranberry bogs. Using similar engines as those for coal mining, these cars haul vines that will be planted on new bogs. The man in the first car is believed to be Russell Trufant of Carver.

Eight

The Savery Neighborhood

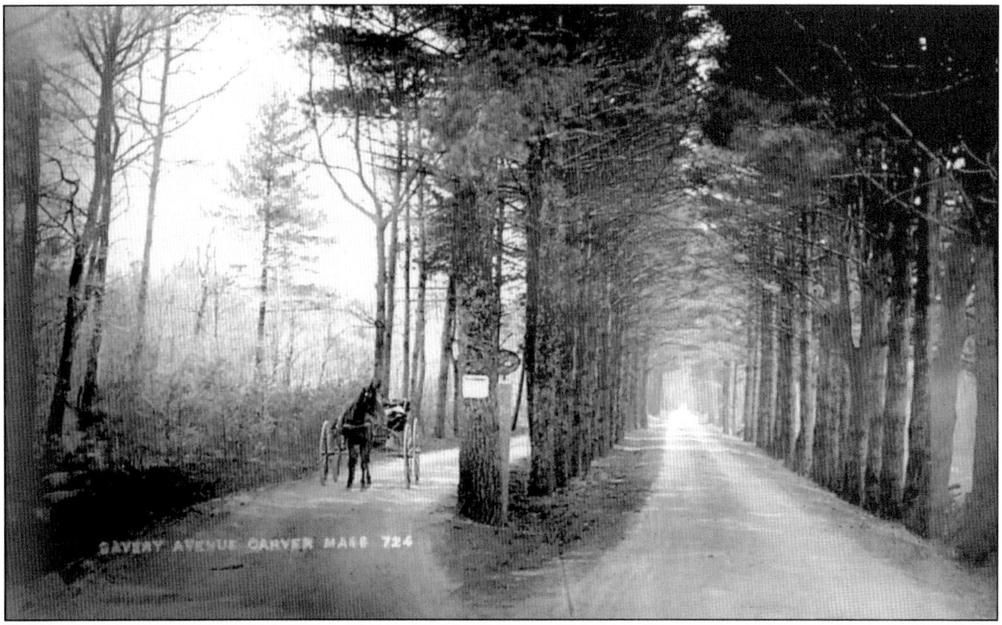

Savery Avenue, believed to be the first divided highway in the United States, is now part of the Savery Historic District in South Carver. Eli Southworth, Jesse Murdock, Thomas Hammond, Tillson Atwood, and Joseph Barrows donated the land for the avenue. William Savery financed the building of the road, providing local men with much-needed work during a difficult economic time. The avenue was completed in 1862.

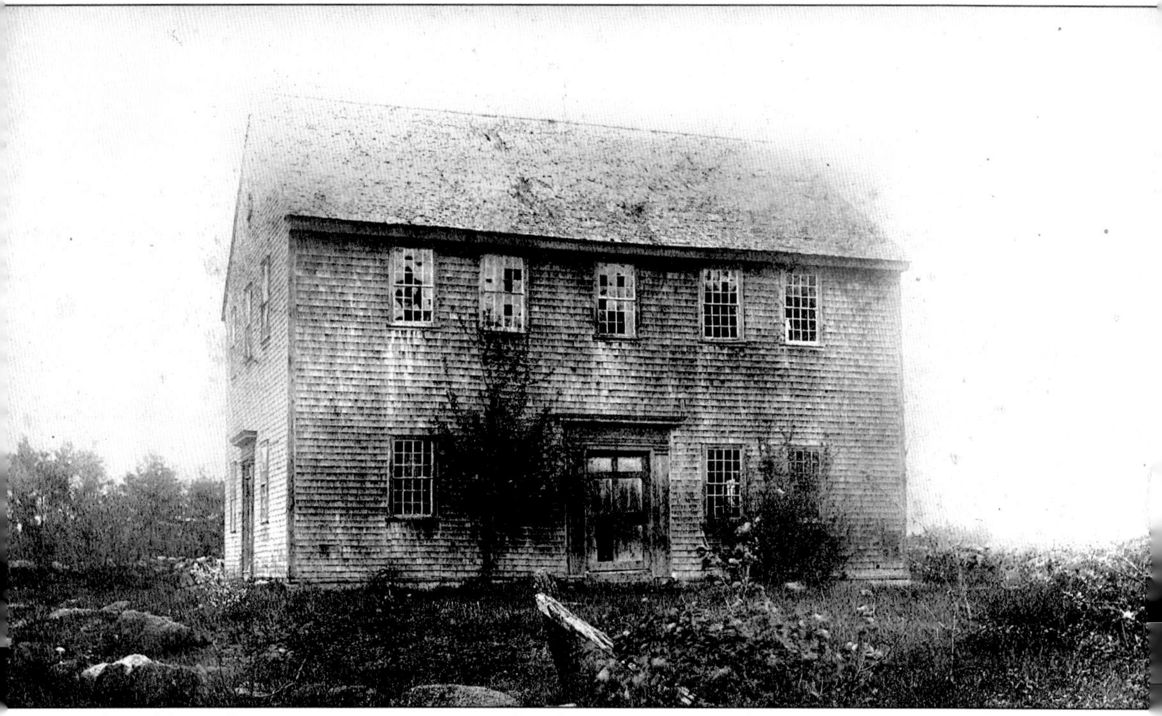

The Old South Meeting House was completed in 1774 to provide a meeting place for the people who lived in the southern part of the South Precinct. The building stood on a hill near the intersection of South Main Street and Mayflower Road. Worship services were held there until 1854, when the building became known as Bay State Hall. It was then used for town meetings, political and social gatherings, and training and storage for the militia. After the Civil War, it was commonly called the Light House, since the light from its windows could be seen from a great distance. The building was taken down in 1890.

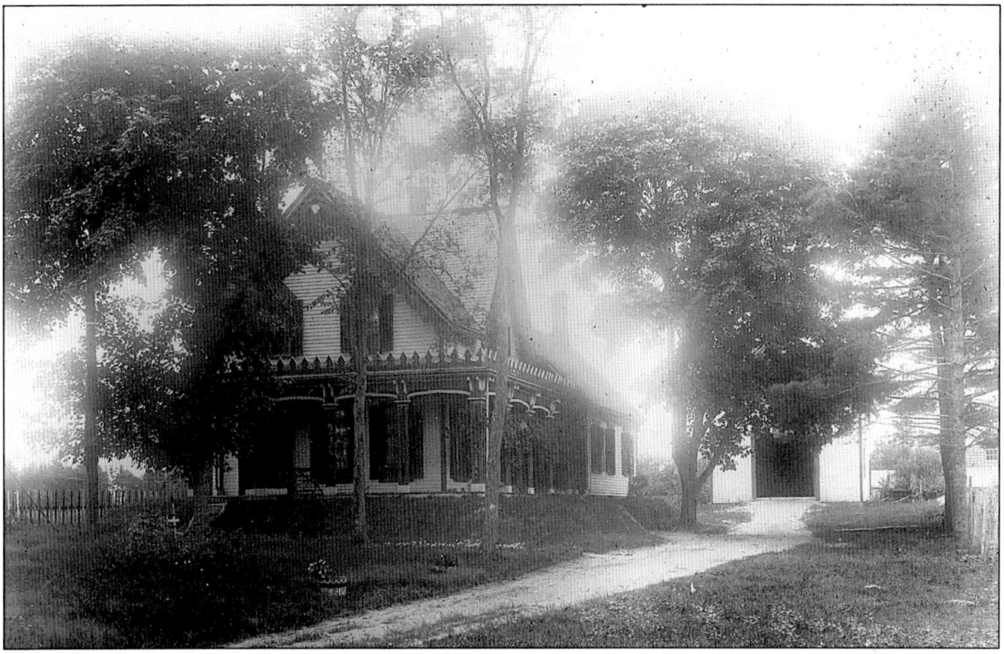

Murdock Villa was built in 1847 by whaling captain Henry Murdock. After Murdock's death, the house was rented by the Savery family to house their guests during the summer. The house was later occupied by Dr. Ellis Cornish and his family. The pitched gables and decorative trim distinguish it from other Carver homes.

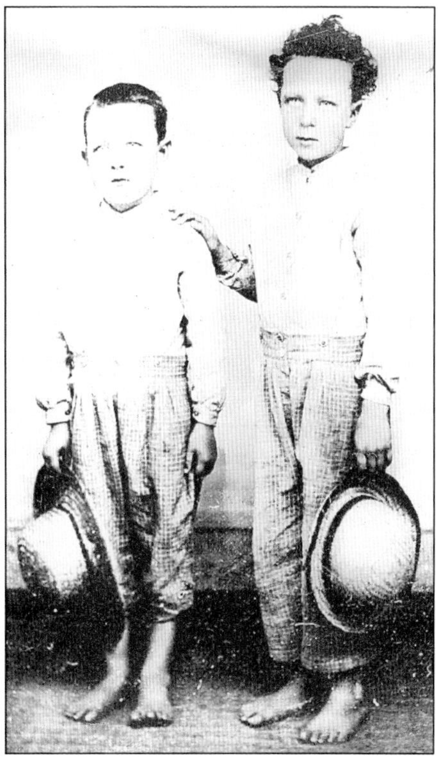

Pictured here are William Murdock (left), age four, and his brother Ira (right), age six, sons of Capt. Henry Murdock. William Murdock grew up in the Savery neighborhood during the active days of the Ellis Foundry and the Shoestring Factory. Murdock eventually moved to New York but wrote numerous letters in the 1940s and 1950s to Carver residents. The letters describe his childhood years in the Savery neighborhood and provide an insight into life in Carver in the late 1800s.

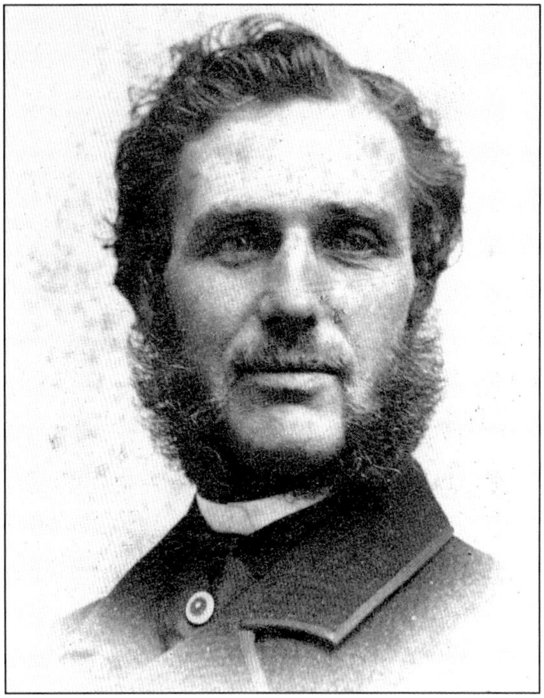

Capt. Henry Murdock (1818–1878) was the captain of a whaling ship. Murdock went to sea at the age of 20 and worked on whaling ships out of Fairhaven and New Bedford. He became a captain in 1853.

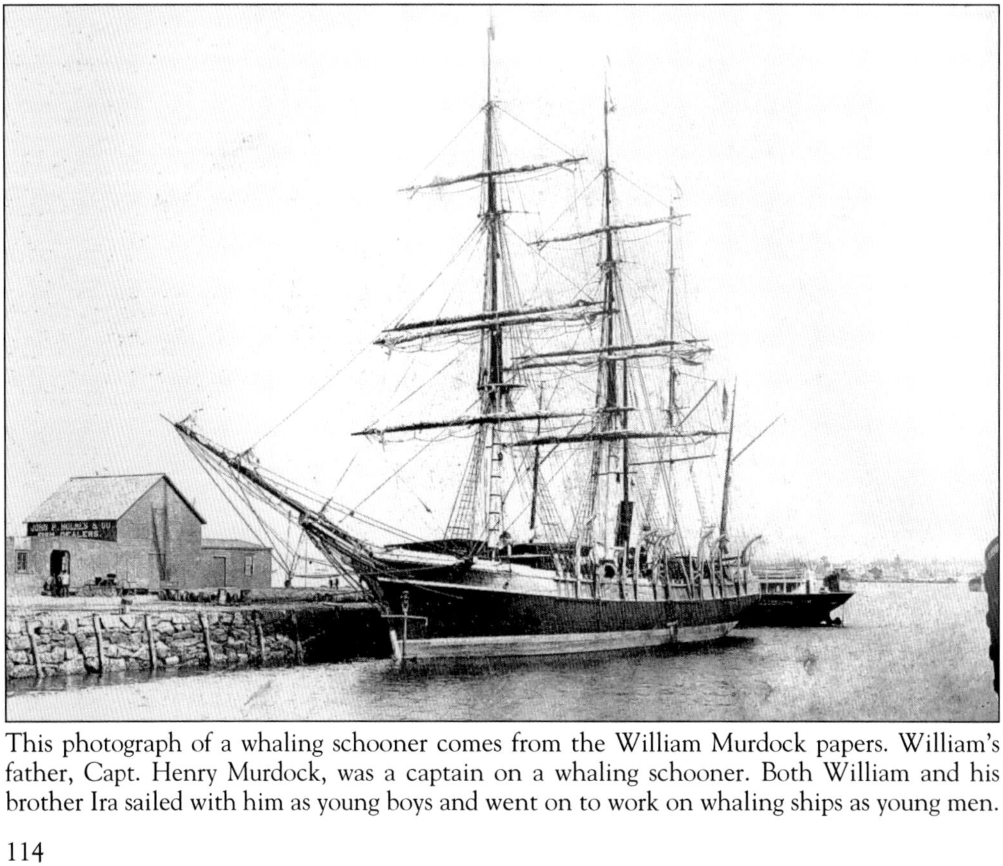

This photograph of a whaling schooner comes from the William Murdock papers. William's father, Capt. Henry Murdock, was a captain on a whaling schooner. Both William and his brother Ira sailed with him as young boys and went on to work on whaling ships as young men.

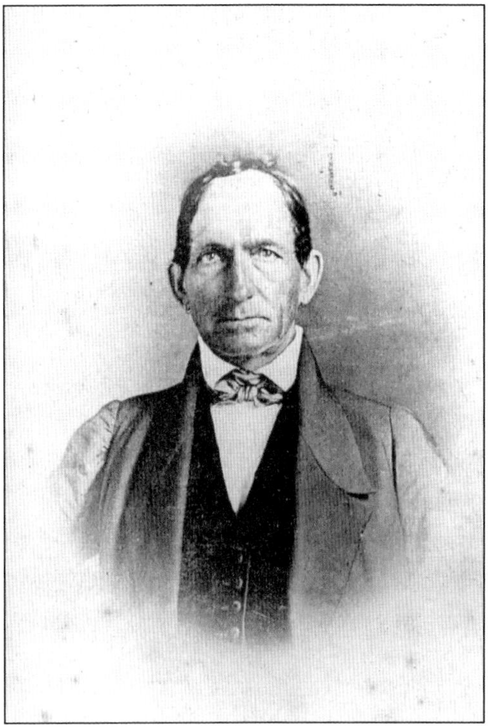

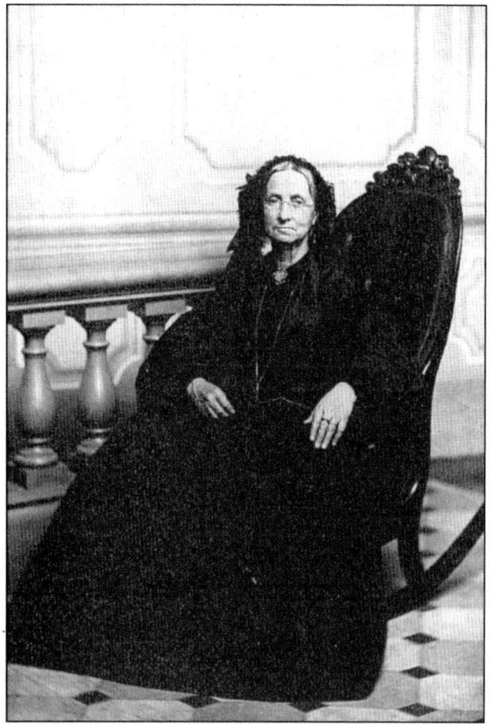

John Savery and Polly Atwood Savery had five children: William, Polly, Hannah, Waitstill, and John, who died in infancy. John Savery Sr. began working in the iron trade in Carver in 1807 and went on to establish other iron works in New York and New Jersey with his son William.

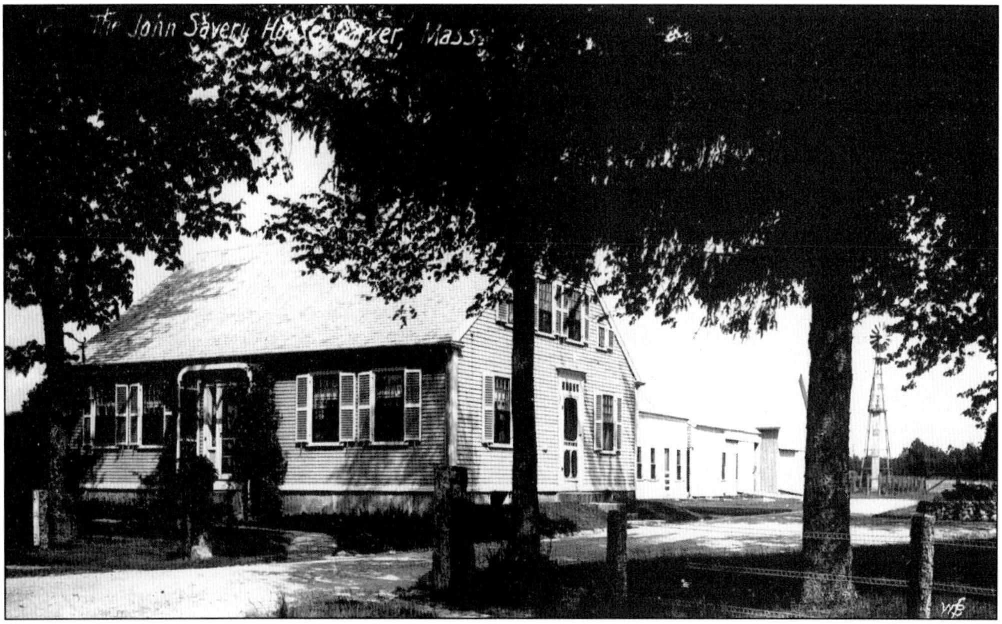

The John Savery house, built in 1830, was first occupied by Savery and his family. The home is located near Savery Avenue. Leyden Cottage is in the back.

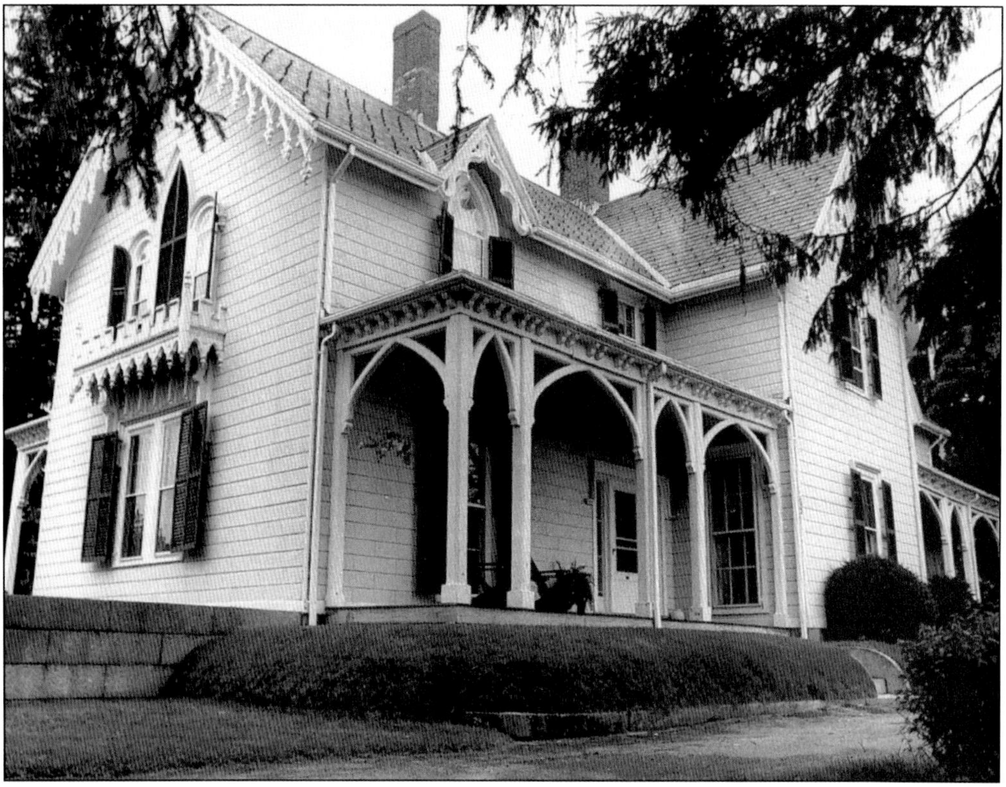

Leyden Cottage is one of Carver's finest homes. William Savery built the home in 1850 as a summer residence but moved there permanently when he retired in 1877. Savery descendants lived in the home until 2001.

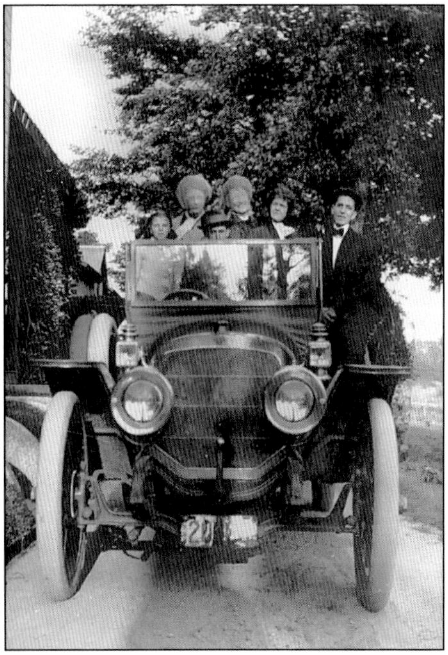

A family sits in a car outside of Leyden Cottage on Sampson's Pond. (Courtesy of Michael Mazalelwski.)

William Savery, the son of John Savery, became involved in business at an early age, working with his father in the iron trade. William was very committed to the town and was influential in the building of the Union Church. He was responsible for the building of Savery Avenue, which was a lasting gift to the town. He also contributed books to all of the schools in town.

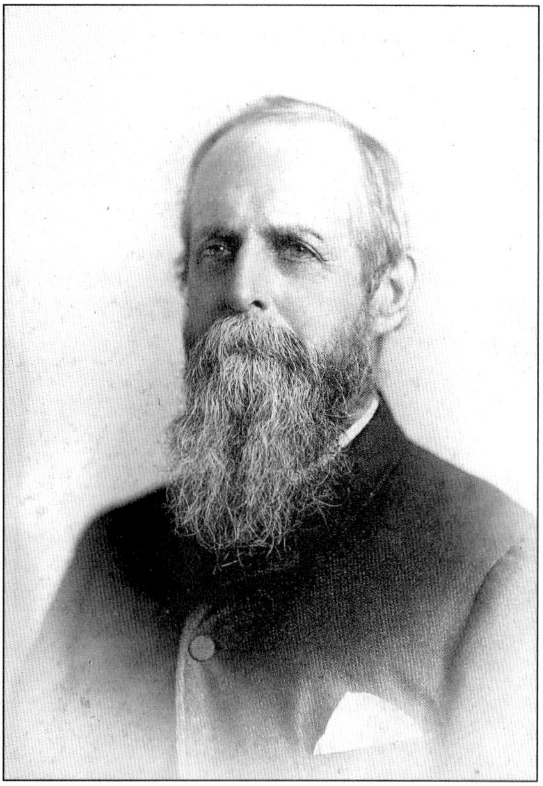

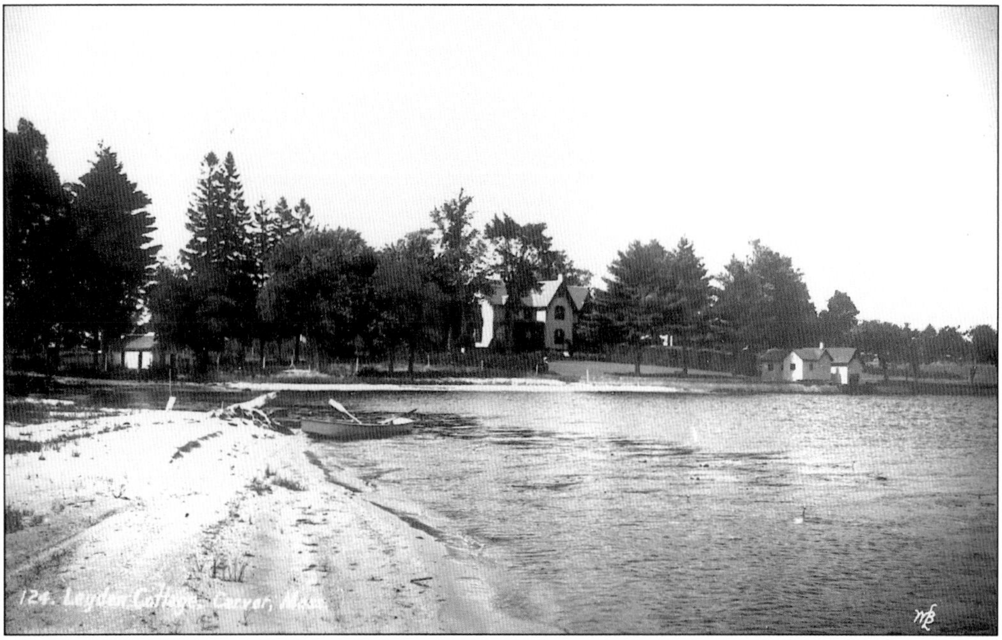

William Savery spared no expense in the building of Leyden Cottage. Local granite was used for the foundation, and Italian artists were hired to paint elaborate murals on the parlor ceiling. Savery's interest in landscaping led to the creation of attractive gardens, paths, and ornamental plantings.

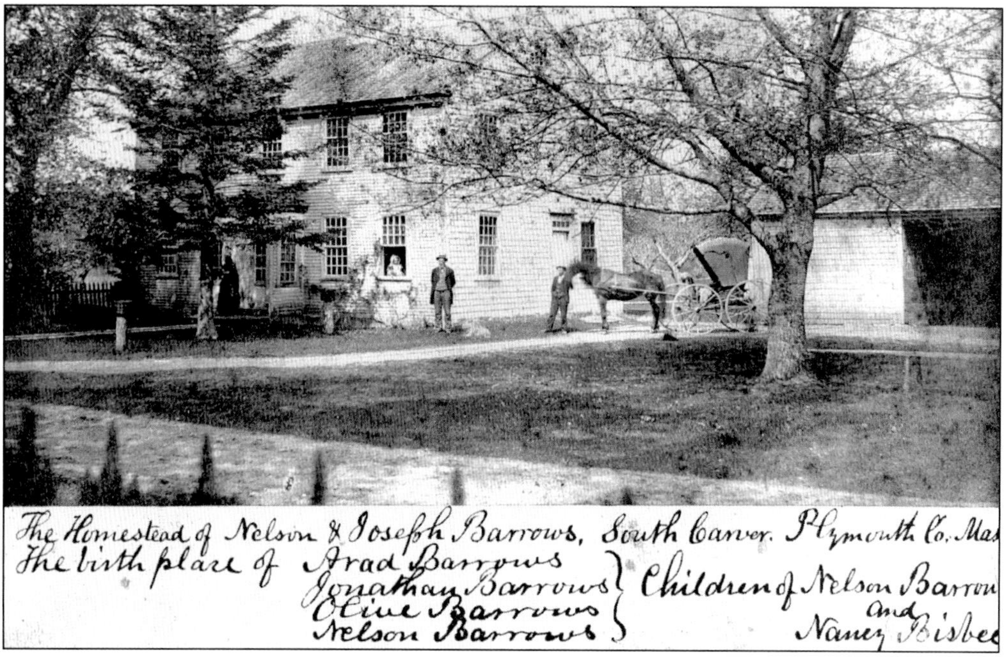

The Barrows house was constructed in 1785. George Barrows's great grandsons Nelson and Joseph, along with John Bent, built a small blast furnace on a brook near the home in 1825, but the venture failed due to a lack of water. The Barrows family was active in town affairs. This photograph was sent to Nelson Barrows by his son Arad. (Courtesy of Peter Fabry and the Bradshaw-Barrows family.)

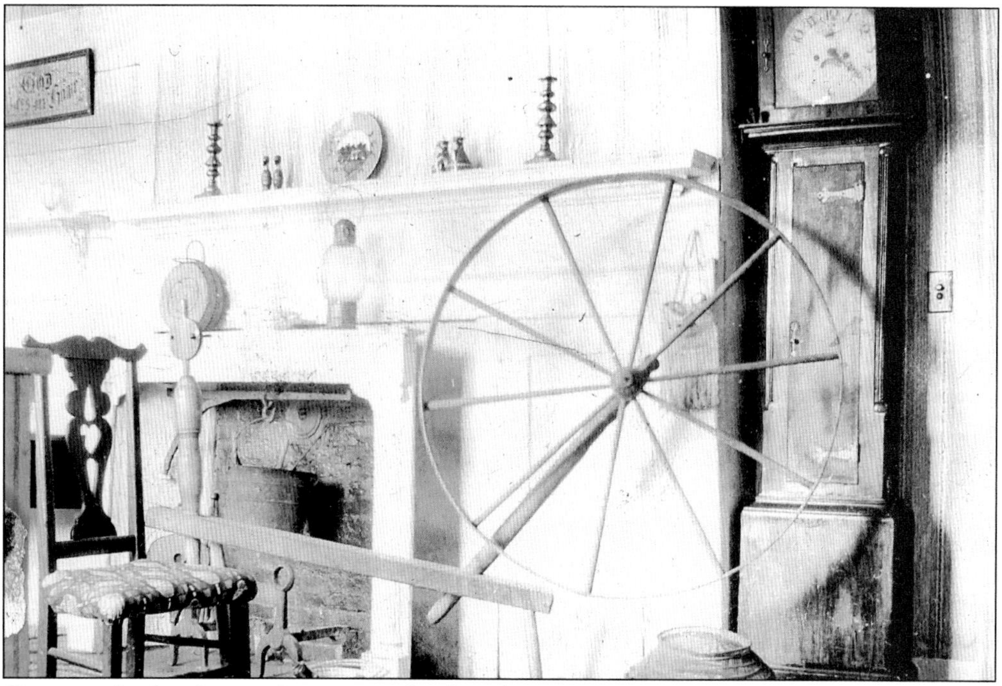

Shown is the fireplace and spinning wheel in the common room of the Barrows house in the early 1900s. (Courtesy of Peter Fabry and the Bradshaw-Barrows family.)

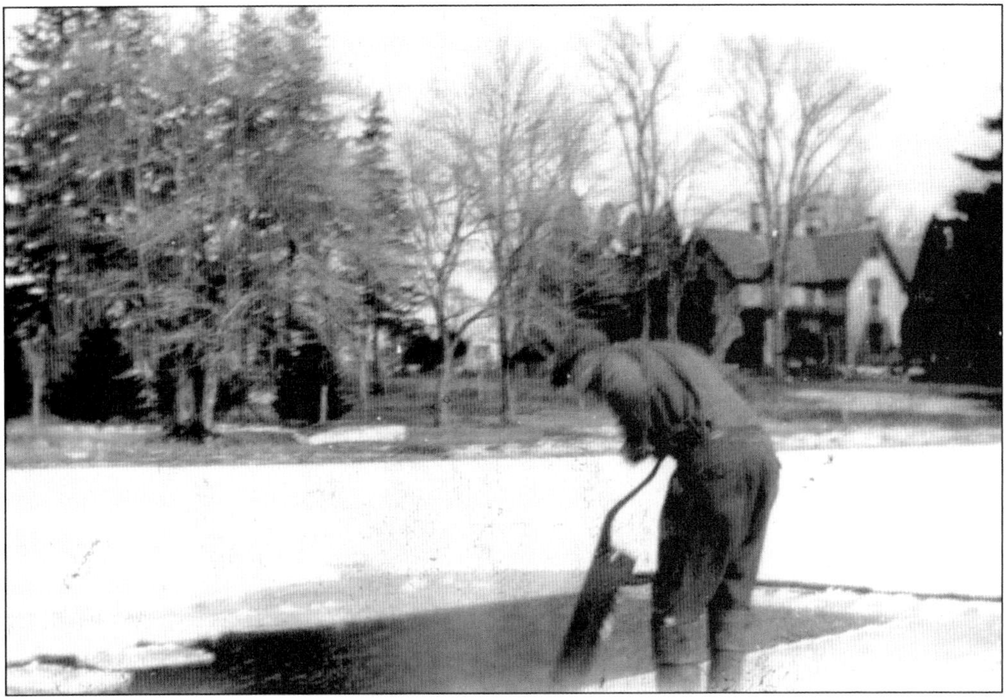

Ernest W. Shaw, nephew of Eliza Bowers, cuts ice for the icehouse on Sampson's Pond. (Courtesy of Barbara Shaw Logan.)

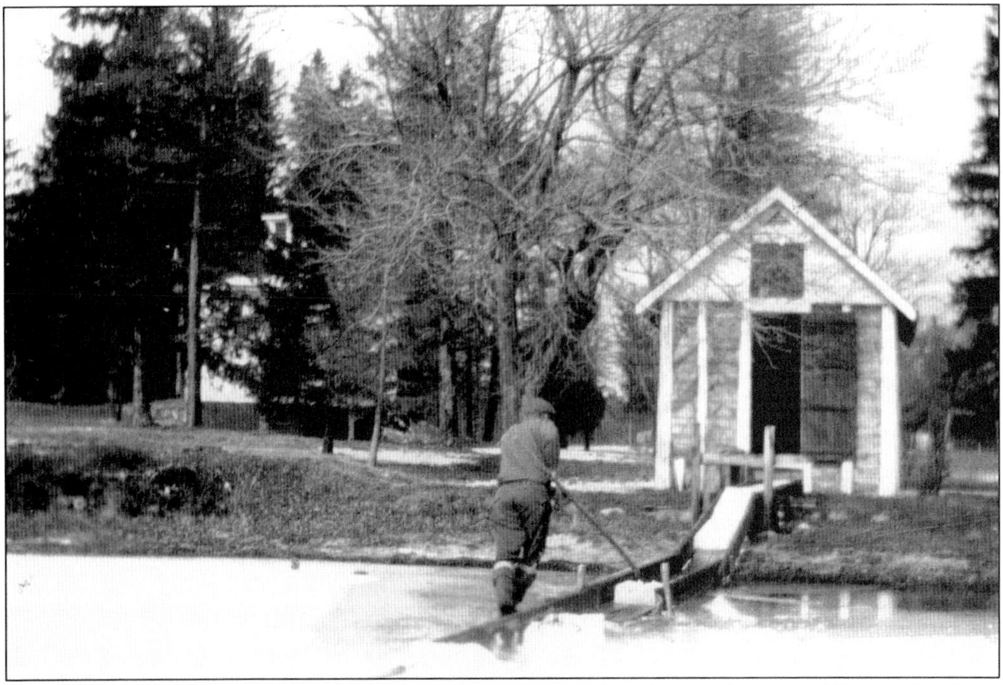

E. W. Shaw pushes ice into his icehouse behind the Larches. Later, the ice will be used to keep perishable food from spoiling in the Shaws' icebox. (Courtesy of Barbara Shaw Logan.)

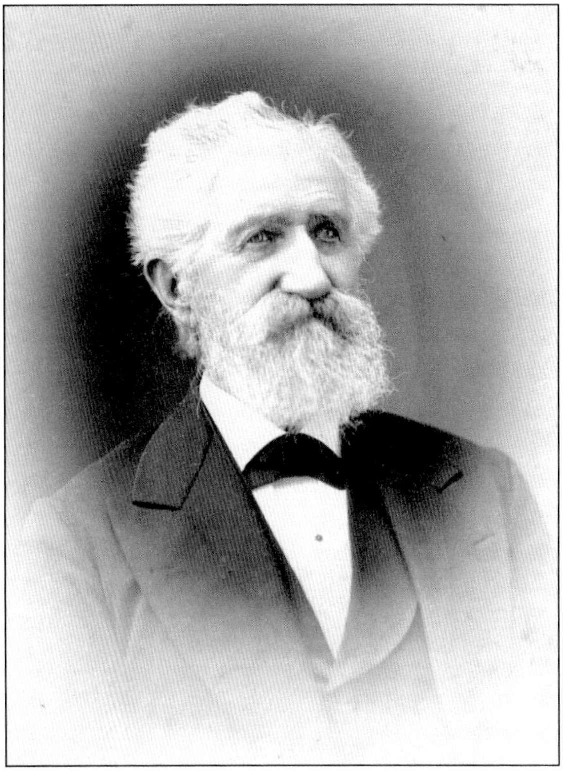

George P. Bowers came to Carver as a young man and worked for Benjamin Ellis. He was a daring and successful entrepreneur and established some companies, which included a manufacturer of hallowware. Bowers built Carver's first large cultivated cranberry bog. He was active in town affairs and married Eliza Shaw after his first wife, Waitstill Savery, died.

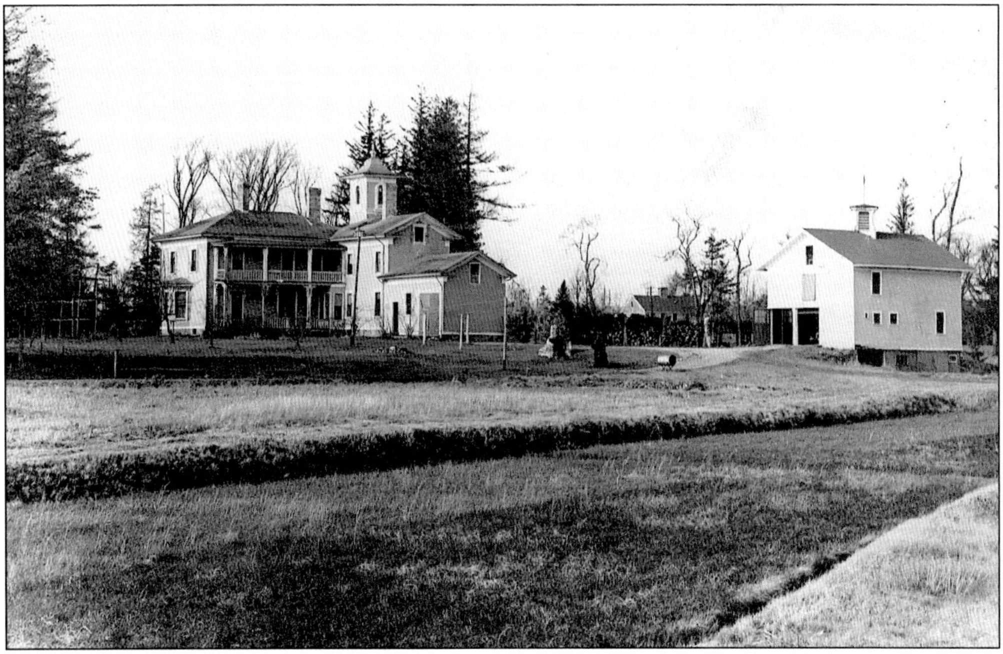

The Larches was built by George P. Bowers *c.* 1852. Located on the northwest side of Sampson's Pond, the property adjoined the Savery estate. Like Leyden Cottage, the home was first used as a summer residence. The house is distinguished by a tower. The several magnificent larch trees that give the property its name have survived many hurricanes.

Eliza Shaw Bowers was the wife of George P. Bowers and the sister of Samuel Shaw. Samuel Shaw was the owner of the Murdock Parlor and Grate Company in Boston, which was originally established in South Carver in 1867.

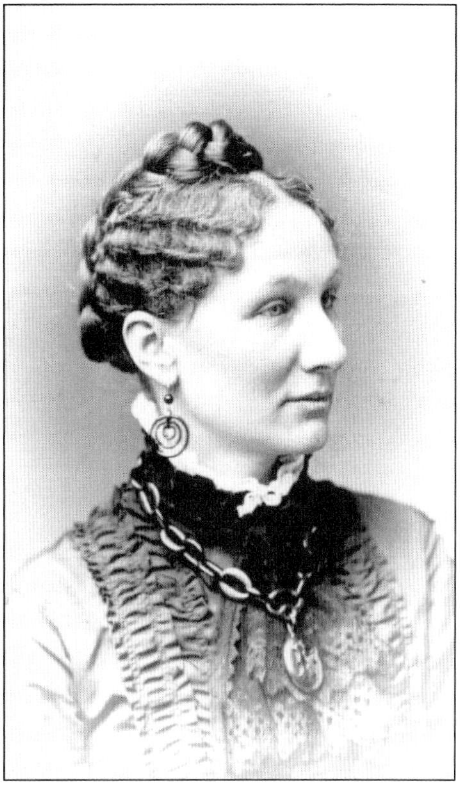

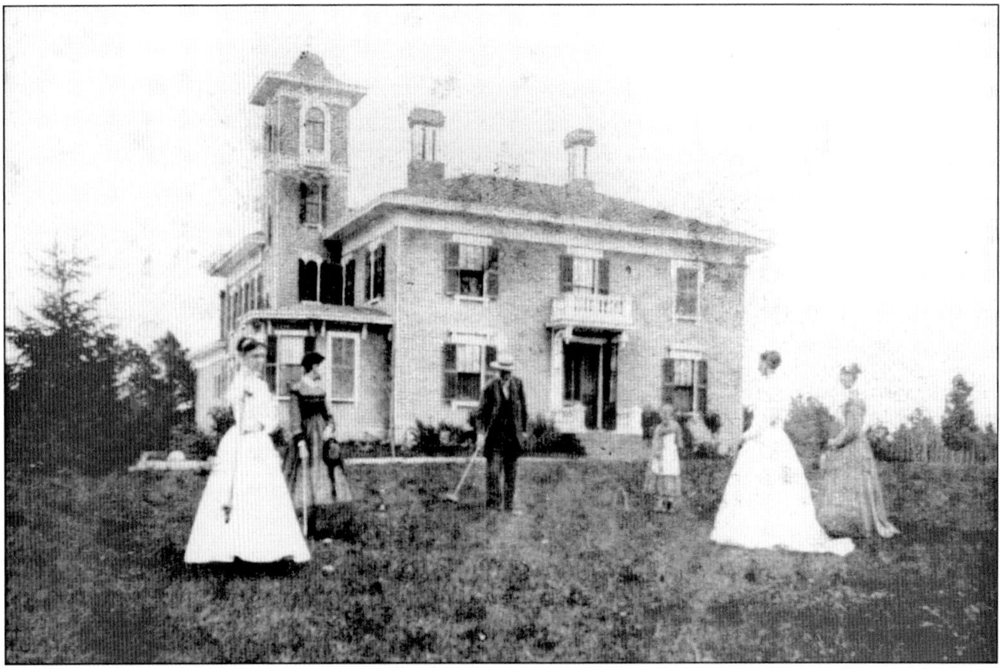

Playing croquet on the front lawn of the Larches are, from left to right, unidentified, Mary Savery Jowett, George P. Bowers, Hattie Savery, Waitstill Savery (Bowers's first wife), and Eliza Shaw (Bowers's second wife).

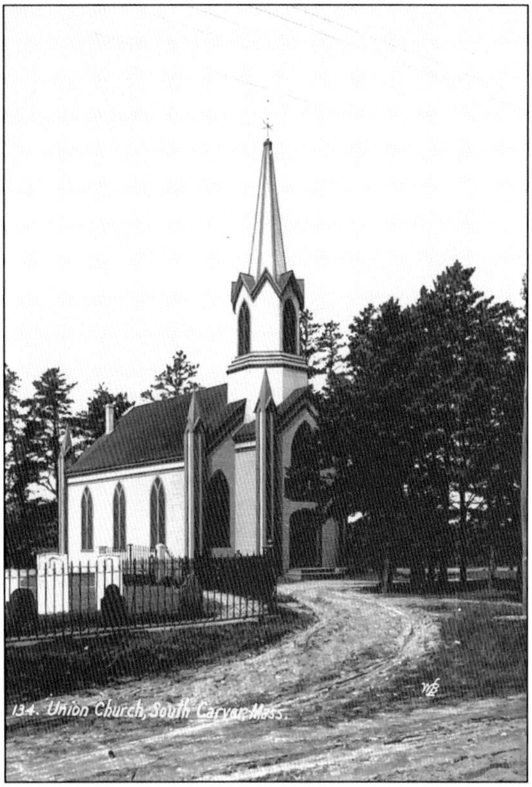

Union Church is believed to be one of the first non-sectarian churches to be built in the country. The rural Gothic-style church was built in 1855, and the proprietors funded the building on the pew plan. William Savery and Jesse Murdock donated a pump organ and a bell, both still in use today.

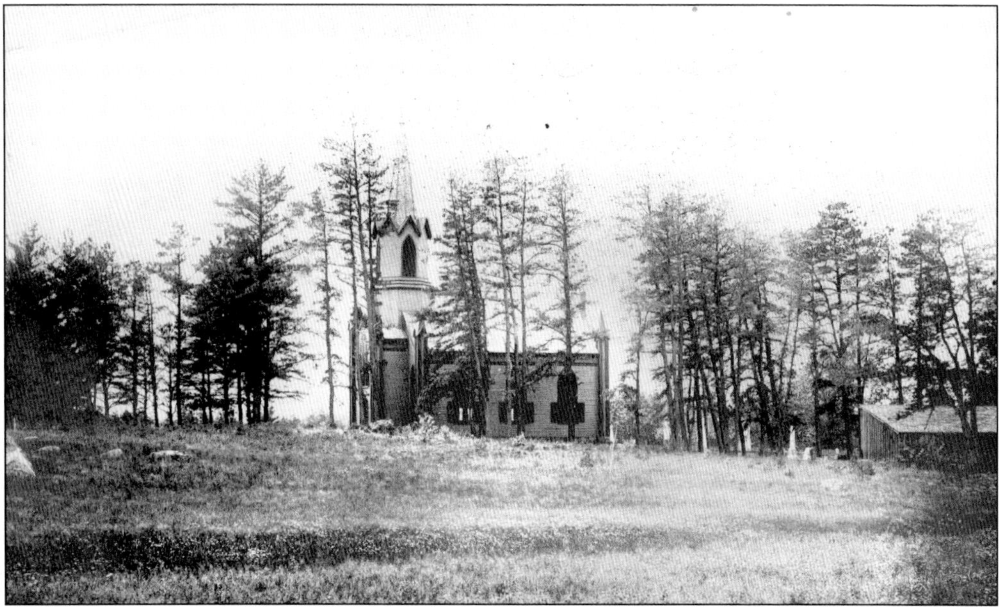

Aside from the year 1865, when the Union Church had a permanent pastor, services were held in the summer by pastors of varying Protestant faiths. Services are still held in the summer, as well as during the holiday season.

Nine

Edaville Railroad

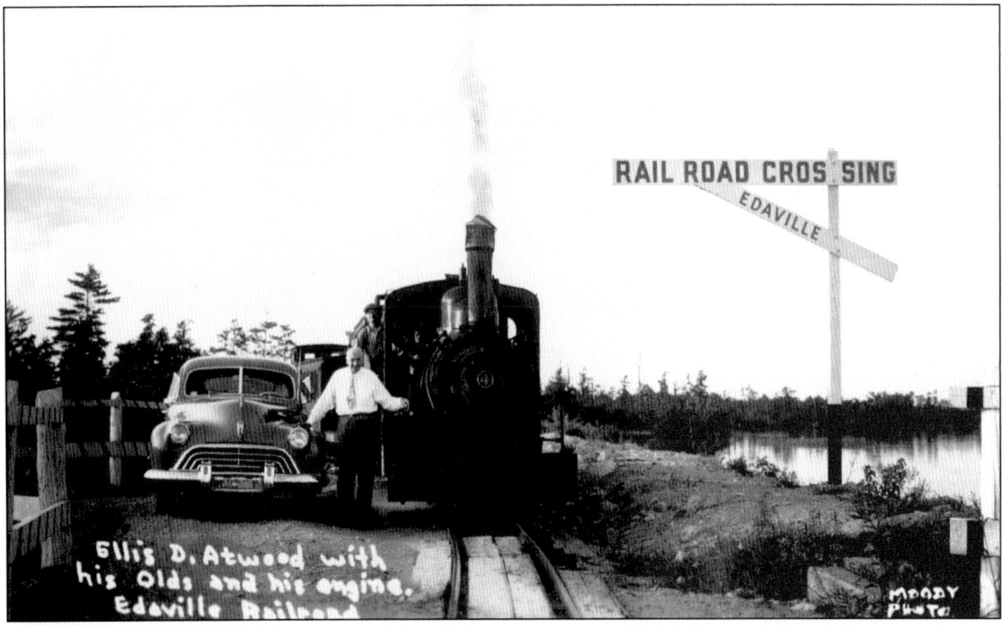

Ellis D. Atwood, founder of Edaville Railroad and a local cranberry grower, stands next to his steam engine, originally used on his cranberry bogs, and his brand-new Oldsmobile. The steam engine eventually became part of the tourist attraction Edaville Railroad. "Edaville" came from the initials in Ellis D. Atwood's name. (Courtesy of the Edaville USA Collection.)

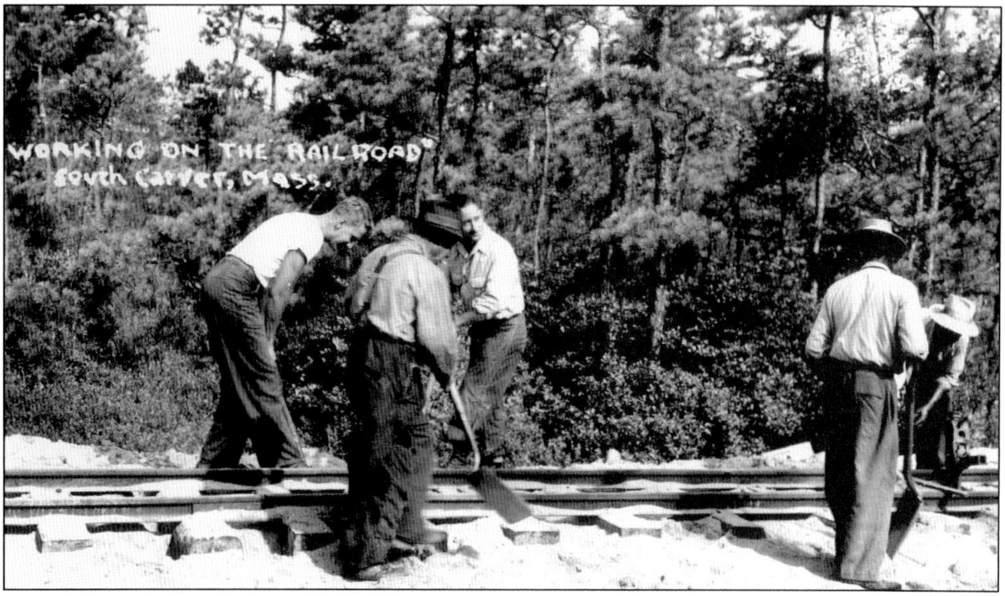

Benjamin Hatch, third from the left, supervises the track crew at Edaville in the 1940s. (Courtesy of the Edaville USA Collection.)

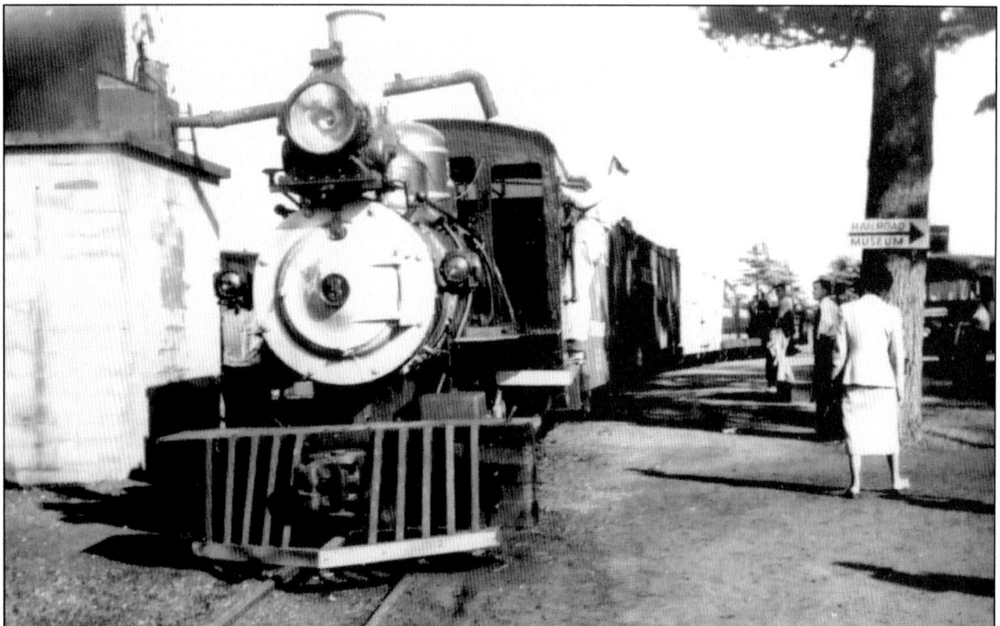

David Eldredge, nephew of Mrs. Ellis Atwood, stands on the water tower on the far left as Engine No. 3 takes on water. Eldredge later became an owner and general manager of the Ellis D. Atwood company. (Courtesy of the Edaville USA Collection.)

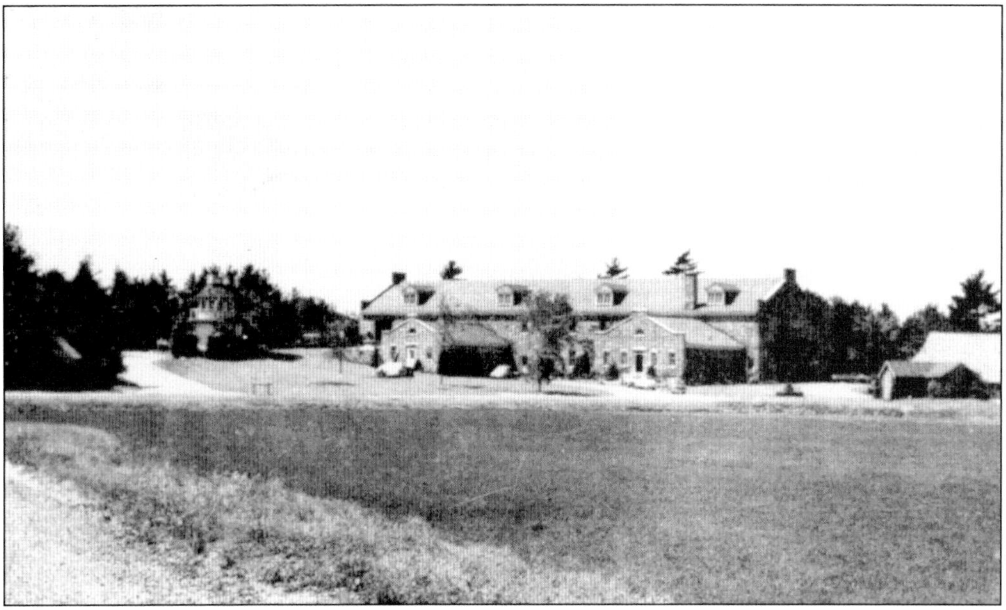

The Ellis D. Atwood screen house was built in 1940 to replace a wooden screen house that had burned. Although most screen houses were made of wood, the design for this building was chosen to resemble the Old State House in Boston and was typical of architecture in 1790, when the town was incorporated. The screen house was the center of operations for the Ellis D. Atwood bog company.

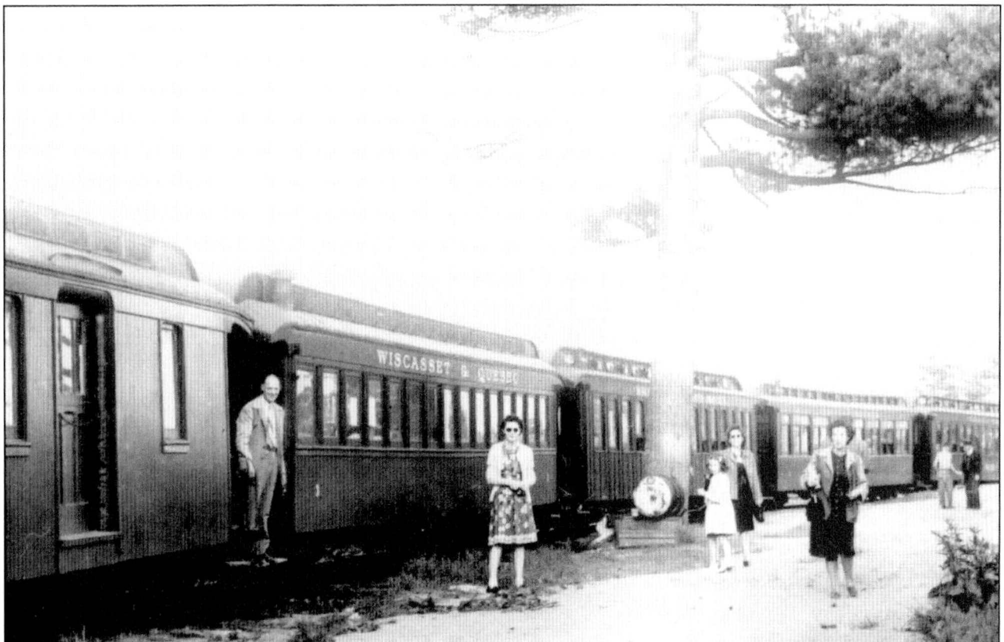

Passengers board the train at Edaville's main station in the 1940s. (Courtesy of the Edaville USA Collection.)

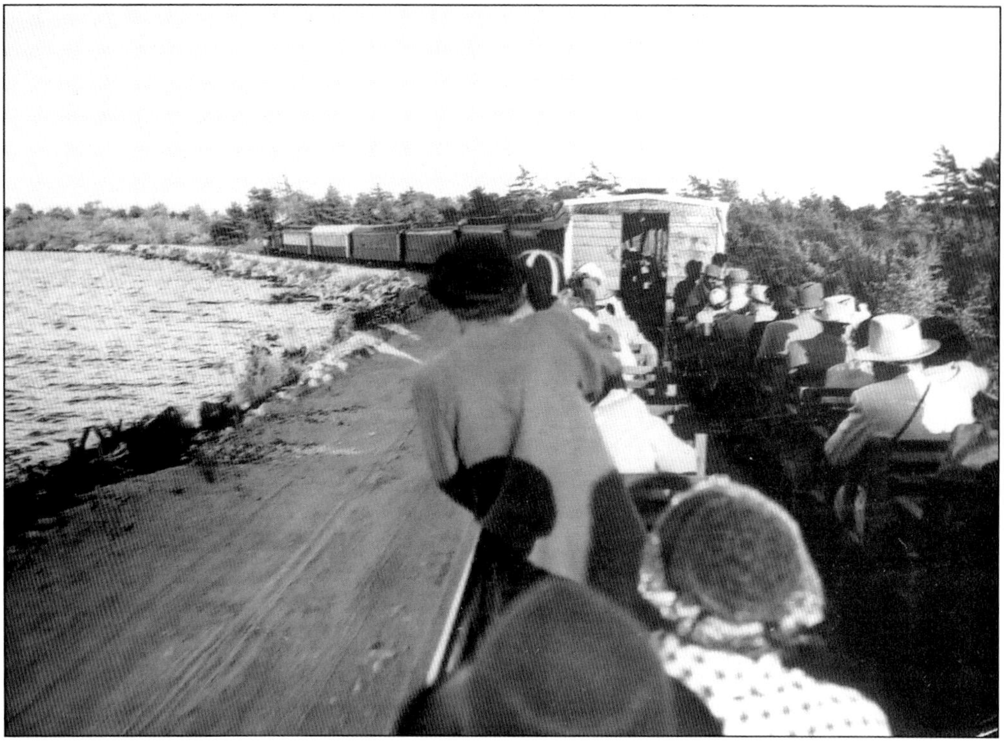

Linwood Moody, a conductor on Edaville Railroad, took this photograph of passengers on an open car as the train passed by the Atwood Reservoir. (Courtesy of the Edaville USA Collection.)

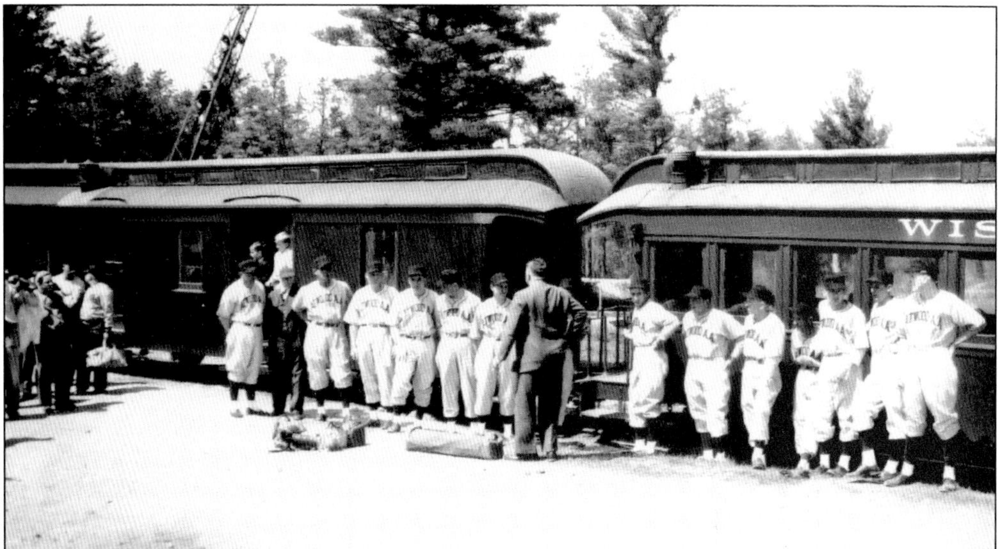

The Atwood AA baseball team poses beside a train at Edaville Railroad before a game. (Courtesy of the Edaville USA Collection.)

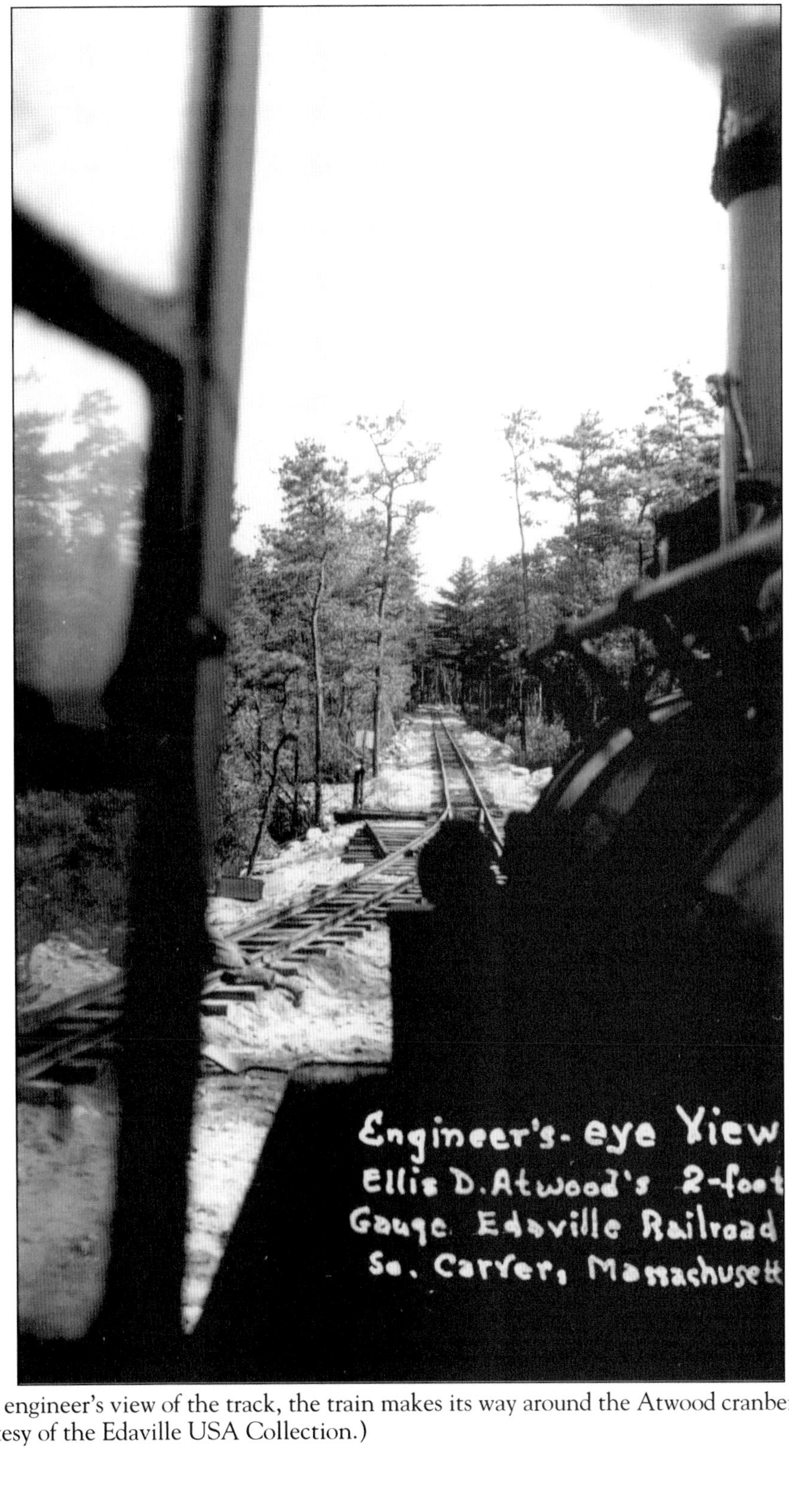

In this engineer's view of the track, the train makes its way around the Atwood cranberry bogs. (Courtesy of the Edaville USA Collection.)

BIBLIOGRAPHY

Braddock, Ellsworth C. *Memories of North Carver Village*. Marion, MA: Channing Books, 1977.

Burrows, Fredrika Alexander. *Cannonballs and Cranberries*. Taunton, MA: W. S. Sullwold, 1976.

Griffith, Henry S. *History of the Town of Carver, Massachusetts: Historical Review 1637–1910*. New Bedford, MA: E. Anthony & Sons, 1913.

Mills, Maggie. "Then and Now." *The Carver Citizen:* Memorial Press Group, 1984–1986.

Murdock, William Bartlett. *Blast Furnaces of Carver*. Poughkeepsie, NY: William B. Murdock, 1937.

Penti, Marsha. *Comprehensive Community Inventory of the Town of Carver*. Carver, MA: Carver Historical Commission, 1980.

Shaw, John A. *Samsons Pond, Indians, and Bog Iron*. South Carver, MA: John A. Shaw, 1997.

Town of Carver Annual Reports, 1881–2002.